Falling Stars

The story of Anzacs from Ukraine

Elena Govor

ALCHERINGA
Canberra, Australia

Falling stars : the story of Anzacs from Ukraine = Падаючі зорі. Анзаки з України.
ALCHERINGA, Canberra, Australia
Second edition 2017

Copyright © Elena Govor 2017 (*elena.id.au*)

Apart from fair dealing for the purposes of research or private study, or criticism or review, as permitted under the Copyright, Designs and Patents Act, 1988, this publication may be reproduced, stored or transmitted in any form, or by any means, only with the prior permission in writing of the publishers. Inquires concerning reproduction outside those terms should be sent to the publishers.

Designed and edited by Raphael Kabo

National Library of Australia Cataloguing-in-Publication entry
Title: Falling stars : the story of Anzacs from Ukraine / Elena Govor.
ISBN: 978-0-9580800-5-7 (paperback)
Notes: Includes bibliographical references and index.
Subjects: Ukrainians--Australia--Biography.
        Immigrants--Australia--Biography.
        World War, 1914-1918----Participation, Ukrainian Australian.

Publication of this book was made possible thanks to financial support from The Karpaty Foundation.

Additional biographical information and archival resources about each Anzac are available online at *russiananzacs.net*.

Cover images: Nikalas Kiva (centre), a Ukrainian Anzac, with his friends Osiph Rinkevich (left) and William Averkoff (right) (Courtesy of Rinkevich family). Below: Poppies are still blooming on the battlefield near Villers-Bretonneux, stained with the blood of the Anzacs from Ukraine. (Photograph courtesy of Jukka Illman). Images on the back cover are courtesy of Peter Tilleard.

Contents

Acknowledgements v
Introduction 1

Part One – From Ukraine to Australia 7
    Ethnic complexities 8
    The roads to Australia 14
    The first to settle in Australia 22
    'Chain migration' and emerging Jewish communities 24
    Ukraine – the Russian Far East – Queensland 28
    Ukrainian émigrés in Queensland communal life 34
    Seamen and tradesmen in other states 39

Part Two – War 45
    Paths to the war 46
    Gallipoli 63
    Egypt & Palestine 68
    Western Front 73
    Blending in 91

Part Three – Life 105
    The Bolshevik shadow in Australia 106
    On land and sea 109
    Becoming Australian 131
    The Second World War 154
    The broken threads 164

Conclusion – the falling stars 167
Notes 169
List of abbreviations 187
Appendix – Biographies 188
Index 233

In memory of Nina Christesen and Professor Harry Rigby,
the founders of Australian Slavonic studies.

Acknowledgements

I am grateful for the support of Oksana Hull, who encouraged me to undertake this project in 2013, and has provided inspiration and valuable advice on many aspects of the research throughout these years. Oksana also drafted the biographical appendix in the book and provided the Ukrainian spelling of Anzacs' names in this section.

I am also grateful to Dr Halyna Koscharsky and Dr Geoffrey Hull for their thoughtful advice and editorial comments.

Dr Kevin Windle greatly contributed to the editing of the manuscript.

The families of the Ukrainian Anzacs were the source of inspiration and support for the publication of this book and generously shared their memories, reflections and images. Among them are:

Jan Rees (Michael Ankudinow's family)
Vivien Brodsky and Warwick Brodsky (Louis Brodsky's family)
Valerie Tereshchenko (Nickefor Domilovsky's family)
Betty Arnold (Dorfman) (Wolf Dorfman's family)
Robyn Dryen (Edward Dryen's family)
Dru West (George Ferber's family)
Richard Goffin (Ben Goffin's family)
Carol McKenzie (Richard Gregorenko's family)
Maree Smith and Annie Smith (family of Osiph Rinkevich, a friend of Nikalas Kiva)
Thelma Webberley (Peter Komesaroff's family)
Jackie Kaminer (George Koty's family)
Svetlana Vishnevaia (Ksenofont Kozachuk's family)
Dorothy Lazarus and Leah Jas (the Lakovskys' family)
Alexander Ouchirenko (John Ouchirenko's family)
Barbara Scott (Feodot Peachenoff's family)
Dane Robilliard and John Piven-Large (Zacharias Pieven's family)
Violet Cotman (Joseph Rudezky's family)
Janice Hunter, Don Hunter, and Dorothy Tober (Albert Michael Tober's family)
Tom Volkofsky (Theofil Volkofsky's family)
Peter Tilleard, Alyn Tilleard, and Carolyn Bur (Tilleard) (Cezar Wolkowsky's family)

I am also grateful for the resources and support of the staff at the National Archives of Australia, Australian War Memorial, the National Library of Australia, particularly its manuscript department and Trove service, and the Queensland State Library, for the digitisation of the *Queenslander Pictorial*, which published photographs of many Anzacs from Ukraine.

My Ukrainian and Russian colleagues, Yulia Prokop, Viktor Kumok, and Dmitry Shirochin, provided assistance in the search for Ukrainian archival records concerning Anzacs' families. My Finnish colleague Jukka Illman visited and photographed several graves of Ukrainian Anzacs in France on my request. His photograph of field flowers on the battlefield near Villers-Bretonneux is featured on the front cover.

And finally, I want to thank my son Raphael Kabo, who painstakingly worked with me on editing and re-editing the manuscript, preparing images, and designing and typesetting the book. Besides his practical help, he provided great support with his enthusiasm, resourcefulness, and deep, unabating engagement with the destinies of the Anzacs.

Introduction

The Ukrainian nation came to global attention only recently, during 2004 with the Orange Revolution, but more so during the invasion of its territory by Russian forces in 2014 and 2015. While Ukraine has had a long historical tradition which can be dated back to Kyivan Rus (882–1240), its present borders within the Soviet Union were established after the Second World War. Its formal independence from the Soviet Union was declared in 1991, and its struggle for true independence from Russia and the forces associated with the Soviet past is ongoing.

By the mid-nineteenth century the territory of present-day Ukraine was divided between two empires – the Russian and the Austro-Hungarian (under Polish administrative governance), and later, after the First World War, between the Soviet Union and Poland. Due to this lack of cohesive state borders, and in spite of a long independence movement, conducted both at home and in the diaspora, Ukraine has hardly been regarded as a nation in its own right by the West. Not surprisingly, the study of the history of its multifaceted connections with Australia, dating back two centuries, has not had a chance to flourish. This history is the proverbial iceberg awaiting its underwater explorer, but even the protruding tip is telling and engaging, as is evident from the following two examples. As early as 1910, Ivan Franko (1856-1916), the famous Ukrainian writer from Halychyna (Galicia), published his translations of a collection of Australian short stories. In the introduction he heralded the emergence of an Australian nation, which was taking shape from 'disparate elements', its development fostered by an 'almost entirely independent political life with a republican form of government and its own parliament, though under an English protectorate'.[1] On the other side of the globe, in 1918, the Melbourne newspaper *Leader* announced to Australians: 'The Ukraine – a new nation arises. An oppressed people break their bonds'. This detailed article was based on a study by an American political scientist, Frederic Austin Ogg,[2] but its publication in Australia heralds the beginning of Australian interest in this faraway nation. Incidentally, the first reference to the name 'Ukraine' in Australian newspapers dates back to 1808.[3]

Ukrainian Anzacs, the subject of our study, are among the hidden facets of Ukrainian-Australian connections. When thousands of Ukrainians came to Australia after the Second World War as displaced persons from war-torn Europe, they noticed hardly any traces of the earlier Ukrainian presence in Australia. In the studies produced by these immigrants, they consistently made the history of Ukrainian settlement in Australia begin with themselves.[4] They were not aware that half a century before their arrival, Australia had become home to several thousand Ukrainian-born people, who toiled right across the land from Cairns to Geraldton, from Darwin to Gippsland, who fought for this country during the First and the Second World Wars, and whose names are commemorated on the walls of the Australian War Memorial, a sacred place of the Australian nation. However, it must be said that there was a good reason for this 'blindness.' Firstly, the number of ethnic Ukrainians was comparatively small, with many leaving Australia after the war. Furthermore, these earlier Ukrainian immigrants from Tsarist Russia had lived under the assimilationist policy of the Russian Empire in regard to its Ukrainian subjects, whose language it banned in printing and education between 1876 and 1905 and again between 1910 and 1917. For these men, 'identity' was perhaps more complex than for the Ukrainians who came after WWII.

The post-1945 Ukrainian community in Australia had a number of distinctive features: its members arrived between 1948 and the early 1950s, as a cohort of displaced persons (DPs) with much in common – they were relatively young, with strong anti-Soviet or anti-Russian political views, and a quite homogeneous Ukrainian identity. All this allowed them to build a strong communal life, centred around churches, Ukrainian schools, and cultural organisations. The impressive legacy of this community's strength is its preservation of its Ukrainian language and identity in their families in the second and even third generation. A historical monument to these émigrés is embodied by the work *Ukrainians in Australia*, encyclopaedic dictionaries, bibliographies of Ukrainian publications, and proceedings of conferences dedicated to the study of the Ukrainian presence in Australia. All these make this community one of the strongest and best represented among European émigré communities in Australia.

Nevertheless, Marko Pavlyshyn in his thought-provoking paper 'How much do we know about Ukrainians in Australia?' mapped out the deficiencies of Australian Ukrainian studies. One of these was the need for 'careful archival research' of the early Ukrainian presence in Australia.[5] Khrystyna Misko's pioneering study 'The pre-DP wave: Rethinking the boundaries of the diaspora' was the first to make use of archival records; it was published in 2000,[6] and the author has recently published *Faded footsteps, Forgotten graves: Queensland's Ukrainian Anzacs*, the story of ethnic Ukrainian Anzacs.[7] An overview by Kalyna Kenez, 'The first visitors from Ukraine', was based mostly on secondary materials.[8] The primary sources used by Oleksandr Savchenko, a historian living in Ukraine, have been limited mostly to the documents of revolutionary émigrés from the Russian Empire.[9] Although Elena Govor's prior studies of early emigration from the Russian Empire to Australia acknowledge the Ukrainian presence, this presence was presented in the general context of multiethnic emigration to Australia.[10]

Studies of Ukrainian emigration to Australia have so far been conducted in the context of exclusively ethnic Ukrainian emigration. This approach might seem paradoxical: while the struggle for independence, for the statehood of Ukraine, has been at the top of the political agenda of Ukrainian émigrés for decades,[11] the understanding of Ukraine as a country with a multiethnic population seems to be beyond the scope of most studies to date; yet the territory of present-day Ukraine has always been populated by different peoples and the present Ukrainian nation is a complex multiethnic entity. While ethnic Ukrainians constitute the core of this nation, it also incorporates other Slavs (Russians, Poles, Bulgarians), Jews, Germans, Armenians, Greeks, Crimean Tatars and several other peoples. Although their co-existence has not always been peaceful, for centuries these peoples have shared the land of Ukraine, loved it as their home, and remembered it when their destinies took them to other parts of the world. When we consider the geopolitical reality of today, within which the independent state of Ukraine enters the European arena, it is timely to expand the focus and to explore the history of Ukrainian presence in Australia in a national, rather than a purely ethnic, framework.

This study is the first attempt to apply this approach, exploring the history of the Ukrainian presence in Australia as a national presence, rather than a more limited ethnic one, through a case study of Ukrainian-born recruits in the Australian Imperial Force (AIF) during the First World War. Thus, the heroes of our study will be, along with ethnic Ukrainian Anzacs, all Anzacs born in Ukraine, or, in a few cases, associated with Ukraine, whatever their ethnic background. The stories of these forefathers of the modern Ukrainian community have been recovered from Australian and some Russian archival records, Australian periodicals, Russian-language newspapers published in Australia, a variety of digital genealogical and military databases, and interviews and correspondence with the descendants of these Anzacs.

In spite of the limitations of many of these sources, the facts derived from them are woven into the story, which will, it is hoped, provide a new brick in the reconstruction of Ukraine's multifaceted history, and of its two-century-long connection with Australia.

As the field of this study – a collective biography of diverse peoples coming from the territory of present-day Ukraine – is a new one, it is important to clarify the terminology used in the book. While the present Constitution of Ukraine applies the term 'Ukrainians' to all its citizens, for reasons of clarity, when writing about people born in Ukraine in the nineteenth century, we aim to distinguish between ethnic Ukrainians and other ethnic groups originating from Ukraine. As will be discussed in the book, at that time in many individual cases there were no clear-cut borderlines between different ethnic groups who had, for centuries, shared the land of Ukraine. A number of factors influenced this fluidity: on one hand, there was the brutal Russian Imperial policy of Russianisation; on the other hand, while people continued to uphold their original ethnic/religious identities, they experienced influences from the predominating Ukrainian or Russian cultures. These processes allow us to speak about cultural integration; the Ukrainian influence was especially strong in rural areas, while Russian culture had a strong influence in industrial and cultural centres such as Odessa and, of course, its influence intensified when the natives of Ukraine moved away from its territory, be it via conscription to the Russian Army or via migration to Siberia and Harbin. Concomitant complex processes occurred on the western territories of present-day Ukraine, at that time under the control of the Austro-Hungarian Empire, where the influence of Polish culture was strongest. The individual manifestations of such multifaceted ethnocultural identities varied, from cases where some Jewish families from Ukraine preferred to use Slavic personal names, to cases where some people of non-Russian ethnic origin associated themselves with Russians. Whenever possible we acknowledge these choices.

Another aspect that requires further clarification is the notion of 'Russian'. A century or more ago, when Ukraine was still deprived of its nationhood, its population were legally nationals of the Russian and Austro-Hungarian Empires, and were seen as such by other nations. The Ukrainian political emigrant and journalist Gregory Piddubny was baffled by this discovery when he landed in Queensland in 1913. 'They called everyone from Russia "Russian"', he wrote about his first contacts with Australians, 'although I was saying that in Russia there are, for instance, Ukrainians, Georgians, Poles and others'.[12] While being dubbed a 'Russian' might be perceived as offensive for a Ukrainian, whose nation experienced a long history of forceful Russianisation, on the side of Australians this was a general practice, without any explicit intent to offend Ukrainians, Belarusians, Jews, or Poles. The word 'Russian' was used by Australians to mean 'Russian national', which covered all people emigrating from the Russian Empire to Australia. Therefore, all Australian official documentation, be it naturalization records, security surveillance dossiers, or army service applications, treated the 'Russian' nationals as a whole, without specifying their ethnicity. This terminology was widely used by the press, the population at large, and, as a result, by some immigrants themselves and by their descendants. In many cases this was due to an acceptance of the dominant cultural conventions, rather than as a conscious surrender of their original ethnic identities. Such usage of the word 'Russian' remains quite common in the English language up to the present, although Russian and Ukrainian languages now consistently distinguish between *Rossiyane* (subjects of the Russian Empire/Federation), Russophones (Russian speaking) and ethnic Russians; this approach is slowly coming into broader usage in English.

Although it might seem natural while writing about historical events to use the terminology of the time, we have decided to consistently distinguish, unless it is obvious from the context, between 'Russians', applying this term to ethnic Russians only, and 'Russian subjects/nationals', which covers all immigrants from the Russian Empire and includes all natives of Ukraine. We hope that the reader will understand the occasional discrepancy this creates when we are writing about a 'Ukrainian Anzac' and quote a police report or the memoirs of his children, where he is referred to as 'Russian' according to the conventions of the time.

While religious denominations on the territory of present-day Ukraine were diverse – for instance, there was more than one Orthodox and Catholic Church – we were unable to reliably untangle this complex matter when speaking about the religious denominations of the Anzacs. The available data, comprised mostly of entries in service records made by army officials, who hardly had any knowledge of non-Anglican and non-Protestant, let alone Ukrainian churches, is scarce and confusing. Thus, we use only the terms commonly accepted in Australia at the time: 'Russian Orthodox', 'Roman Catholic', and 'Jewish', without applying more precise Ukrainian terms; this is a matter for future research based on Ukrainian records.

Names of Anzacs and other Ukrainians are used in the book in the forms in which they were used in Australia. Thus, we do not convert Thomas to Khoma or Toma, John to Ivan or

Jan, George to Yuri (Юрій), Peter to Petro, etc. Neither do we unify variations of the same name; thus we have Nikalas for one Anzac and Nicholas for another, Wolf and Wolfe, Afanasey, Afanasy, and even Alfroniza. If some individuals used several versions of their forenames and surnames, we use, in order of availability, those under which they were naturalised in Australia, then those they used most consistently, and finally those under which they served in the army. The Ukrainian versions of names, including their forms in Ukrainian script, are provided in the biographical appendix compiled with the assistance of Oksana Hull. In the appendix we also reconstruct the original Russian, and, where possible, Jewish names of the Anzacs.

Ukrainian place-names are transliterated from Ukrainian, accompanied in some cases, in the first instance, by a transliteration of the Russian variant of the spelling, which was commonly used in English until recently. The transliteration is based on the Ukrainian National transliteration, 2012.[13] Several BGN/PCGN conversions are observed, such as spelling Odessa rather than Odesa, and Donetsk rather than Donets'k.[14]

The system of transliteration used in the references is based on the Library of Congress transliteration for Ukrainian.

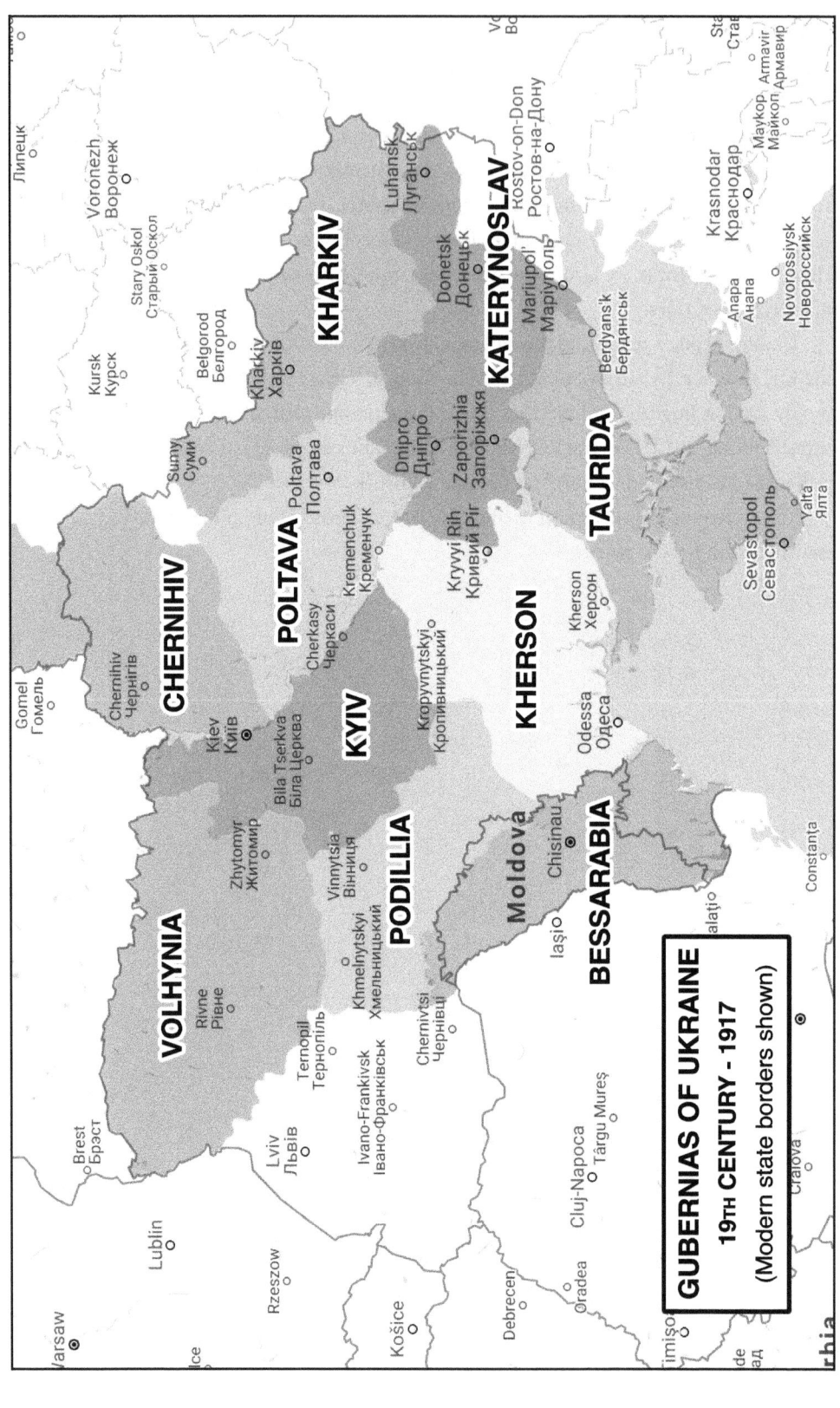

ONE

FROM UKRAINE TO AUSTRALIA

Ethnic complexities

How many Anzacs from Ukraine were there? To find them it is necessary to sift through over a thousand service records of Anzacs from the territories of the Russian and Austro-Hungarian empires. Yet this remains a difficult question to answer, and we have to accept that we will never have absolutely exact statistics. In many cases we have to speak of approximate percentages and tendencies, because for a number of men there are no data. Nevertheless, we can provide some statistics, although with reservations. We have determined that 134 men born on the territory of present-day Ukraine, or associated with it, enlisted in the AIF during the First World War. All but one came from provinces (*gubernias*) that were then part of the Russian Empire; the single man who came from the territory of the Austro-Hungarian Empire was Elias Lebovitz, of Jewish origin, born in Lviv, but he claimed his parentage to be from Kyiv. For three of them we do not have any data about their birthplace besides 'Russia' (i.e. the Russian Empire), but the names of two of them (Efim Maximenko, Isaac Micolazyk) suggest they were most likely Ukrainians. Morris Rothstein's place of birth was recorded as the non-existent 'Cherkavosk',[1] the format of which nevertheless suggests that it is quite likely a Ukrainian placename as well.

In a number of other cases, although the placenames are similarly corrupted, it is possible, with a degree of certainty, to establish their original spelling. These misspellings can be explained by the fact that the main document from which we derive this information – 'Attestation paper of persons enlisted for service abroad' – was often filled in by a recruiting clerk by ear and, unless the birthplace was a well-known port like Odessa, it was often recorded in a highly idiosyncratic way. For instance, Albert Michael Tober's place of birth was recorded as 'Weongn, Russia', while his father's address appeared as 'Bulu, Russia' and only another version of this mysterious place in another enlistment form, where it was recorded as 'Volleen', helps us to guess that all three were attempts to record the name of the Ukrainian province of Volhynia (Volyn)! Jacob Leffow's 'Chanakow' and 'Charnagow' must be Chernihiv (Chernigov in Russian). Wolfe Hoffman's 'Achvato', 'Chashwatte', and 'Chachewato' turned out to be Khashchuvate (Khashchevatoye) in Podillia (Podolia) province. The place of birth of William Whynsky (who served as Whnsky, his surname was also recorded as Whensky), was noted down as 'Russia, Vehesky'. Since the surnames Vynsky and Vensky exist in Ukraine, and William was 'Roman Catholic', the chances that he was Ukrainian or Polish-Ukrainian are quite high.

In some cases, our Anzacs made their own contributions to this geographical confusion. For instance Matfeus Oleinikoff consistently, in his applications for naturalisation and for enlistment in the army, gave his place of birth as 'Moscow, Russia', but when a policeman came to interview him he noted that Matfeus was born in 'Poltavia, Moscow, Russia'.[2] Given his surname, it is very likely that Oleinikoff was born in Poltava province in Ukraine and used Moscow as a well-known place to avoid complicated explanations. Jack Vengert, in different documents, provided a variety of birthplaces: 'Kieff near Vladivostock', 'Odessa' and 'Kieff'. Carl Kills similarly had a variety of birthplaces: 'Libau' at enlistment and 'Woeskonecy now Poland' in his naturalisation. His father's address was recorded as 'D. Waskovea, Wolanskay G[ubernia] Russia', which suggests that their roots were from the same Volhynia province, rather than Libava. The 'D.' in 'D. Waskovea / Woeskonecy' most likely stands for *derevnia*, i.e. village. The probable location is Voskovtsy village, near Kremenets in the south-east of Volhynia province. Likewise, Afanasey Korniack seems to have struggled for many years to convey the name of his native place: 1915 'Torilesk', 1916 'Boritz', 1924 'Warsaw'; 1925 'Poritsk near Odessa', and 1930 'Ivanitch, Poritzk', which must all stand for Porytsk near Ivanychi, in the same Volhynia province.

Not surprisingly, many opted simply to give their place of birth as Odessa, which was known all over the world. For instance, George Malisheff enlisted as a native of Odessa, but from his will we learn that his brothers lived in 'Niurafskou Manor' in Yampil county in Podillia, which makes it quite likely that he was born there as well. John Cherpiter (or Cherpita) gave his place of birth as 'Cameno, Odessa, South of Russia', probably aiming to indicate his Ukrainian identity. 'Cameno' could be Kamianets-Podilskyi as, according to the 'Memory of the People', the Second World War database,[3] a number of men with the surname Cherpita originate from villages in this province, and indeed his wife's statutory declaration made after his death reveals that his father Mitrofan lived in Kamianets-Podilskyi.[4] Thus, the disproportionate dominance of Kherson province – the location of Odessa – in Table 1 might well be the result of this preference for Odessa as a recorded place of birth.

The confusion over the place of birth of John Sepscak might be due to political circumstances. In his enlistment documents and application for naturalisation he consistently gave his place of birth as simply 'Russia', although in a newspaper advertisement he added an unidentifiable 'Romen, Russia', but policemen during the naturalisation interview recorded that he was born in 'Hopszywnica, Russia'.[5] 'Romen' could be the Ukrainian town of Romny, while 'Hopszywnica' could be Polish Koprzywnica in the province of Radom, in which case Romen could be a misspelling of Radom. His alien registration records may shed more light on his origin. There his nationality was initially noted as 'Austrian', but crossed out and replaced with 'Russian'. If indeed he was born in Koprzywnica, which was in Russian-ruled Polish territory, but very close to the Austrian border, it is quite possible that he took precautions not to be identified as an Austrian subject, which would have resulted in detention as a Prisoner of War (POW) by the Australian authorities. Nevertheless, his reluctance to give his place of birth as Poland, and his religious denomination being listed as 'Greek Church', i.e. Russian Orthodox, make it likely that he was a Ukrainian.

The ethnic distribution of Ukrainian-born servicemen poses even more difficulties, although we have a number of sources of information for this purpose. Two major indications here are the serviceman's name and his religion, which in a number of cases were supplemented by his own direct or circumstantial evidence.

Jewish Anzacs are the easiest to distinguish here: their religion was usually, although not always, recorded as 'Jewish' or 'Hebrew'. Out of 51 recruits born in Ukraine whom we can identify as Jewish, at enlistment three gave their religion as Church of England, another three as Lutheran, Protestant and Salvation Army, one as Roman Catholic and three as Orthodox. The latter might be converts coming from assimilated families in the southern provinces of Ukraine. The former (Anglican and Protestant) probably did not care much about religion at all, and on enlistment stated the same religion as their Australian mates.

It is also easy to distinguish six foreigners who were born, or claimed to be born, in Ukraine. Alexander Barr Winning and Roland Arthur Cooper were British; Lamotte Alexis Sage and Christian Rink were French; Emile Auguste Tardent was Swiss; Joseph Rudovsky, who later gave his name as Mikulicic-Rodd, was a Croat. These foreigners did not have Russian citizenship and the degree of their assimilation into the surrounding Slavic culture varied. Roland Cooper's parents, for instance, lived since their childhoods in different parts of the Russian Empire, where their parents were engaged in business. Roland spent his early childhood in Russia, where his father worked as an engineer, but in 1909 the whole family moved to Sydney, severing their Russian connections. Alexander Winning's family lived for over ten years in Ukraine, where his father James worked for a geological company collecting exploratory core samples; he died when Alexander was just three and his mother returned to England, later moving with the children to Australia, which also terminated their Russian connections. On the other hand, the Tardent family, whom we shall meet later, had long-lasting connections with Ukraine and Russia, which continued after their emigration to Queensland.

The five Germans whom we distinguish among the Ukrainian-born Anzacs – Jacob Leffow, Alexander Sast, Jack Vengert, Albert Michael Tober, and Alexander Spisbah – were Russian subjects whose families had most likely been living in Ukraine for generations and were fully assimilated. Tober's granddaughter has vague knowledge of his origins: 'my father used to say that his father's father was German and his mother was Irish and he was born in Russia', although, as we have seen, this was in fact Volhynia in Ukraine.[6] One more person with non-Slavic ethnic heritage among our Anzacs was Cemon (Simon) Afendikoff, born in Odessa. He had a Greek-derived surname, but, like Ukrainian Germans, the Afendikovs could have been assimilated into the surrounding Slavic culture for generations.

The remaining 71 recruits can be broadly categorized as Slavs; they include people of Ukrainian, Russian and Polish ethnic origin. It is not always easy to draw an exact ethnic border between them, because, as noted above, the south-eastern provinces of modern Ukraine have experienced migration and resettlement since the late eighteenth century. At the same time, the people of Ukraine were often subjected to Polonisation or Russification. For some this process resulted in the loss or suppression of their original culture; many others developed and maintained double (and sometimes even triple) ethnic identities. Rural people would have expressed their cultural identity through their mother tongue and their own customs so long as they remained in their local areas, only gradually becoming immersed in Polish or Russian language and culture if they moved to the cities to study or work, or were conscripted into the Russian army.

Theofil Volkofsky from Lypky near Skvyra (south-east of Kyiv) was one who followed this pattern. His son Tom initially responded to my question about his father's ethnic origins by saying, 'The family had been Polish and had moved to Kyiv in Ukraine. They were Catholics.' Further probing revealed, however, that Volkofsky had become Russified as a student at a teachers' college, abandoning his Roman Catholicism at the same time as he was exposed to contemporary Russian ideas, 'all the talk of evolution and writings of Dostoyevsky and Tolstoy', as his son Tom put it.[7] Theofil's brother, Cezar Wolkowsky, was remembered by his grandchildren as 'Russian'. In the popular mind, Poles were associated with the Roman Catholic church, whether they lived on the territory of Poland or Ukraine, but this was of course not always the case, and Volkofsky undoubtedly experienced a strong Ukrainian influence. Indeed, a postcard in Cezar's archives reveals that the name of their sister left behind in Ukraine was Ganya, which suggests Ukrainian rather than Russian or Polish ethnicity. But the memories of Cezar's grandson Alyn testify that the brothers indeed had multiple ethnic identities. When after the Second World War their third brother, Wojciech, joined them in Australia, 'they used to have major arguments, as Cezar would speak in Russian, and his brother [Wojciech] would get very angry, saying "Speak Ukrainian!"'[8]

Another case is James Theodor Gretchinsky, who was born in Horodia, in Chernihiv province not far from the borders of both modern-day Belarus and Russia. When in Australia, he applied to become an interpreter in the military censor's office, stating that he spoke 'Russian, Polish, and Courland, and one or two Russian dialects, also French and Japanese'. By 'Russian dialects', he obviously meant the Ukrainian and Belarusian which would have been spoken around him while he was growing up. His ethnic origin is further complicated by a tale, popular among the Grechinskys in Horodia, that their ancestor was a Greek priest, Jacob, who came to Nizhyn in the time of Catherine the Great.[9] But whatever was his ancestry, the Australian James Gretchinsky, in spite of his knowledge of Ukrainian and Belarusian, was predominantly Russian in culture. His father, Fedor Pavlovich Grechinsky, was a doctor (probably the brother of another doctor and writer, Vasily Pavlovich Grechinsky) and James himself received a good education in Moscow. His religion was listed as Greek.

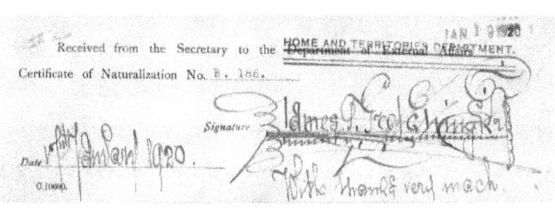

Gretchinsky's signature testified that he was a man of letters (NAA)

Untangling the ethnicity of Slav Anzacs from Ukraine, we cannot always rely on surnames as a reliable indicator of their ethnic heritage. For instance, the Platonoff brothers,

Thomas Platonaff and George Platonoff, came to Australia in 1911 from Siberia with their parents. Their surname is typically Russian, but some investigation uncovers a more complex picture. While Thomas never bothered to record his birthplace in Australian documents as anything more than 'Russia', George's place of birth was recorded as 'Hovro, Ukrahenka, Russia', while their father Stephan gave his place of birth as 'Ukrainka' in Kherson province. The place of their birth could be Novoukrainka, a township south-west of Elisavetgrad (now Kropyvnytskyi) in Kherson province, as George's mysterious 'Hovro' might be Novo written in the Cyrillic script! Further probing in the Australian documents leads us to discover that George's and Thomas' mother's surname was Odarchinko, which sounds undoubtedly Ukrainian. Similarly, Nicholas Roomianzoff's 'Russian' surname Rumiantsev is at odds with his mother's 'Ukrainian' surname, Ohota. Considering that he was one of the few who, in his enlistment documents, gave his place of birth as 'Little Russia' rather than simply 'Russia', and obviously wished to convey that he was different from ethnic Russians, we might consider him to be Ukrainian. On the other hand, Paul Drachuk, who was born in Kishinev (now Moldova), had a characteristic Ukrainian surname ending in '-uk'. It is tempting to consider him Ukrainian, but from an interview with his family still living in Moldova it becomes clear that, in spite of the Ukrainian surname, he was a Russified Moldovan and thus remains beyond the scope of our study. At the same time, George Didenko, an Orthodox adherent from Akkerman in Bessarabia (most of which is now in Moldova), was most likely a Ukrainian.

Another telling case is that of George Malisheff, who later stated that his true name was Petr Fedorovich Checkman. Neither of these names – Malisheff or Checkman – is 'typically' Ukrainian, and the fact that he claimed to be born in Odessa might suggest that he was an ethnic Russian or a Russified Jew. But the Slavonic names of his brothers, which appear in his will, and the fact that they lived in a village in the heart of Podillia province suggest that they might all be Ukrainians.[10] Indeed, the 'Memory of the People' database lists a number of people from Podillia with the surname Chekman as Ukrainians.[11]

In rare cases we can obtain testimony about self-identification from our recruits themselves. Thus Zacharias Pieven from Chernihiv, applying for naturalisation, stated: 'I am by birth a Cossack'. He put a full stop and then added 'Russian'.[12] Considering that he had a typical Ukrainian surname (*piven* in Ukrainian means 'rooster'), and that the naturalisation form forced him to provide his national, rather than ethnic background, we are fully entitled to consider him Ukrainian. Indeed an entry in his Russian passport shows that he was a Cossack from the township of Saltykova Divitsia in Chernihiv province.[13] William Kolesnikov and Stephen Provaka (he served under his original name Stepan Proiavka) from Surazh in the same Chernihiv province should be outside the scope of our study, as Surazh is now on the territory of the Russian Federation, but the fact that they consistently claimed Kyiv as their place of birth in their naturalisation records might indicate that they associated themselves with Ukraine. This assumption is reinforced by the fact that Proiavka had a 'Ukrainian' surname and the population of Surazh was a mixture of Russians, Ukrainians and Belarusians. All this supports our decision to include them in this study.

The national and ethnic status of Gregory Jakimov, who was born and grew up in Kamianets-Podilskyi, turned out to be surprising. He was obviously a Slav of Orthodox religion who grew up in the Ukrainian culture. During the war he served in the AIF as a Russian subject, but, when becoming naturalised in 1922, he stated that both his parents were 'Bohemians', i.e. Czech, which is why in his Australian naturalisation papers he formally renounced his Czecho-Slovakian, rather than his Russian, nationality.[14]

Attestation papers included a compulsory question on religious denomination, which might be helpful in untangling ethnic complexities. In the case of Slavs the information provided by this question is unfortunately more often confusing than clarifying. This could have resulted from communication difficulties between enlistment clerks and the Russian-born recruits. It is also likely that many clerks had little knowledge of the Eastern Churches. The commonly used term at this time to describe any member of the Eastern Orthodox Church, irrespective of location, was 'Greek Catholic', in reference to the church's origins in the Greek-speaking parts of the Holy Roman Empire. (This term would have been quite confusing for Ukrainians, as in Ukraine the Uniate Greek Catholic Church exists along with the Russian Orthodox Church). Enlistment clerks followed this practice to some extent in recording religious persuasions. Thus Vasily Kavitski and Peter Kusmin (whose original name was Samuel Zadorohney) from Kyiv province were listed as Greek Catholics. Sometimes the enlisting clerks even confused the Greek Orthodox and Roman Catholic Churches, recording as 'Roman Catholics' natives of the Russian Empire who certainly must have been Russian Orthodox. This relates, for instance, to the above-mentioned family of Platonoff from Novoukrainka: one brother was recorded at enlistment as 'Greek', the other as 'Roman Catholic'. Nicholas Gulevich from Odessa was recorded in one attestation paper as 'Greek Church' and in another as 'Roman Catholic'. Furthermore Efim Maximenko was recorded first as 'Greek Roman Catholic' and then as 'Roman Catholic (Greek)'. It is likely that all of them were in fact Russian Orthodox. The case of Stephen Surovsov from Klimov in Chernihiv province further confirms this supposition: as a new arrival in Australia, he enlisted in the 1st AIF as 'Roman Catholic', but when he joined the 2nd AIF during the Second World War and could communicate well in English, he gave his religious denomination as Russian Orthodox, which must have been the correct denomination all along. The denomination for six of our Slavs was also recorded as Church of England. As was often the case with Jewish recruits, they either did not care about religion or could not communicate their situation at enlistment.

Keeping in mind all these reservations, we can estimate that among the above-mentioned 71 Slavs, about 51 were ethnic Ukrainians, at least 3 were Poles, and 17 were ethnic Russians or Poles with predominantly Russian culture, including one 'Bohemian'. Khrystyna Misko in her study identified 60 Anzacs as Ukrainian.

Territorial distribution according to place of birth, subdivided by the major administrative unit in the Russian Empire – province – is as follows:

Table 1. Ethno-territorial distribution of Ukrainian-born Anzacs

Province	Ukrainians	Other Slavs, Germans, Greeks	Jews	Western Europeans	Total
Bessarabia	1	-	-	-	1
Chernihiv	8	4	1	-	13
Katerynoslav	2	-	8	1	11
Kharkiv	-	2	-	1	3
Kherson	10	11	22	4	47
Kyiv	11	4	4	-	19
Lviv	-	-	1	-	1
Podillia	6	1	5	-	12
Poltava	2	-	1	-	3
Taurida	1	1	5	-	7
Volhynia	6	2	3	-	11
Unidentified	4	1	1	-	6
Total	51	26	51	6	134

Sources: Estimate based on data in service records and naturalisation files.

The roads to Australia

Looking at these numbers, the question arises: why and how did all these future Anzacs land in Australia? The Ukrainian presence in Australia has a long history, which still awaits a comprehensive study. Here we will consider the prevalent pattern of Ukrainian immigration in the late nineteenth and early twentieth century by examining the cohort of men who were to become Anzacs. Their immigration by year is presented in Figure 1 (overleaf).

These statistics make it obvious that while the numbers were initially low, starting in 1910 there was a rapid increase in the number of arrivals. These grew steadily up to the beginning of the First World War, which halted all immigration and significantly reduced commercial sailing in Australian waters. These immigration statistics for Anzacs born in Ukraine coincide with the general pattern of emigration from the Russian Empire to Australia in the first two decades of the twentieth century.[15]

Emigration from Ukraine to Australia before the First World War followed several distinct routes. Unlikely though it might seem, the most common route was via Siberia and the Russian Far East. Nearly half of the natives of Ukraine arriving in Australia in 1910-1915 took this route. The growth of emigration through the Far Eastern ports was fuelled by various factors,

Figure 1. Arrivals of Ukrainian-born Anzacs in Australia, 1882-1918

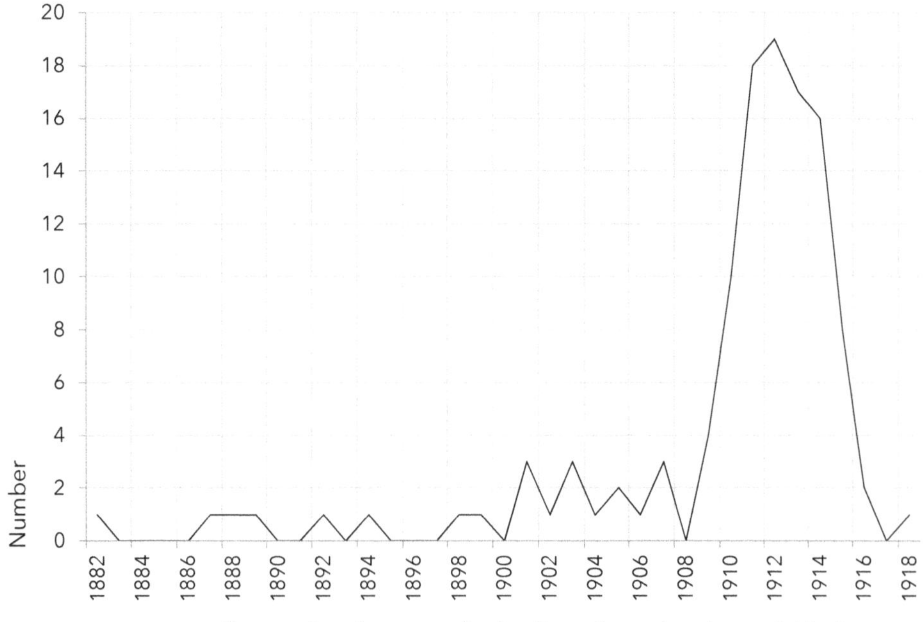

Sources: Data from naturalisation files, alien registration, and shipping records

including the opening up of the Russian Empire's eastern frontier provinces in the latter part of the nineteenth century, which coincided with increased mobility within the Empire. The year 1905 brought renewed change in social and political conditions in the wake of the first Russian revolution, the end of the Russo-Japanese war and the completion of the Trans-Siberian railway. A highly fluid population had now become attracted to Russia's eastern provinces and, with the opening of the railway, the movement of people across Russia was simplified; this mobility was also increased as a result of the Stolypin land reforms, which allowed peasants to leave their village communities and seek employment elsewhere. The majority of those migrating were young men seeking adventure or new lives, those escaping their old lives for political reasons, and those avoiding conscription in the dreaded Russian army, but whole families also moved to the East.

In those years the fame of Australia as a 'working man's paradise', a nation of socio-economic bounty, political freedom, and abundant land allotments, was on the rise. This determined the choice for many potential emigrants from the Russian Empire, a choice encouraged to some extent by the activities of emigration agents in Far Eastern ports and the increasing availability of regular steamship services to Australia. These emigrants usually came via Harbin and the Japanese port of Moji, from where Japanese steamships plied the Australian route, calling at Darwin, Cairns, Townsville, Brisbane, Sydney and Melbourne. They experienced difficult and uncomfortable voyages, usually in the lowest class available (costing 120 roubles, or about £12, from Harbin to Brisbane), on ships such as the *Kumano Maru*, *Nikko Maru*, *Yawata Maru*, *Eastern*, *Empire*, and *St Albans*. Almost all of them disembarked in Brisbane.[16]

A red page of life
Theofil Volkofsky's secret

A hundred years later the long train ride across Siberia to the eastern ports has taken on all resonance of an ancestral journey, lingering in the memories of the descendants of the Ukrainian Anzacs as a symbolic rite of passage. To them the Trans-Siberian Railway replaces the long sea voyage from England to Australia in the British tradition. Theofil Volkofsky 'got on the Trans-Siberian Railway and he became a telegraphist there', his son Tom recalls.

> Everything was in Morse code in those days. Dad was quite good at all that. He worked on that for some time. Then he took up a farm in Siberia somewhere … but … a Siberian tiger came and got over the cow yard. It kind of took the joy out of his cattle-farming and he decided to move on a bit further. He ended up in Vladivostok. From there he went through China to Japan. He liked the idea of Canada and he liked the idea of Australia. Both these governments seemed to be promising to him and so he actually tossed for it. He said, 'Heads I go to Australia, tails I go to Canada'. And it came down heads for Australia.[17]

Indeed, as in any traditional ancestral journey, life seemed filled with endless promise and the entire world lay within their grasp. Alas, or perhaps luckily, Tom, an Australian boy who grew up in Dubbo, never knew what really happened to his father in that fairy-tale Russian land of Siberia.

In 1912 Theofil had just been released from Waterfall Hospital near Sydney, where he was confined with consumption. Lonely, jobless, and penniless, he was walking the streets of Sydney when he came across a sympathetic journalist who recorded the story of his misadventures – 'A red page of life' as he called it.

Theofil's story started 'in a village in Little Russia, one of the provinces verging on the Crimea', according to the journalist's explanation of Russian geography for the Australian reader. While working as a teacher, Theofil confronted a Russian Orthodox priest who had punished an indolent 'small golden-haired girl', beating her with a thick ruler until 'a final lash across the head split the unfortunate child's ear from the top to the bottom'. Volkofsky's Tolstoyan attempt to reason with brute force brought him into trouble and he had to leave his position. With no prospects in his native Lypky he made for Siberia. In Achinsk he trained as a telegraphist and was put to work at a station on the Trans-Siberian railway somewhere near Petrovsky Zavod in the Chita area.

This was the time of the Russo-Japanese War and the Russian Revolution of 1905, when the workers in this area established the so-called Republic of Chita, controlled

Telegraphist seized by soldiers as seen by an Australian artist (The Sun, 1912)

by their labour organisations. To quash the social unrest and railway strikes, which affected the movement of troops to the front, the army sent a punitive detachment led by General Paul Rennenkampf, who had a number of suspects shot without trial as his train travelled east. Volkofsky was suspected of passing on 'revolutionary telegrams' and ordered to provide the names of revolutionaries. To save himself he began writing down every name he 'could remember having seen on the tombstones in the cemetery of his native' Lypky. This did not help and he was dragged off for execution, stripped of his clothes, thrown on the snow and lashed with a knout. After thirty lashes he lost consciousness; presumed dead after eighty lashes, he was left in the snow in a pool of blood. Only when Rennenkampf's squad had left was he brought inside and hours later regained consciousness. A local doctor was too frightened to treat him, and he was rescued and nursed back to health by a nomadic 'Mongol' tribe which inhabited the territory south of Chita. Returning to Russia, he moved to Vladivostok where he worked as a navvy on the railway and contributed to two local newspapers. As the tide of revolutionary sentiment ebbed and the newspapers were closed down, he found himself under police surveillance and realised that the time had come for him to flee the country for good.[18] The rest of the story, about the tossing of the coin, was more suitable for the ears of his children...

Volkofsky's case is a telling one when we consider the distinction between political and economic emigration. Most likely Volkofsky was not a member of any political party: he was not arrested and exiled, and he cannot be found in the databases of political prisoners. Nevertheless, his departure from Russia, whatever he would later say about tossing a coin, was a political escape. And at the very beginning of his journey stands the figure of Tolstoy, and Dostoevsky's moral dilemma of the happiness of mankind weighed against a single tear of a child, and the little girl in a Ukrainian village beaten by the priest.

Direct emigration from Ukraine to Australia via Odessa or European ports was far less common than emigration across the Russian Far Eastern borders. While there exist only a few records of future Ukrainian Anzacs embarking on this direct voyage, there are a larger number of cases of Jewish families leaving for Australia, and some of them, for example the Lakovsky family, lived in Odessa at the time of their emigration. Others came from the Jewish farming colonies in the provinces of Katerynoslav (Ekaterinoslav) and Taurida.

Some Jewish emigrants came to Australia as a result of a two-stage migration via other countries. Families influenced by Zionism, which offered the prospect of a utopian life in Palestine, travelled there at the end of the nineteenth century, while others chose England or America, and it was from these countries that their sons, taken there as children, embarked on a new journey, by choice or by chance, to Australia. While emigration via the Russian Far East contributed to the Russification of the Ukrainian natives, whether Ukrainians or Jewish, this two-stage migration had the opposite effect: the young were influenced by the culture and language of the first country they reached with their parents. For example, Max Perlman from Odessa wrote: 'I left Russia with my parents for Jerusalem when I was 3 years of age'. After 13 years in Palestine he came to Perth aged just 16.[19] Harry Sadagoursky was a child when his family landed in Western Australia in 1912 after thirteen years in Palestine. The case of Lion Harlap was similar: he was taken by his parents to the farming colony of Rehovot in Palestine as a baby, and even claimed later that he was born in Rehovot rather than Odessa.[20] He had also come as a teenager to Western Australia, where his married sister had settled two years earlier. Elias Lebovitz, when enlisting in the AIF, gave his place of birth as 'Palestine, Lemburg, Austria', although his application was accompanied by a certificate from the Russian consul stating that his 'parents were Russian subjects born in Kief, Russia'.[21] He obviously felt an affinity with Palestine where he grew up, rather than with Lviv (Lemberg) where he was born. Similarly, Frank Goldstein from Ruzhyn and Wolfe Greenstein from Odessa emigrated to England as children with their families and grew up there as fully assimilated Britons before finally settling in Australia.

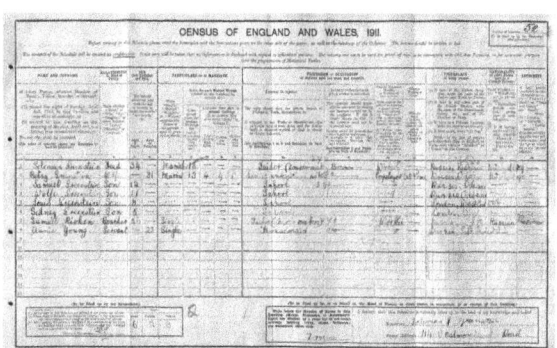

Odessa as a place of birth figured in the British census of the Greenstein family (UK National Archives)

Finally, a significant proportion of the Ukrainian-born Anzacs landed in Australia as seamen. About one third of them were employed in seafaring-related occupations as sailors, firemen, ship's carpenters, marine mechanics or electricians. Although later some gave their occupations as labourers or miners upon enlisting in the AIF, their tattoos, painstakingly described by the recruiting officers, betrayed their seafaring past. They had either been discharged or had deserted their ships. With the outbreak of the war, vessels were often stranded in Australia and their crews dismissed. Ukrainians, along with Russians, Poles and Ukrainian Germans were the most numerous in this group. Some of the seamen were Jewish, although this was not a trade usually associated with Jews from the Russian Empire. Many of them were from Odessa, or at least claimed to be. Ukrainian-born seamen arrived in Australian ports from all over the world: Ksenofont Kozachuk came from Canada, Denis Papchuck from South America, Alexander Belfort and Alexander Popow from New Zealand, and many – like John Ouchirenko, Ben Goffin, Albert Morozoff, Joseph Kleshenko – arrived from the USA.

While for Anzacs from the Baltic territories and Finland the choice of a seafaring profession was commonplace, for Anzacs from Ukraine it could carry a hint of romance, which would explain why we find among seafarers a number of young men from well-off or middle-class families, who often went to sea when their fathers died. Alexander Popow, for example, born in Hlukhiv (Glukhov) in Chernihiv province, was the son of a general in the Russian army and had studied electrical engineering at the University of Liège in Belgium. Another case is that of George Kamishansky, born in Kerch, whose work in Australia as a seaman on coastal ships belied his origins. His father, Petr Konstantinovich Kamishansky, who grew up in Podillia, was a St Petersburg court prosecutor who had committed some kind of legal infraction and had been sent into internal exile. However, because of his high social standing, he served out this exile as the provincial governor of Viatka.[22] Like Popow, George Kamishansky was well educated, and knew French, German and English. Boris Poselnikoff, from Odessa, came from a military family: his father was a colonel in 'the 3rd Sharpshooter regiment'.[23]

Two seamen from Odessa
Ankundinow's and Brodsky's stories

In 1938 one former seaman and Anzac, Michael Ankudinow, wrote to the military authorities applying for a replacement copy of his discharge certificate in his peculiar English: 'Loss occured on Track shivting camps from one to another state traveling cary a swag looking another camp and jobs'.[24] He sounded and looked like a typical Australian swagman, and no one could guess that this was once a boy with 'a good education, with tutors and at school',[25] and that his stepfather, a doctor and philanthropist, was a member of the Vladivostok city council and owner of several Vladivostok newspapers. The further the tides of life took Michael away from his prominent and happy family, the hazier his past became. By 1938 there seemed to be nothing fixed or permanent about it: not his name (in Australia he was also known as George Wilson, alias Callahan), nor his place of birth (he chose freely between Vladivostok, St Petersburg and Helsinki), nor even his date of birth (there are six different dates between 1879 and 1901!), let alone a place of abode.

Michael Ankudinow (left, back row) with his family in Vladivostok, c. 1911 (Courtesy of Jan Rees)

Only by establishing contact with Ankudinow's relatives was it possible to discover his origins. It turned out that he was born in neither Vladivostok nor St Petersburg, but in Odessa. His mother Aleksandra was from Poltava in Ukraine. She was married to a Mr Zverkov and lived in Odessa; she had two children, Aleksandra and baby Michael, when her husband suddenly died. To support her young family Aleksandra opened a dress salon in Odessa.[26] Rescue came in the form of marriage to Georgy (George) Evseevich Ankudinov, a doctor assigned to the Black Sea Fleet and based in Odessa. He grew up in Revel (Tallinn) in a cultured, well-to-do Russian-Baltic German family, in a house full of music and arts, and received a good education as a surgeon at the Kronstadt Naval Hospital. On marrying Aleksandra, Georgy adopted her children and gave them his name. Shortly after marriage he resigned his commission and the young family set off to Vladivostok.[27] Their great granddaughter Jan Rees tells about their life in Vladivostok:

> George became a very successful doctor and with the support of his wife, became involved in many charitable works. They opened children's shelters, which eventually became orphanages for the homeless. Alessandra encouraged higher education for girls, helped establish a High School and was an active member on the Board of the Vladivostok Women's College. [...] In 1900, George built a 30-bed private hospital, and opened a charity clinic for patients who were unable to pay. [...] He also opened a venereal disease clinic to treat sailors in the Russian Imperial Navy. The financing and support of his enterprises were all his own effort. [...] During the Russo-Japanese War he was mobilized as a reserve doctor and treated the wounded, both the Russians as well as the captured Japanese. After the War, he was recognized by the Japanese government for his compassionate treatment of their citizens. [...] In 1912, for services to the community, both husband and wife were decorated by the Czarina of Russia and were

knighted. George became involved in various Government and Council Boards for the benefit of Vladivostok.

George and his wife Alessandra established a happy home life. A large home was built at Sedanka, just outside Vladivostok for their large family – 6 children of their own and the 2 whom George adopted. The girls had a governess to supervise their education, the boys a tutor with a nanny for the babies. The children were taught music and the arts.[28]

According to family tales, 'one winter, when he was 16 or 17, Michael became restless and, finding life very restrictive, ran away to sea by joining a tramp ship in Vladivostok Harbour. He was later found to be settled in Australia'. A tramp ship, explains Jan, is 'a commercial vessel that has no regular schedule but takes on and discharges cargo whenever hired to do so'. This indeed was the type of ship on which many Ukrainian-born Anzacs had experience of service.

Michael returned home at least once, as a photograph taken in about 1911 has survived, showing him with his family. But this quiet life was obviously not for him. He himself later stated that he served in the Russian army and then went seafaring, spending time in China, Japan and the United States until he landed in South Australia in 1912.[29]

For Louis Brodsky, another sailor from Odessa, it was the miserable conditions of life in Russia that drove him to seek his fortune at sea. Alexander, Louis Brodsky's son, only ever saw his grandparents in an old photo, and to him they 'appeared to be short-statured folks in poorish circumstances. They looked as though they might have unwillingly endured the eternal dread of pogroms and an extremely selfish aristocracy.' Louis might have been escaping family circumstances as much as social conditions, but perhaps there was a streak of restlessness, too. According to his son,

> Dad reacted adversely to discipline, 'clearing out' from home when he was 9 and again when he was 11. There was always something gypsyish about him for he preferred to wander than to be static, and even at an early age his will was strong and his spirit very mercurial. He used to tell us about how he hid in ships' holds, where his only 'companions' were squeaking rats, and his main food, mouldering potatoes.

Whatever the exact reasons, Louis took that familiar path down to the ships and the sea, choosing this tough, dangerous life over remaining a poor Odessa Jew: 'he preferred to try his luck than to knuckle down in Odessa'.

One of his favourite yarns was, - Alexander continues, - how he went to a wealthy uncle - a tea and sugar merchant - and announced that he was determined to see the world. 'Good luck', said the rich man, tossing his hopeful nephew a rouble (about 20 cents)! Dad would chuckle and his twinkling eyes would crease, as he relived that hopeful moment. His mother begged that he would settle down to home and schooling, but Dad's mind was made up. He spent a considerable part of his adolescent years at sea, travelling the Baltic, the Bay of Biscay, the Mediterranean and even the Atlantic, in appalling freighters and even more terrible weather. He made our skins creep with his description of how he was washed overboard in stormy weather off the French coast, only to be luckily tossed back onto the welcome deck by a returning wave.

What set Louis apart from many others who went to sea was his 'role of a keen critic and reformer'. His exposure to the appalling conditions under which seamen lived and worked awakened a social conscience that never left him - and it was that commitment to a spirit of justice and freedom for the under-privileged, rather than the Jewish traditions in which he grew up, that he carried with him to Australia and passed on to his sons.[30]

The first to settle in Australia

Although most of the Ukrainian-born future Anzacs arrived within a period of a few years preceding the war, some of them landed in Australia much earlier and we will begin our narrative with their stories.

The first to arrive were probably the Polish family of George Marion Tchorzewski, who was a young boy when his family landed in Rockhampton, Queensland, in 1882. His parents, Ignacy Tchorzewski and Emily (née Kozlowska), settled at Bingera Plantation near Bundaberg, and established a sugar cane farm. Their second son Władysław was born there, but died in infancy. Being one of the first settlers in the area, Ignacy earned respect among local farmers and was registered in 1901 as a Justice of the Peace. In 1892, when George was naturalised, his occupation was recorded as sugar planter in Burnett Heads.[31]

The family of Emile Auguste Tardent, a Swiss Anzac born in Mykolaiv (Nikolaev) on the Black Sea, had long and diverse connections with Ukraine. The head of the family, Henry Alexis Tardent (1853-1929), a journalist, horticulturist and public figure, was born in a French family in Le Sépey in Switzerland. From his teenage years he travelled and studied in Halychyna, Ukraine and Bessarabia, learning German, Polish, Russian and Latin, and made a living by tutoring. He graduated from Odessa University, becoming a language teacher in Mykolaiv high school. His elder children, including Emile Auguste, were born in Ukraine. In 1887 the Tardents moved to Queensland, attracted by favourable accounts of the young colony. Here Henry Alexis established a farm and co-operative winery at Roma, later using his agricultural experience to manage an experimental state farm and championing the progress of agriculture as agricultural editor of the pro-Labor *Daily Standard* (1913-29). He also edited several local newspapers, was active in different cultural societies, and published a number of pamphlets.[32] Along with the promotion of Australian-French and Australian-Swiss ties, he was an ardent supporter of immigrants from the Russian Empire when they began arriving in Queensland in 1909. In particular, he was instrumental in the establishment of the first Russian colony in Wallumbilla in 1910, which included a number of Ukrainians.[33]

Tardent family in Toowoomba in 1905 (J. L. Tardent, The Swiss-Australian Tardent Family History and Genealogy)

In 1909 one of the first Ukrainian political immigrants in Queensland, Anthony Pashinsky, said how glad he was to meet Henry Tardent in the land office in Brisbane. Tardent, who had no opportunity to speak Russian for several years, confessed to the new arrival from the land of his youth:

> I love Russia with all my heart and am deeply fond of the Russian people, but as for your government! ... It is leading a splendid, wealthy and powerful country into poverty and decay. When I was a teacher in Russia I always felt deeply indignant when I saw the senseless regime it imposed on educational institutions.

His sons, born in Ukraine and Australia, later to become Anzacs, were raised by him as free men.[34]

Alexander Boronow from Odessa came to Australia in 1889 after a few months in Scotland. His tattoos suggest that he had experience as a seaman, but after landing in Sydney, he moved to the Bundaberg area in Queensland and found employment as a cane cutter. Isaac Woolf from Uman in Kyiv province came at the same time and worked as a cobbler in South Australia. Lamotte Alexis Sage from Odessa had French ancestry; his father's name was Louis and sister's was Dolora. Nevertheless, Lamotte's religion was recorded as 'Slav', which must have meant Russian Orthodox; he claimed three years' service in a 'Cossack Regiment', while his sister lived in Archangelsk. All this suggests long-standing connections with the Russian Empire. On landing in Albany in Western Australia, in 1898, he found employment in the south-western areas of the colony, working as a 'timber-cutter', 'sleeper-carter' and 'hewer' on the construction of the railway lines.[35] Christian de Rink, a mechanic, arrived in Sydney in 1899; on enlisting in the AIF, he gave his birthplace as Odessa, a claim supported by the Russian consulate, which obviously took him for a Russian subject. In 1930, however, when applying for naturalisation, he stated that he was born in Bordeaux, France, of a French father and Romanian mother. 'My parents left France when I was very young and we have resided in Odessa, Canada, England and Australia,' he wrote. We may add that subsequently he was recognised as a German, convicted in Adelaide as Schmidt and stated in his alien registration that he was 'Christian Lawrence Smidt Rinkoff (known as Rink)'. Whatever his ethnic origin, his connection with Odessa, where he was apprenticed to a man named Kochura for 6 years, seems to be true. His Orthodox religion also suggests a connection with Ukraine. In Australia he worked in the industrial centres of Broken Hill and Newcastle as an electrician and mechanic.[36]

Two future Ukrainian Anzacs arrived in Australia in quite an unusual way: they deserted from the cruiser *Gromoboi*, of the Russian navy, which visited Australia to take part in the celebrations for the Federation of the Australian colonies in 1901. One of them was Alfroniza Morozoff from Odessa,[37] who changed his name to Jack Morris. He is in all probability identical with Aphonasiy Cardapolop, i.e. Afanasy Kargopolov, whom the Victoria police listed as a deserter from the *Gromoboi*. By the time of his enlistment in the AIF, he was working as a bridge carpenter at Bunyip Swamp in Gippsland, Victoria. His mate Huon Pollejuke/Pologouck (known as Jack Pollock) at the time of desertion was recorded by the police as Ivan Polyxhonk;[38] his original name can be reconstructed as Ivan Poleshchuk. He was from 'Ollenow, Podolia' and worked as a cook in Melbourne.

MISSING from the russian warship *Gromoboi*, the undermentioned sailors :—Aphonasiy Cardapolop, Phedor Colbin, Alexander Tzerkovnicoff, Vlas Malycheff, Nicolay Bazloff, Ivan Polyxhonk, Vasyly Sysoief Dondkyn—none of them speak English.— O.4984. 27th May, 1901.

Advertisement in the Victoria Police Gazette, 1901

'Chain migration' and emerging Jewish communities

While these first arrivals came to Australia as individuals, each with his own story and reason for emigration, the first decade of the twentieth century brought groups of immigrants with shared patterns of movement and settlement, forming emerging communities of Ukrainian-born people.

The earliest of these communities consisted of Jews from Odessa and the Jewish farming colonies of Novorossia, who sailed from Odessa to Egypt, where they boarded ships bound for Australia. Their first port of call in Australia was Fremantle, the major port of Western Australia, a state where rapid economic development began only in the 1890s, with the discovery of gold in Kalgoorlie and Coolgardie. The first of these émigrés probably landed there due to a shortage of money, which did not allow them to sail on to the more populous states of Victoria and New South Wales. Their relatives and friends followed them, and the community began to grow. Later, after establishing themselves in Western Australia, some of these first settlers moved on to the eastern states.

Among these first Jewish-Ukrainian settlers in Western Australia were several families of future Anzacs. Dorothy Lazarus, a niece of the Lakovsky brothers, relates the circumstances of her family's departure from Odessa. They had, she says, earlier moved from Katerynoslav 'to Odessa, because there was more education and music for the children. Grandfather at 21 built a hotel in Odessa, he had about 250 employees. ... My grandfather spoke Russian and Yiddish. Because my mother was 14 when they came out, she had wonderful memories of Russia, as they were very wealthy people and had a very good life in Russia.' With growing social unrest the situation changed. When her grandfather witnessed the brutal repression of rebel soldiers and sailors in Odessa, 'he said to the family, "If they are doing that to themselves, what will they do to the Jews? Let's get out of here". So my grandfather paid fares for the whole lot of the relatives and brought them to Australia, to Perth.'[39] In fact the grandfather, known in Australia as Tom Lachovsky, came to Australia well ahead of the brutal crushing of the revolutionary rebellion in Odessa in 1905, portrayed by the noted film director Sergei Eisenstein in *The Battleship Potemkin*, but in Dorothy's memory events were obviously jumbled. Another granddaughter of Tom, Leah Jas, has a more precise timeline of their emigration: 'My grandfather came first to Australia. Grandfather arrived at Perth in 1899 and had a sister named Shaffer who was already here. Grandma had to wait a year and decided to come by herself with the children.'[40] Shipping records show that the grandmother 'Pascha' came to Australia with her children in 1903. We may note that the Slavonic forms of their names, which they kept in Australia, suggest their profound assimilation into the Russian-Ukrainian world of Katerynoslav and Odessa. The process of Tom's family's settlement in Australia is recounted in his obituary:

> Like many of his countrymen, Mr. Lakovsky found an attraction in the boom days of many of the Australian mining locales. Arriving in Perth, W.A., in the year 1900, he immediately proceeded to Kalgoorlie, where the rest of his family came to take up residence. Alternating between Kalgoorlie and Perth, Mr Lakovsky then proceeded East to Broken Hill which was then sufficiently attractive to hold him for several years. Broken Hill at this time enjoyed a population of over 40,000 souls. The Great East called strongly, however, and the year 1912 saw the Lakovsky family domiciled in Sydney.[41]

Tom worked as a grocer, providing supplies to the mining towns of Kalgoorlie and Broken Hill.

The other West Australian arrivals were the Lebovich, Rappeport, and Zines families. Aaron Lebovich, who came with his family in 1903, was from the Stavropol area, although his son Morris, who would die on the Western Front, claimed to be born in Odessa when he enlisted in the AIF. Aaron worked as a fish merchant in Perth and later, like Lakovsky, moved to Sydney. The Rappeport family from Nikopol ran a fruit shop, while Max Zines from Kamianets-Podilskyi, according to his naturalisation papers, was a 'marine dealer'. The family of Harry Sadagoursky came from Odessa; by 1917 he was living in Perth with his parents, working as a carter.

At the time of landing in Fremantle, the Lakovskys' sons, the future Anzacs Edward and David, were 10 and 5 respectively; Morris Lebovich was 8, Samuel Rappeport was 14 and his brother Lionel 16. Leaving fears of pogroms behind, they grew up just like other ordinary Australian city boys, with the same pursuits and interests, and undergoing the same military training compulsory for Australian boys at the time. The difference for these Jewish boys was that in Australia they had the benefits of a better start in life and a better general education than would have been their lot in the then Russian Empire. There their parents were limited to occupations connected with commerce, which they often continued to practise in Australia. By contrast, the sons mastered a broader variety of trades: Morris Lebovich was a saddler, Samuel Rappeport was a bootmaker, Joseph Morris Zines a tailor. The question of identity was probably of little concern for most of this younger generation: for them, 'Russianness' and 'Jewishness' were already giving way to a sense of being Australian – or being 'British'. This probably explains why at enlistment Edward stated that his denomination was 'Salvation Army' rather than Jewish.

In the following years, the Ukrainian Jewish community in Western Australia continued to grow. The new arrivals engaged in a combination of traditional urban trades and others more suited to the pioneering Australian outback. Thus, while Saul Haiff from Odessa worked as a tailor in Perth, Wolfe Hoffman from Podillia was a labourer and a mill hand at Jarrahdale, and Samuel Mackomel was a blacksmith. They were joined by Max Perlman and Lion Harlap from Palestine and Israel Feldman from Egypt. Perlman worked as a marine dealer, Feldman as a marine collector, while Harlap was first employed at a mill in Big Brook, but later sold fruit in Perth.

We can see similar tendencies in the south-eastern states. The pioneer of emigration here was Edward (Abram) Dryen, whose family lived in the Jewish farming colony of Veselaya in Katerynoslav province. Landing in Adelaide in 1894, he soon moved to the rapidly growing mining town of Broken Hill, where he kept a shop. His relatives on his mother's side – the brothers Albert and Samuel Harold Krantz from Novopavlivka – came ten years later. Thirteen-year-old Albert learnt the trade of carpentry in a Broken Hill mine, while Samuel, after four years in Broken Hill, moved to Perth, where he worked in a hotel. Similarly, Israel Heselev followed his brother Benjamin to Broken Hill; their family was from Uspenivka and Huliaipole (Guliaipole) in Katerynoslav province. While Benjamin managed a cake shop, Israel mastered the profession of 'machinist'.

But the major centre of Ukrainian Jewish emigration in the south-eastern states was Melbourne. Chaim Freedman, an Australian-born historian of Jewish emigration, dates the first arrivals in Melbourne from Jewish farming colonies in Katerynoslav province to 1883.[42] This was a chain of family emigration that lasted for several decades. Two future Anzacs came with this wave, Woolf Zmood and Peter Komesaroff, both from Andriivka near Berdiansk in Taurida province. Unlike young settlements in Western Australia and Broken Hill, Melbourne had a long-established Jewish community with a significant proportion of Ukrainian-born Jews. Unsurprisingly, young Zmood and Komesaroff had no chance to move outside the traditional Jewish occupations and were employed as drapers and commercial travellers, which, however, allowed them to acquaint themselves well with the country. The Heselev family from Broken Hill probably moved to Melbourne for its status as a cultural hub, as both brothers became musicians there.

Young Pinkhus Komesaroff (sitting left) with his elder siblings in Berdiansk, two years before his departure for Australia (Courtesy of Komesaroff family)

The cultural potential of Melbourne played an important role in the life of Reuben Laman Rosenfield, an Anzac connected with Ukraine who would attain the rank of major, the highest among our Anzacs. Reuben was born in 1872 in Raseiniai in Lithuania, but a few years later his family moved to Simferopol in Crimea. Here Reuben's younger siblings were born, and here he studied at a 'Government school' (most likely this was Simferopol high school or Gymnasium). His family associated themselves with Simferopol, which allows us to consider him one of the Anzacs from Ukraine. When Reuben was sixteen his family emigrated to Melbourne. Reuben was the eldest of six children. When they landed in Melbourne none of them 'could speak a word of English'. Reuben, like his father, was to become the family's breadwinner and he was apprenticed to a saddler. But this was not enough for his curious mind, which had been awakened at school in Simferopol, and he 'entered the Working-men's College, where he spent his evenings in the study of English, Latin, Algebra, Euclid and kindred subjects, working during the day at his trade and studying at night', as his first biographer tells us.[43] After three years of study he matriculated in all subjects and entered Melbourne University to study medicine. He made his living by private tutoring and remained passionately focused on his studies. Five years later he successfully graduated and received his degree in medicine. The help of several kind people – Jews and Christians alike – during those hard years prompted him to help the underprivileged through his work.

Ukraine – the Russian Far East – Queensland

A significant proportion of the Ukrainian-born Anzacs – about 47 men – came to Australia, mostly Queensland, from the Russian Far East and we will look more closely at the specific characteristics of this group. Ethnically, the majority were Ukrainians, who numbered at least 28 men; Jews numbered 11, or one quarter. The rest were Russians and Poles, and one Russified German. Jewish emigrants within this 'Far Eastern' exodus were distinguished by a significant degree of Russification. For instance five of the eleven Ukrainian Jewish Anzacs, when enlisting in the army, stated their religion as non-Jewish, which indicates either their rapid assimilation or indifference to religion. Many of them came from cosmopolitan Odessa in the wake of pogroms in the Pale of Settlement. Russification affected other migrants from Ukraine as well; many had lived for a long period in Siberia, the Russian Far East or Harbin. Their confused statements of their places of origin, such as 'Kieff near Vladivostock' and 'Poltavia, Moscow', mentioned above, might be an indication of this trend. Some, belonging to the Ukrainian families who migrated to Siberia or the Russian Far East in the late nineteenth century, were born in these parts and had no direct connection with Ukraine. For instance, Maxim Svinaboy, a man with a typically Ukrainian surname, claimed to be born in Vladivostok and as such is not included in our statistics.

Conscription for service in the Russian army, along with socio-political changes in the country, had a significant uprooting and assimilating effect on the future Anzacs. As AIF enlistment forms included a question about previous military service, we have rich data about the Russian army service of our future Anzacs. Thus John Kachan from Berdychiv (Kyiv province), Afanasey Korniack and Marian Pshevolodskey from Poritsk and Bilka in Volhynia province, Egnaty Sologub and James Gretchinsky from Konotop and Horodnia in Chernihiv province all fought in the Russo-Japanese War. According to an Australian newspaper, Gretchinsky was 'a sub-lieutenant in the Russian army'.[44] Often the veterans of the war stayed in the Russian Far East after discharge from the army and later emigrated to Australia. George Malisheff from Podillia served five years in the Russian army. James Cochura from Malomikhailivka (Katerynoslav province) served for three years in the Russian Foot Guards, coming to Australia from Vladivostok. Sebastian Radetsky from Lidykhiv in Volhynia served in the army for two years. The heads of three Ukrainian families who took land in Central Queensland – Stephan Platonoff, Matfeus Oleinikoff, and Feodot Peachenoff – also had army experience. From stories like Wolf Dorfman's, we can see that conscription usually had the same uprooting effect on Jews as it did on others. Dorfman failed to return home to Rivne (Rovno) in Volhynia, remaining in the Far East after his period of service; in 1915 he emigrated to Queensland.

Sometimes service in the Russian army was cut short or avoided altogether. Aaron Lemish from Vyshnivets in the same Volhynia province deserted soon after conscription and fled to Australia from Harbin. The one-year term of Alexander Sank's service, followed by his immediate departure to Australia, suggests that its termination might have been on his initiative. Moisey Kotton from Kremenchuk in Poltava province, when applying for naturalisation in Australia, wrote to the Australian authorities: 'Since I arrived in Australia I lived under the name of Max Kotton. The reason I done so was the fear of being send back to Russia: I have not done any crime except leaving the country, which is a crime itself according to the Russian law.'[45] He left Harbin for Brisbane in 1912 at the age of 20, on the eve of conscription. Two years later his brother Samuel followed him at exactly the same age. The reluctance of Jews to serve in the Russian army was quite understandable: besides forced assimilation, they often endured mistreatment and humiliation.

The major centre of the Russian exodus via the Far East was the rapidly growing Russian town of Harbin, established on Chinese territory as a service centre for the Chinese Eastern Railway. Besides being a centre of employment associated with the railway and thus attracting businessmen, traders and labourers of all kinds, it also enjoyed relative political freedom and racial tolerance. These factors influenced Jewish migration there in the wake of pogroms in the Pale of Settlement in the early 1900s. Unlike Slavs from Ukraine, who were mostly single young men, half of our Jewish Anzacs went to Harbin with their parents and siblings, which was the case, for instance, of Alexander Sank, George Ferber, Moisey Kotton, and Leon Rothman. Samuel Trager, who would later enlist in the AIF, came to Brisbane with his parents and four siblings.

Although family resettlement among Ukrainians was less common, some did go to the Far East with their families. Thus, the aforementioned three ex-servicemen Platonoff, Oleinikoff, and Peachenoff moved from the Far East to Australia with their wives and children. Young

Alexay Ostrinko (Osmirko) came to Brisbane at the age of 17 to join his married sister Paulina Loss-Pavlenko, who arrived a year earlier; they were from Monastyrysche in Poltava province. Constantine Pinkevitch's family from 'Jelejnetz' (Il'intsy?) in Kyiv province stayed behind in Harbin; the father of Peter Kusmin, 'John Zadorohney' lived in Vladivostok; the mother of Leonard Noweetsky, who was born in Zmerynka in Podillia, lived in Khabarovsk, the capital of the Russian Far Eastern Primorsky (Maritime) province. The wife of Egnaty Sologub, who came to Australia in 1912, stayed in Sosnovka, in Spassk *volost* (county) of the same province; this area, south of Vladivostok, was another centre of the exodus to Australia.

The social and professional backgrounds of this wave of immigrants were diverse: along with peasants and labourers, many had some form of trade, mostly in a technical field, which was not surprising due to frequent prior employment on the Trans-Siberian railway. For instance, Chernihiv Cossack Zacharias Pieven started his career as an apprentice fitter in the shipbuilding yards in Odessa; then he moved to Nizhni Novgorod in Russia, where he worked as a fitter in mechanical workshops in Sormovo, and finally in 1909 he moved to Harbin, where he was employed by the Harbin railway workshop.[46] Pshevolodskey was a carpenter, Sologub a bridge carpenter, Nikalas Kiva a tinsmith, Pinkevitch a turner, Gulevich a fitter, Sank a motor mechanic, Korniack a machinist, Andrew Snegovoy from Odessa and Joseph Rudezky from Skvyra (Kyiv province) listed their trades as motor driver or chauffeur, and Gretchinsky was an electrical engineer. The latter, working at the Bingera sugar cane plantation in 1913, applied for the position of a chauffeur, recommending himself as 'young, steady, and sober, practical all round'.[47]

 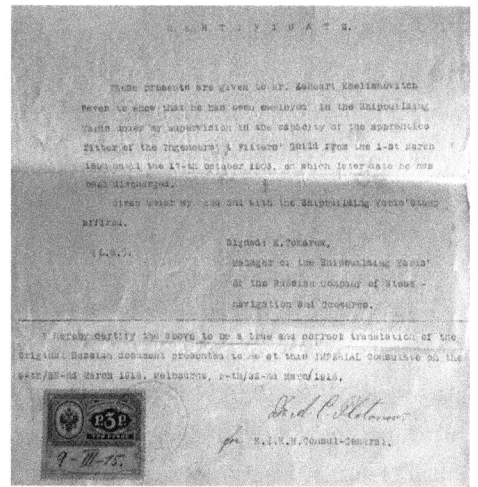

Left: Zacharias Pieven, an employee of Harbin Railway workshops
Right: Employment reference from Odessa certified by the Russian consulate in Australia (Courtesy of Piven-Large family).

Only a few had white-collar work: Noweetsky was a draughtsman, while Nicholas Fedorovich from Odessa and Richard (likely Erofei) Gregorenko from Karapyshi near Kyiv gave their occupation as clerks; Andrew Kovalevsky from Blahovishchenka in Katerynoslav province was probably a clerk too. The service sector was not large either: Vengert was a cook, George Ferber was a draper, Joseph Vurhaft a gardener, Alexander Rayzner from Odessa was a tailor. The latter belonged to a small group of future Anzacs who had professional experience in Asia beyond the Russian sector surrounding Harbin. Rayzner lived in Hong Kong for four years after leaving Russia; Dorfman travelled in Germany, Austria, the USA, China, Japan and the Philippine Islands. But Yur Kivovitch, brought up in Odessa, had the most impressive record: he was engaged in trade in South China, India and Hong Kong, and when enlisting in the AIF he claimed to have 'diplomas as an interpreter in Russian, Arabic, Turkish, German, etc., also a working knowledge of French, Italian and Spanish'. In another document it was noted that he knew 'Russian and subsidiary Slav languages', which meant most likely Ukrainian.[48]

Arriving in Brisbane, the Ukrainian émigrés were housed for a few days in Emigrant House on Kangaroo Point and then had to take any available job. Tom Volkofsky relates the hard times experienced by his father Theofil: 'He could not speak a word of English and he had to take labouring jobs. He got work on the railways, just laying sleepers … It was terribly hard work, he got as much as 200 blisters on his hands doing this work'.[49] In general, non-English speaking immigrants at that time were offered almost exclusively labouring jobs, and 'pick and shovel' work on railway construction became the most common employment for our cohort of immigrants. For instance, George Malisheff was, upon arrival, working for six months on the Evergreen-Cooyar railway.[50] Nicholas Gulevich, in spite of his training as a fitter, upon arrival 'worked on the Kannagur and Blackbutt railway line', north-west of Brisbane, and then found a job as a tailer at a sawmill near Benarkin in the same area.[51] Feodot Peachenoff from Bratske in Kyiv province, who came in 1911, leaving his family behind in Russia, found employment on the same line, the Benarkin railway extension where Gulevich was employed. Within four months he moved north to work on the Booyal railway extension in the rapidly developing cane growing area near Bundaberg; only 16 months later he earned enough money to pay for tickets for his wife and daughter. The Platonoff family (father and two sons) who came a month after Peachenoff, immediately set off for the Cordalba-Dallarnil railway construction in the same area of Bundaberg. Stephen Loosgie (Lushchik) from Voloskivtsi in Chernihiv province likewise worked on the railway. John Mamchin's railway experience is glimpsed in the words of his medical report, in his AIF service record, which indicates that in 1915 he developed 'rheumatism while working in water on [a] railway line'.[52]

Many Ukrainians worked in the mines. Gregory Piddubny, a journalist who was born as Tolmachev in Kharkiv province, in his book *Midiani Zagravy,* described his experience in the Mount Chalmers copper mines, where he met some fellow-countrymen.[53] Among the miners were a number of future Ukrainian Anzacs. Afanasey Korniack, landing at Townsville, set out a few weeks later for one of the most remote areas of Queensland, Cloncurry and Friezland (later renamed Kuridala). This was the centre of copper mining, with several smelters operating in the area. He would work there until his enlistment in the AIF. We have little information about Egnaty Sologub's initial employment in Queensland, but he enlisted in the AIF at Cloncurry, where he was obviously working or attempting to find employment at the mines. Stephen Surovsov found employment at the Balgowan Colliery near Oakey, west of Toowoomba. Constantine Pinkevitch worked for four years in another mining hub, Mount Morgan near Rockhampton, where the mines produced gold, silver and copper. Stephen Provaka, after working for several months in Jandowae, probably building a railway there, moved to Mount Morgan and became a miner.

In general, accidents in the Australian mining industry were quite common at the time. For example, James Cochura, who came from Vladivostok to Sydney, initially moved to the remote mining town of Cobar in central western NSW. Within a few months he had moved to West Maitland in the Newcastle area and was working in a coal mine in Kogarah. In a mining accident there, he severely injured his right thigh and fractured his skull. Notes taken in the military hospital during the war briefly described his ordeal:

> unconscious for some hours (3 or 4) woke in Hospital and remained there 2 weeks and went back to work at Mine. Skin [on the skull] grew together in 6 weeks – then began to lose work owing to headache and giddiness.

He continued to have severe headaches, but had to continue working. When he had recovered somewhat he moved to another mining town, Broken Hill, where a community of Russian and Ukrainian-born émigrés was growing.[54] Maxim Shular from Sosnytsia in Chernihiv province, had injured his knee at work in Mount Morgan mines. Theofil Volkofsky, after his baptism in Australian working conditions on railway construction sites, worked in opal mines in Lighting Ridge, NSW, and eventually developed tuberculosis.

Another common occupation was cane cutting in Northern Queensland. This was a hard seasonal job, but high wages attracted many to test their endurance. Among our group the cane cutters were Nicholas Fedorovich, a man with literary talents educated at a university, who worked in the Cairns area, and James Gretchinsky, another cultured man who worked at a plantation near Bingera. John Kachan, Andrew Kovalevsky, Leonard Noweetsky, Nicholas Roomianzoff, and Nickefor Domilovsky, who enlisted in the AIF in sugar cane areas, were probably also cane cutters. Thomas Pesmany from Hlukhiv in Chernihiv province worked in the Bundaberg area as well, later moving to Melbourne and Sydney.

In those years the swagman, a seasonal labourer, was a characteristic feature of the Australian socio-cultural landscape. It is quite possible that some among them were Ukrainians who ventured to the interior of the country. For instance, Andrew Snegovoy wrote in his naturalisation that he worked 'at country nearly all over Queensland'.[55] George Ferber, a Jewish youth from Melitopol, at first worked in the traditionally Jewish occupation of a draper, but when enlisting in the army he claimed to be a stockman – a common outback trade. Another Jewish youth, Max Kotton, after trying a number of jobs in South Queensland, finally settled in the small township of Naughtons Gap, near Lismore in NSW. He worked as a carter, winning the love and respect of local farmers.

A few future Anzacs, after several years of hard work in railway construction or cane cutting, managed to save enough money to buy a farm, usually a sugar cane plantation. Thus Nicholas Gulevich by 1914 was already a sugar cane farmer at Figtree Creek near Cairns, as was Constantine Pinkevitch. A group of Anzacs-to-be with families took up land in the sugar cane growing area around Cordalba in 1912-1913. The heads of three of these families had previously served in the Russian army. They were Matfeus Oleinikoff (who had eight children), Feodot Peachenoff with one daughter, and Stephan Platonoff with two adult sons.

Only a few, with a trade that was in demand, could secure employment in the cities. For instance Alexander Sank, a motor mechanic, wrote in his autobiography that he worked as a driver and a sailor, as well as in factories and workshops.[56] Yur Kivovitch, a 'linguist', worked for a while as a subcollector of customs in Townsville and then as a refreshment room keeper. Marian Pshevolodskey probably worked as a carpenter in Brisbane, while Leon Rothman worked as a jeweller.

Still, some managed to find their fortune in their new homeland. In 1927 Theofil Volkofsky could proudly say: 'I landed in Australia without money or knowledge of English, yet I worked myself from a pick and shovel man to a station owner',[57] but behind those simple words lay some hard times. After his arduous experience in railway construction and in the mines, as his son relates, he

> moved down to Sydney. He always liked fishing and he got work in the fish-market in Sydney, […] but he thought he wouldn't do that all his life.
>
> He heard that in western New South Wales there were jobs on properties, so he thought he could have a look at that. He got on the railway and went out to Bourke. Arriving in Bourke, he only had a shilling in his pocket. Somebody told him there was fish in the Darling River, so he went and bought a fishing line, just because he wanted his own food. He went down to the river and he caught a magnificent, big Murray cod, which he took back up to the hotel and he sold it to the hotel and bought some more fishing lines … he could see this fish would be popular in Sydney, so he started sending them to Sydney.
>
> This was very successful, so successful he sent to Europe for Cezar, his brother, to come out, and he came out and they worked on it together. They had as many as 50 fishing nets and 200 fishing lines in the Darling River at one time … The farmers started to go crook, they reckoned the sheep were not able to get down to the river bank. So he moved to an island in the Darling River to upgrade his business. They made their own fishing-boat out of local trees, using carved limbs for the frame.[58]

Ukrainian émigrés in Queensland communal life

Stories of individual outback success like that of Volkofsky aside, we might note that the characteristic feature of Ukrainian émigré life in Queensland was its communal nature. Intermingled with Slavs and other peoples from the Russian Empire, they came to Australia from the Russian Far East often in groups, setting off together to look for employment or congregating with their compatriots upon arriving at the mines, railway construction sites or cane plantations. At this point we will look more closely at the socio-economic and cultural networks which incorporated Ukrainian émigrés in Queensland before the First World War.

During the years 1909-1915, about three thousand émigrés departing from Harbin and the Russian Far East via Japan landed in Queensland ports, mainly in Brisbane.[59] The total number of arrivals from Russia to Australia during these years was over six thousand, but it should be noted that each year about 30 per cent of these left Australia,[60] so the total number of Russian-born émigrés in Queensland probably never exceeded three or four thousand, in spite of claims by the Russian consul Alexander Abaza that the population of Russian nationals in Queensland stood at five thousand.[61] Whatever the number, at a conservative estimate Ukrainian-born émigrés amounted to at least 30 per cent of them, and Slavs among the latter accounted for 75 per cent; most of these Slavs were ethnic Ukrainians.[62]

The numbers of Russian born émigrés in Queensland were high enough to establish a vibrant communal life, in which Ukrainians and Ukrainian-born people played an important role from the very beginning. Their presence was noted in the first report on the establishment of the Russian Association in Brisbane during the Christmas holidays of 1911. Having decided to celebrate Christmas according to the Gregorian rather than the Russian (Julian) calendar, on Christmas Day the émigrés attended the Greek Orthodox Church service in St Luke's Church, conducted in 'two Russian dialects' as well as English and Syriac. On 27 December they held a concert in St Mary's Parish Hall at Kangaroo Point. 'Two sets of national songs were sung', noted the reporter, 'those of North and South Russia – the dialects being widely different. In fact, the people of these countries may be said to be almost of different nationalities. In the crowd last night it was an easy matter to pick out the fair skinned Northern man or woman and the dark haired Southerner.'[63] The Australian reporter was obviously describing the Ukrainian presence, but did not know how to name this nation and its language. The highlight of the concert was 'a little drama attributed to the great Russian poet [sic] Gogol', a writer beloved by both Russians and Ukrainians, 'which was acted with ability'.

Although the rapidly growing community of immigrants in Brisbane cherished their ethnic identities, be they Ukrainian, Russian, Polish or Jewish, there was a significant sympathy towards internationalism, proletarian internationalism moreover, which allowed all these ethnic groups to intermix. Symptomatically, the name of the major émigré association founded in Brisbane in December 1911 was changed by January 1916 from *Soiuz russkikh emigrantov* (the Union of Russian Emigrants) to *Soiuz rossiiskikh emigrantov*, which can be translated as the Union of Russian-born Emigrants. Later it was renamed to *Soiuz rossiskikh rabochikh* (Union of Russian-born Workers). The more elegant translation of this name, Union of Russian Emigrants/Workers, is somewhat misleading, as its founders intentionally replaced the word *russkii* (ethnic Russian) with the word *rossiiskii* (the adjective derived from the name of the country *Rossiia*/Russia) to avoid limiting the nationality of its members to ethnic Russians only. The use of the word 'emigrants' rather than 'immigrants' in the Union's name is noteworthy as well, revealing this group's characteristic emphasis on their exodus from Russia rather than their settling in Australia. To add to the confusion, it should be mentioned that in English this Union was usually referred to as the Russian Association. The Jewish association was accordingly named the Jewish Workers' Association, and admitted as members only proletarian Jews from the territory of the Russian Empire.[64]

The good wages that many émigrés enjoyed from labouring jobs allowed them to provide financial support to Union initiatives. From as early as 1913, the Union planned to open its own premises.[65] This eventuated in 1915 when rooms opened on Stanley Street, providing a place for weekly meetings and lectures as well as a growing library, which numbered 1000 volumes by 1916. Besides books, many of which were donated by the émigrés or bought overseas, the library subscribed to a number of Russian periodicals, published its catalogue and mailed the materials on demand to readers far from Brisbane. Russian libraries were also established in Melbourne, Sydney, Ipswich, Cairns, Port Pirie, Broken Hill and other places.

Ukrainians actively participated in Union activities from the very beginning but, disappointed that its library stocked only Russian-language books and periodicals, formed the Ukrainian Workers' Circle (Український робітничий гурток) in 1915.[66] From its inception, the Circle aimed to meet the cultural needs of Ukrainians all over Australia. The news of its formation was accompanied by a note informing Ukrainians that 'The Circle's library has books, journals and newspapers in the Ukrainian language, which are sent on demand all over Australia'.[67] Like the Union of Russian-born Workers, which combined political and cultural activities, the Circle had a strong political and class-oriented bent alongside its cultural agenda.[68] The activists who facilitated the work of the Circle were Gordon Melashich, Gregory Piddubny and Gregory Harchenko. The highlight of its activities was the performance in 1915 of Taras Shevchenko's historical play *Nazar Stodolia*, directed by Sergey Alimoff, a political émigré from Kharkiv. Among the actors were Harchenko and Melashich, as well as Mrs Rudovskaya and Mrs Gorbun. The profits from the performance were used to support the Circle's library and political prisoners in Russia.[69]

The Ukrainian journals and magazines that the Circle's library stocked were mostly émigré publications ordered from Canada and the USA. Letters intercepted by Australian censors list a number of such orders from Piddubny to the USA and Switzerland for *Haydamaky* and *Narodna Volia*.[70] The library also subscribed to the Canadian periodicals *Robochyi Narod, Chervonyi Kobzar, Novyny*,[71] *Rada* (Kyiv), *Ukrains'ke zhittia* (Moscow), and *Robitnyk* (Detroit).[72] By August 1916 the library boasted 40 Ukrainian titles.[73] Ukrainians responded to this initiative well, as may be seen from a list of donors to the Ukrainian library from Cairns, published in January 1917 in the Brisbane Russian newspaper.[74] The library was originally located in Brisbane, but in 1916 it moved with G. Melashich to Cobar, and in February 1917 from Cobar to Sydney. By that time it held more than 100 volumes of 'the best Ukrainian writers' and received 'newspapers of International orientation'. It sent books to Ukrainians all over Australia. G. Melashich was still the Circle's secretary.[75]

Another organisation in which Ukrainians took an active part was the Society of Support for Political Deportees and Prisoners in Russia, established in Australia in 1913. In 1914 one more political organisation, with a specifically Ukrainian focus, was established in Brisbane, named the Group of Support for Russian and Ukrainian Socialist-Revolutionary Parties.[76]

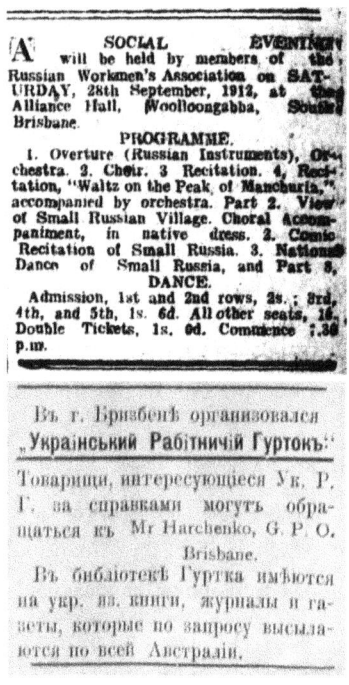

Top left: Ukrainian performing arts, disguised as 'Small Russian', played an important role in the activities of the Union of Russian-born Workers (The Telegraph, 1912)

Bottom left and right: The Union newspaper informed its readers about the activities of the Ukrainian Workers' Circle

The communal nature of the early Ukrainian and other émigrés in Queensland manifested itself in different forms, not only politically. As we have seen in the examples of our Anzacs, the majority in the first years after their arrival led a nomadic life. During the early 1910s it gradually assumed a regular pattern. In summer they congregated in Brisbane for the Christmas break. These reunions held the attraction of opportunities to meet their compatriots, enjoy cultural and social activities organised by the Union of Russian-born Workers, and sometimes indulge in gambling. In the first months of the new year, when money ran out, they moved to the country to build railways, and further north to cut cane. Those with a trade or business skills remained in Brisbane. Some, finding only short-term employment, would return to Brisbane a few months later to recuperate and renew acquaintances again, but their largest gatherings would await the next Christmas festivities. Gradually an infrastructure which catered to their needs grew up on the south bank of the Brisbane River, in the areas adjoining the Immigration Depot on Kangaroo Point. The area of settlement of Russian-born émigrés (mostly Russian, Ukrainian and Jewish) extended from South Brisbane between Merivale and Stanley Streets, and continued to the neighbouring suburb of Woolloongabba along Stanley Street and Logan Road, with a considerable Jewish enclave on Deshon Street known as 'Little Jerusalem'.[77] By the time of the war, natives of the Russian Empire comprised the fourth largest émigré community in Brisbane.

Half a dozen Russian boarding houses grew up around the Union headquarters, which were situated on Stanley Street, between Russell and Glenelg Streets. The Ukrainian presence within them was quite significant. George Kelemnuk from Podillia opened his boarding house and canteen, proudly named 'Moscow', next to the Union. Benjamin Barcan from Białystok likewise enjoyed the advantages of this location. In 1915 the advertisement for his business read: 'After a meeting at the Union do not forget to call in to the Russian tailor, right opposite Malinowsky's fruit-shop on Stanley St'. Simon Malinowsky, the owner of this shop, was from Kamianets-Podilskyi. The 'Adelaide' boarding house, popular with émigrés, and John Shouiupoff's shop were a block to the west of the Union along Stanley Street. Two blocks to the east was Paul Stoopachenko's boarding house (Stoopachenko was from Poltava). The 'Kiev' boarding house was further south-east in Woolloongabba.

Russian, Ukrainian, and Jewish businesses grew up nearby. A Russian family from Odessa with the English name Douglas opened a 'Russian' fruit and grocery shop on the corner of Melbourne and Hope Streets and supplemented their income with several boarders. The shop of Stephen Dimbisky, another native of Kamianets-Podilskyi, was on Stanley Street. Panteleimon Brovkoff from Podolsk offered his skills as a carpenter; Nicholas Shlensky mended Russian boots in the premises of his Victoria boarding house on Albert Street, while Efim Crafti, a former political prisoner from Sevastopol in Ukraine, had a well-established furniture business in the 'Coupon' shop in Fiveways, Woolloongabba. Crafti also sold tickets for steamboats returning to Russia and worked as an interpreter.

The presence of new arrivals from the Russian Empire was so noticeable by 1915 that many local businesses in the South Brisbane and Woolloongabba area started catering especially for them. The Signal Cash Store on Logan Road, Woolloongabba, for example, advertised delivery of 'fresh herring from Riga', and stocked 'especially for Russian customers sunflower oil, bay leaf and pork lard'. Other businesses – chemists, a dentist, a hairdresser, a jeweller, a photography studio, a hardware store, etc. – employed Russian-speaking shop assistants. Thus, émigrés from all over Queensland could send their orders to the chemist in Russian and have the necessary medicine dispatched to them. Similarly, Joseph Mirgorodsky from Melitopol, the printer of the first Russian newspaper in Australia, also owned a bookshop that sold Russian-English dictionaries with delivery to the railway construction camps. A few bookshops ordered Russian books by demand and stocked Russian gramophone records.[78]

Russian newspapers published in Australia, in spite of their obvious pro-socialist tendencies, were instrumental in uniting Russian-speaking émigrés. Through them, émigrés could learn of the local workers' movement and international affairs. They also provided a platform for correspondence from Russian speakers all over Australia, for debate on burning issues such as conscription, and even for poetry. At least one third of the newspapers' space was devoted to advertisements concerning social meetings, parties, and picnics, as well as for businesses providing services to the community.

The Union of Russian-born Workers, like the Ukrainian Workers' Circle, supported an active cultural life. It had a theatrical committee, which arranged performances during the community's Christmas gatherings. The Jewish Workers' Association also produced several Russian-language plays as part of its holiday entertainment. Sometimes Slav and Jewish socialists clubbed together to raise money and put on shows. In 1915 they jointly organised a masked ball with prizes for the best 'ideological' costume. Russian revolutionary songs were also in demand, but it would be unjust to portray such events as purely ideological. Above all they were about socialising and fun. Australian newspaper reports described in detail such exotic 'Russian' entertainments as *balalaika* concerts, while Vladimir Nasedkin, a political emigrant from Ukraine, remarked of those years that 'to marry, especially after the perfect evenings organized by the Russian colony, was not in the least difficult as the [Australian] girls dreamt of Russian dances and songs'. In many cases, these 'Russian' songs and dances were in fact Ukrainian. In Melbourne, the community of immigrants from the Russian Empire organised a Russian musical circle and balalaika orchestra.[79]

Looking at this young multiethnic community, we might wonder about the ethnic and cultural identities of our heroes – who among them was Ukrainian or Polish, who was Russian or Jewish. These identities were often not as clear-cut as we modern historians would like them to be. Piddubny, a political émigré who carried his Ukrainian identity through years of Russian exile and was always on the lookout for his compatriots, wrote that in Australia 'Ukrainians mostly speak among themselves in a characteristic Russian-Ukrainian 'industrial' jargon, a mixture spoken by the workers and employees of the [Chinese] Eastern Railway and industrial towns in Ukraine'.[80] If we are to add to this their acceptance of being named 'Russians' by the Australian public and the authorities, one might believe that their Ukrainian identities were rapidly dissipating. In many cases this was not true. In spite of the Russian Empire's long history of Russianisation, which for instance prohibited education in Ukrainian, and the nation's rapid industrialisation, which uprooted the most active Ukrainians from their ancestral homes, they preserved an affinity with their traditional culture. We can witness this in the snippets of information that appear in the Australian sources about their life in the new land of Australia, be this Ukrainian folk songs and dances, socialist periodicals published by numerous Ukrainian exile communities in America and Europe, or simply their time spent camping together while working in the mines or cutting cane.[81] Jews from Ukraine settling in Brisbane after a period spent in Siberia or Harbin experienced similar processes of influence by the dominant Russian culture, while maintaining connection with their Ukrainian-based traditional Yiddish culture. Characteristically, Jewish émigrés from the Russian Empire (many from Ukraine), feeling themselves alien among the English Jewry of Brisbane, organised their own Deshon Street Synagogue.[82]

The future Ukrainian Anzacs were part of this Russian-Ukrainian-Jewish world rapidly developing in South Brisbane. The trial by fire of their multifaceted ethnic identities was to be the melting pot of army service.

Seamen and tradesmen in other states

In the south-eastern states, the presence of Ukrainian-born immigrants was probably not significant enough to be described as fully formed communities, only 'emerging communities' similar to the loose-knit Western Australian communities discussed above. The largest number of Ukrainian-born future Anzacs outside Queensland was in New South Wales, especially in Sydney. We can name at least 25 men who congregated in this state on the eve of war; ten more were in Victoria, nine in South Australia, and five in Western Australia. As in Queensland, these were mostly new arrivals who disembarked there in the early 1910s, and as in Queensland they were mostly Slavs, with Jews comprising a little over a quarter of them.

The characteristic feature of this group was the prevalence of seafaring occupations. Many of them, having arrived just a few years before the war, continued working on coastal vessels, not staying long in any one place. When the war began, some were stranded in Australia. It is interesting to note that at least three Ukrainian-born men, when enlisting in the AIF, gave their address in Sydney as 233 Commonwealth St, Surry Hills. They were Jacob Leffow from Chernihiv, Cemon Afendikoff from Odessa and Daniel Rodenko from Kharkiv; the latter however was rejected by the army due to lack of English. All were seamen, and we can suppose that this was the address of some sort of seamen's boarding house.

Among the sailors, we find several young Jewish men with a peculiar pattern of immigration: they had usually settled in America with their parents as children, and signed on as crewmen on ships which took them to Australia; among them we find George Koty from Kyiv and Morris Rothstein from 'Cherkavosk', ship's painter Ben Goffin from Tulchyn in Podillia and marine mechanic Alexander Belfort from Odessa.

Seamen often had to be versatile to survive and, when stranded on shore, took a variety of different employments. The history of Boris Poselnikoff is typical of this group. He went to sea when his parents died; in 1912, as a sailor aboard a Russian sailing ship, he disembarked in Newcastle, aged 22. There he stayed for two months and worked on fishing boats, then spent four months in inland New South Wales working on farms. On returning to the coast, he signed up as a sailor on a German ship leaving for Hamburg, and came back to Sydney nine months later. He then decided to try his luck in Melbourne, where he found a job as a scaffolder, applying the skills he had learned on the masts and spars of sailing ships. Then followed a new contract on a German ship to London. In May 1914 he returned to Melbourne and resumed his scaffolding job there. Clearly finding that his long Russian surname was difficult for foreigners to pronounce, he changed his name to Robert Nicholson. Joseph Kleshenko from Dubno in Volhynia, unlike Nicholson, aimed to stay in Sydney when he arrived from San Francisco in 1912, taking whatever chances came his way: first he found work on a merry-go-round in Manly, then worked as a deck-hand on Manly Ferry steamers, then as a tram conductor.

A few like Poselnikoff/Nicholson tried farm labouring jobs in the country. William Kolesnikov arrived in Fremantle aboard the Russian tramp steamer *Neva* in 1907, and first set off to Narrogin, where he was employed clearing land. He then moved to Kalgoorlie, where he worked at mining and gardening, then to Perth, where for a year he worked in cafés before finally taking a job at a bark mill. George Kamishansky, after landing in Melbourne in 1913, set off to Wanalta rural district near Echuca, probably finding some work on a farm there, but three months later he took a seafaring job with an interstate coastal service. Frank Dynowski, born into a well-to-do Polish family in Kyiv, after studying for three years at Leipzig University, came to Australia in 1914 and worked as a labourer at Bugaldie, north of Dubbo. Cezar Wolkowsky joined his older brother Theofil Volkofsky in Bourke on the Darling River, where they set up their fishing business; he arrived on the day war broke out in Europe and at first did not think it would affect them. Albert Morozoff from Odessa deserted from a Norwegian ship in Port Adelaide during the war and enlisted in the army after a short stay at Murray Bridge in South Australia.

In a few months Cezar Wolkowsky will change his smart Australian clothes to an army uniform (Courtesy of Peter Tilleard)

Ivan Rossoggsky, a young Ukrainian seaman, came to Australia not long before the war and found employment at Glenrock station near Moonan Flat, northwest of Newcastle. He learnt English as he went, picking it up from the local people. When he joined the army, an officer recorded his name as 'Rossoggsky', noting 'Cannot spell in English'. His place of birth was recorded as Odessa, but on the same form, when the officer gave up trying to write the address of his next of kin, Ivan himself wrote in Russian 'Vyndery, Cherson Province, P.A. Rossovsky', which suggests that his surname was misspelt, while the place of his origin might have been the township of Bendery. In spite of all these language difficulties, he seemed to fit well in the rural milieu, being 'of a jovial disposition, hard-working, and honest, and liked by all who knew him'. Later his local friends remembered that he was 'familiarly known as 'Pedro''. This is an interesting testimony, reflecting perhaps the process of Ivan's assimilation into the outback world: losing his distinctly Russian/Ukrainian name Ivan, he acquired a new one, Pedro, which still retained a hint of otherness, reflecting how Ivan might have appeared in the eyes of his new friends.[83]

Ivan Rossoggsky's attestation paper (NAA)

Others, like those who arrived in Queensland, sought work in the mines. Ksenofont Kozachuk from Kosivka near Skvyra, Kyiv province, arrived in Sydney in January 1914 from Canada, probably as a seaman. His acquaintance with New South Wales began with mining in the coal fields of Kurri Kurri, near Newcastle. A few months later he migrated to the mines at Mount Morgan in Queensland and worked there for eight months before leaving to cut cane in Bundaberg. From there he moved back to Mount Morgan, but soon left for the Helensburgh and Cobar mines in NSW. By the new cane cutting season he was back in Queensland, working on sugar cane farms near Cairns. Peter Kusmin was working as a coal miner in Newcastle at the time he joined the army. Joe Felipor (whose name was actually Filipov) from Odessa set off to the gold mine at Day Dawn in the deserts of Western Australia. Another miner was Mitrofan Koropets from Dobrotove in Chernihiv province, who worked in New South Wales.

Several seamen who landed in South Australia went to work at the smelters in Port Pirie. Among them we find Alexander Sast from Odessa, Carl Kills from Volhynia, Vasily Kavitski from Olshanskaia Slobodka in Kyiv province, and Joseph Rudovsky, a Croat posing as a native of Odessa. A 'Russian Workers Group' with a library was organised there not long before the war, and among its leading members was a Ukrainian named Sebastian Radetsky. Australian newspapers reported that in June 1914 'A meeting of the Russian Club was held at Port Pirie West […], when Mr. S. Radetsky presided over an attendance of between 40 and 50 members.' The meeting condemned an order which banned members of the radical Industrial Workers of the World from speaking in the streets. 'We show our internationality and identity of interests by taking our places in the fight to help the I.W.W. in their struggle,' stated the resolution of the meeting, probably drafted by Radetsky.[84]

As with the Queensland émigrés, only those few with an adaptable trade were able to afford city life. The engine fitter Efim Maximenko, who had been an apprentice on the railways in Russia, worked in Sydney; Morris Saffar from Volhynia worked as a mechanic in Perth, and John Cherpiter as a boot-maker in Adelaide. Sydney also allowed several future Jewish Anzacs to find a market for their skills: Hyman Broon and Abraham Smoishen from Kherson, and Morris Leneve from Kyiv worked as tailors; Isaac Chain from Odessa was a cigarette manufacturer, Frank Goldstein from Ruzhyn was a jeweller, and Wolfe Greenstein from Odessa mastered the printing trade. By the time war came the Jewish seaman Louis Brodsky was a family man: he ran a shop 'with a big 2/6d sign on the window' for 'clothes cleaning and dyeing', as his son Alexander remembers, and there 'Dad twirled his black moustache and ranted about socialism with his friends'.[85] Unlike the more nomadic Ukrainians, Jewish men tended to settle permanently; nearly all of them had families of their own or, like Greenstein, lived with their parents.

Some of our Anzacs, although claiming white-collar or blue-collar occupations at enlistment, probably did not manage to find such employment in Australia. This might be the case with the mechanic Ivan Gorodezky from Lipivka near Kamianets-Podilskyi and the clerk Dermy (Demetry) Morozoff from Kharkiv. The only exceptions were Alexander Winning, the Englishman born in Kharkiv, who worked in Perth as a draughtsman, and Roland Arthur Cooper, born in Mariupol, with the same occupation in Sydney.

As in the Queensland group, many arrivals in the southern states had experience of service in the Russian army and especially navy. Three seamen from Odessa had naval experience: Alexander Sast claimed to have served for five years in the Russian Navy in the Baltic; Walter Pivinski had served two years, and Albert Morozoff seven, adding that he had fought in the 'Balkan War'.

The case of Elias Jacob Serebrennikoff is interesting in this respect. He was born in a Jewish family in Mikhailivka near Melitopol; his father was probably Iosif Vladimirovich Serebrennikov. The family was emancipated: the children studied in Russian high schools and Jacob's elder sister Berta participated in the revolutionary movement. When enlisting in the AIF, Jacob gave his religion as Greek Orthodox and his occupation as clerk, but his medical records indicate that his original profession was that of a botanist. Alongside this rare profession, he had a lengthy military record. During his five-year service with the Russian Dragoons, he was engaged in suppressing the Boxer Rebellion in China in 1900 and fought in the Russo-Japanese war. When enlisting in the AIF, his rank was recorded as sergeant major, although later he was described in Australian newspapers as a colonel.[86] Another colonel was the German Alexander Spisbah, who came to Albany, WA, in 1911 as a German national, but later consistently claimed to be a Russian born in St Petersburg and was finally naturalised as a Russian born in Kharkiv. He was indeed a colonel while living in St Petersburg, working as an accountant in the Quartermaster service of the Army headquarters in 1909. For some reason he left his comfortable position and in 1910 went to Liverpool in England with young Lydia Batoulin from Orenburg. They married in Liverpool and, with a newborn son, sailed to Australia, where Alexander found employment at Mornington Mill south of Perth.

While many of these men probably thought they had found new lives, new communities and new friends in Australia, events unfolding in distant Europe were about to change their worlds forever.

Enlisting in the army in Cairns, Nickefor Domilovsky (top right) did not forget his family in the village of Stavishche in Ukraine. Together with this photograph, he sent them a block of chocolate with gold hidden inside, which saved his sister Matryona's family during WWI. (Courtesy of Valerie Tereshchenko)

TWO

WAR

Nikalas Kiva (right, standing) with his friends Osiph Rinkevich (standing), William Averkoff (sitting left), and Constantine Diachkoff, while training in the camp in Brisbane (Courtesy of Rinkevich family)

Paths to the war

At the outbreak of the First World War there were certain political similarities between Ukraine and Australia. Both were part of empires – the Russian and Austro-Hungarian in the first case and the British in the second – and their people had to follow the paths chosen by their rulers. At the same time, patriotism and propaganda in both countries conspired to make this war a people's war. Four hundred thousand people in Australia and millions in Ukraine enlisted in the army or were otherwise affected over the course of the conflict. But there were important differences. In Australia, this war, named the Great War, became a keystone of national history and an important factor in uniting the new nation, which had been formed just thirteen years earlier from six British colonies. In Ukraine, the revolutions of 1917 and Russian withdrawal from the war in 1918 were followed by the formation of a short-lived Ukrainian state and the destructive Civil War of 1918-1921. While in Australia the war and its participants were remembered, studied and cherished, in Ukraine, as in Russia in general, it was forgotten for decades, overshadowed by the Civil War, the famine of 1932-33 and terror of the 1930s unleashed by Stalin, and the Second World War. It is only recently that Ukrainian historians have turned to this important page in Ukrainian history.

While in Ukraine – as in the Russian Empire as a whole – men were conscripted to the army, in Australia overseas service in the army was voluntary; nevertheless, some Ukrainian-born men enlisted in the AIF. As mentioned above, by the outbreak of war there were at least a thousand natives of Ukraine residing in Australia; 134 of them enlisted. The proportion joining the army was not high compared with, for example, the Latvian community.[1] However, their enlistment in Australia's volunteer army is an interesting phenomenon, and one which merits investigation, as far as the documents permit. Their motives for enlisting were diverse – as diverse as were these immigrants themselves.

About a quarter among them – mostly Jews – were naturalised, which indicates that by the time of the war they had made Australia their home. Now, many of them sought to join the Australian Army. Characteristically, these were the same Jews who had fled Russia in order to avoid conscription there. Max Kotton, who had left Harbin to avoid conscription and was working as a carter at Naughtons Gap, NSW, made several attempts to join the AIF when war broke out. When he finally succeeded the local newspaper reported: 'Mr. M. Kotton, who succeeded in passing the medical test, is a naturalised Russian, and is only 5 ft. high. The minimum height is 5 ft 2 in, and Mr. Kotton was pleased when he was admitted as a bugler. He is very anxious to get to the front.'[2]

It was quite natural that among those young men who had come to Australia from Ukraine as children in the years before the war, a feeling of duty towards their new home had developed, mingled, perhaps, with a spirit of adventure. Peter Komesaroff, for example, came to Australia at the age of 14 with his siblings, and lived in Melbourne 'with his sister and brother-in-law and worked in their drapery shop', according to his daughter, 'until he ran away to New South Wales, put his age up to 22 years and 10 months, and enlisted in Cootamundra. How they could have believed him is amazing! In the only photo existing of him in uniform he looks like a boy scout.'³ Komesaroff was then only 17. Nineteen-year-old Leon Rothman was discharged in Brisbane as 'under age', at his parents' request. Samuel Trager enlisted in Sydney, far from his parents, who lived in Brisbane, on two occasions, in 1915 and in 1917; first as a native of Mykolaiv, and then as a 'natural born British subject' born in Brisbane. Although in 1915 he was just 16, in each case he gave his age as 21 years and 1 month, as after that age a would-be recruit did not need his parents' consent.⁴ Young Harry Sadagoursky from Odessa, at the opposite end of Australia, in Perth, rushed to enlist in August 1914, but was rejected because he had 'under chest measurement',

Peter Komesaroff (Courtesy of Thelma Webberley)

i.e. was too lean. He tried his luck again two years later, stating that he was 21 years and 11 months old, but several months later we was discharged as 'under age', as he was in fact only 18.⁵ Roland Arthur Cooper, who moved with his parents to Australia at the age of ten, was a teenager at the outbreak of the war. He served in the Militia in Sydney before his parents allowed him to enlist in the AIF in 1917, at nineteen. Wolfe Greenstein, born in Odessa in 1899, could hardly wait until he turned 18; he joined the AIF in June 1918, not long before the end of the war. Among the young recruits we again meet our acquaintances: the Lakovsky brothers and Morris Lebovich from Sydney, 18-year-old George Platonoff from Cordalba, who enlisted before his elder brother Thomas, Joseph Zines from Perth, and Alexander Sank from Rockhampton.

On the other hand, several of the oldest Ukrainian natives, who came to Australia in their youth, did their best to reduce their age at enlistment. Thus George Tchorzewski, a cane farmer from Burnett Heads, claimed to be born in 1876, though according to his naturalisation he was born in 1870; had he revealed his true age, he would not have been accepted. Alexander Boronow, another cane farmer from North Queensland, stated when naturalised that he was born in 1859 or 1861, but in the army he tried to pass for a man born in 1872; he

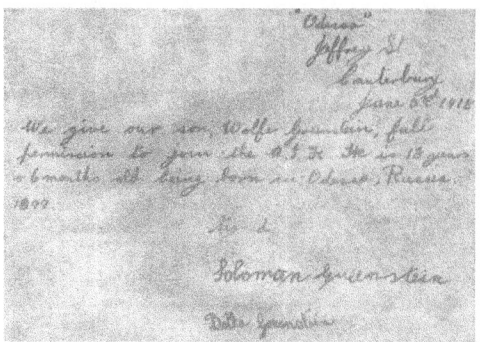

Young Wolfe Greenstein managed to get his parents' permission to enlist in the AIF only at the end of the war (SL NSW)

never reached the front, being discharged as medically unfit six months later. Christian Rink also claimed to be 12 years younger. The determination of these men to enlist in the AIF might well have been due to Australian patriotic feeling.

This was clearly the case with 36-year-old Emile Auguste Tardent from Ipswich, who had four young children by the time he enlisted. His father Henry Alexis Tardent supported the cause of the war, and the sentiment was shared by his family: three of his sons and a nephew joined the AIF. We learn about young Thomas Pesmany's efforts in support of the war from a newspaper report about a garden party at Kedron in Brisbane in June 1915, where he took part in a featherweight wrestling match, all proceeds from which went to the Red Cross Society.[6] Two months later he enlisted in the army himself. David Borszcer, a Jewish musician from Bershad in Podillia, came to Australia in June 1915 with the Belgian Band with the purpose of raising money for the Belgian Relief Fund. A number of the members of this band were Russian nationals, and Russian music, including Tchaikovsky's '1812 Overture', featured as highlights of their programs.[7] Borszcer stayed in Australia and enlisted in the AIF in April 1916; he was not accepted for overseas service but was assigned to the Australian Light Horse Band, based at Menangle Park near Sydney. The Heselev brothers also played in patriotic concerts,[8] and Israel Heselev joined the AIF himself, but his service was not long: he was discharged a month later.

Several Slavs from Ukraine might have been driven to enlist in the first months of the war by familial traditions and ties, the legacy of their own military or naval service, and sympathy towards Russia's war effort. Among such early recruits were George Kamishansky, Alexander Sast, James Gretchinsky, Alexander Popow, Robert Poselnikoff/Nicholson, and Jacob Serebrennikoff. From Ivan Gorodezky's application for the AIF in early 1916, we learn that his father was serving on the Eastern front at that time. Curiously enough, the two who had deserted the Russian Navy in 1901, Alfroniza Morozoff/Morris and Huon Pollejuke (he served as Pologouck), hurried to enlist soon after the news of the Gallipoli landing reached Australia.

Australian newspapers were quick to use the enlistment of natives from Ukraine for patriotic propaganda. Thus, a local correspondent from Cordalba praised 'Private M. Oleinokoff, a Russian, who has seven children, but having been a soldier in his homeland he decided to join the A.I.F. and fight for the British Empire. Having made Cordalba his home, and having become a naturalised British subject, he was willing to leave all and go and fight for freedom and country'.[9] But in some cases it would probably be an exaggeration to speak of patriotism, be it towards Australia or Russia. These men were doing their duty in a more down-to-earth way. For them it would have been dishonourable to sit out the war in Australia while their brothers in Ukraine served in the Russian army and their countrymen and friends were joining the Australian Army. Oleinikoff's enlistment followed that of his friends from Booyal – the Platonoff brothers and Feodot Peachenoff. Like others of different backgrounds or nationalities, some Ukrainians would join up in groups: in January 1915 Nickefor Domilovsky from Stavishche near Kyiv and Nicholas Fedorovich enlisted together in Cairns, while in April 1915 a group of seven Russian-born émigrés enlisted together in Rockhampton. That group included three Ukrainians: Joseph Rudezky, Nicholas Roomianzoff, and Leonard Noweetsky, as well as the Belarusians Usten Glavasky and Andew Jabinsky, the Ossetian Thomas Habaeff and George Vasilieff, a Russian. Two young Jewish men, George Breitman and Yur Kivovitch, enlisted on the same day in August 1915 at Holsworthy near Sydney, although it is hard to say if they were friends. Stephen Provaka joined the AIF in February 1916 with another group of Russians in Rockhampton.

There were others with more of a taste for adventure, and questionable military careers. For the 33-year-old Jewish seaman Louis Brodsky, a family man with 10-year-old twin sons in 1914, the spirit of adventure was probably the driving force. 'Dad, ever restless and stirred by thoughts of adventure in the War, made many efforts to enlist,' his son remembers. 'He ... was repeatedly rejected because of his poor teeth and campaigned against the Army authorities so

Matfeus Oleinikoff (QP)

Stephen Provaka (QP)

vigorously that he won newspaper publicity. He contended that there must be many able-bodied men, similar to him, being rejected for this comparatively minor defect; and he finally won approval from the authorities to create and establish a corps of men rejected only for poor teeth.'[10] His successful enlistment would result in an unexpected turn in his restless life.

Louis Brodsky in uniform with his twin sons (on the right) among family members (Courtesy of Vivien Brodsky)

Joseph Kleshenko, a 22-year-old seaman who landed in Sydney in 1912, joined the AIF no less than seven times. Records held in the National Archives of Australia register his military career as that of three separate men, and some detective work was needed to determine that all were the same man, by comparing signatures and physical descriptions. He first enlisted in November 1914 as Joseph Noyland, a Russian subject born in Dubno. The application was filled in by a recruiting clerk, but when the time came for 'Noyland' to sign, he apparently forgot the name he had chosen for his new identity and wrote: 'Joe Neyman'. He was assigned to the 6th Light Horse Regiment, but then disappeared without a trace, and in the chaos of the first months of war the army obviously had no time to look for him. Nevertheless, by the time of his fifth enlistment, this mythical soldier from the 6th Light Horse had assembled quite an interesting biography for himself. According to Kleshenko's interview with a newspaper reporter,

> Corporal Kleshenko, with the Sixth and Seventh Light Horse, was eventually ordered to Gallipoli, and effected a landing, at Gaba Tepe at midnight on April 27. They charged the

Turks with fixed bayonets, and fought till 4 o'clock in the morning. The fighting was terrific, the enemy being three to one.

'I had been thoroughly trained in the use of the bayonet in the army of my own country, and had a big pull over the Turks. I got the first one in the neck and threw him back, no more anyone to trouble. I accounted for three before I got this' (showing a scar on the back of the right hand, through which a bayonet had been driven.) He was taken to Malta for treatment, but was able to return to the firing line in three weeks. After a day and a half in trenches he received three bullet wounds in the right leg. These necessitating eight weeks' treatment in the military hospital at Alexandria. He was given the choice of a trip to Australia or some other part. He selected Australia.[11]

While 'Corporal Kleshenko' was bayoneting Turks in Gallipoli, the real Kleshenko enlisted once again, in January 1915, this time as Joseph Klinetinko from the same Dubno. On the third occasion, in June 1915, he signed as Joe Klestenko, but the recruiting clerk wrote his name as Kleshenko, and on subsequent occasions he stuck with this name. More than once a period of his army service ended with a bout of venereal disease and discharge, accompanied by the note 'unlikely to become an efficient soldier' or 'services no longer required', but he rejoined again and again at different recruiting offices. An obvious adventurer and troublemaker, he had a mark from a bullet wound on his ankle. This went well with the tales he told the recruiting officers: that he had served not only in the Russian army, but also in the American army for nine months; he even claimed to have received the bullet wound in the Russo-Japanese war. This seems unlikely as he was born in 1892; later, however, it became a 'Gallipoli wound', although it is unlikely that he ever served there.[12]

Such individual cases aside, many among the Ukrainian-born Anzacs may have enlisted for pragmatic reasons. For the majority, who were unemployed, hungry, without social or family networks, the army seemed to offer immediate relief from hardship. It provided meals, clothing, accommodation, and a generous payment of 8 shillings a day, which for a worker was a good wage to help save for the future or support their families in Ukraine. The situation for some was very hard indeed. George Didenko, when applying for his consular letter, could not afford the photograph which the consul demanded he attach to his certificate; moreover, he had broken his right wrist a few months earlier and could not pay for treatment, so was in constant pain. He was discharged from the army because of this injury, but re-enlisted five months later and reached England, where, a year and a half after the incident, it was established that the fracture had not set.[13] Others, having been rejected on medical grounds, chose to remain in the army on home service, which provided employment. Sam Clesner, a printer from Odessa, who came to Australia in 1914, worked for a while for the Headquarters Staff Printers. Edward Dryen, who came to Australia as a child in 1894, mastered English and served for five years in the Royal Australian Garrison Artillery, enlisted in the Australian

Edward Dryen (courtesy of Robyn Dryen)

Permanent Military Forces and served in the Instructional Corps with the rank of acting staff sergeant major.[14]

The seamen, who comprised nearly a third of our Anzacs, often joined out of necessity. Most of the Russian subjects arriving in Australia after August 1914 were seamen, as ordinary immigration of labourers and tradesmen had virtually ceased. Because of the war and the threat to shipping, trade declined; many ships terminated their voyages in Australia and the whole crew would often be discharged. In other cases, seamen who had deserted and found themselves without work had to join the army after a period of self-awarded shore leave. Some did not look for alternative employment at all: Ben Goffin, a ship's painter, arrived in Melbourne from the USA in February 1916 and joined the AIF the same day. Phillipp Gorbach from Odessa and Peter Tkachuk from Dubno joined the army within two months of their arrival. It took other seamen, including Cemon Afendikoff, Albert Morozoff, Alexander Belfort, Walter Pivinski and John Ouchirenko from Odessa, as well as Morris Rothstein from 'Cherkavosk', a little longer to decide to enlist.

Ukrainian sailors wishing to enlist enjoyed a certain advantage over others: the nature of their work meant that they were physically strong, had already picked up some English, learnt how to handle bullies and follow orders, – in a word, they were eminently suitable material for the Australian Army. For Ukrainian civilians of peasant or working-class backgrounds, the situation was different, as may be seen from the case of Platon Beloshapka.

The hungry 'German' in the bush
The story of Platon Beloshapka

Platon Beloshapka, born in Kyiv, came to Australia via the Far East. Before that he had served in the Russian army, though since his service lasted only 18 months it is quite likely that he deserted and chose to try his luck in Australia, like many other Ukrainians. On 10 November 1912 he disembarked in Brisbane from the *Yawata Maru* with two dozen of his compatriots, among them two future Anzacs - Egnaty Sologub, a Ukrainian, and Nicholas Tupikoff, a Russian. According to the AIF attestation papers he was a labourer, and indeed his uneven signature on his application form indicates that his hand was more accustomed to a shovel or an axe than a pen. The signature reads 'Ploton Beloshapka'; the recruiting officer nevertheless recorded his name as Plonton Beleshapka.[15] During the following two decades in Australia, he would accumulate over a dozen different aliases emerging from similar misunderstandings. T.A. Welch, the Russian Consul in New South Wales, recorded Platon's surname in March 1916 as Bjelaschapka. Other instances show spelling variations: for example Plation Beloshoplia (1916 Wollongong Police); Platonff Belashopkr (1916 Holsworthy internment camp); Plontonbb Beloshapka (*Brisbane Courier* 1921); Platanoff Belashapha (*Western Star* 1922). Unfamiliarity with non-English names even resulted in his surname and Christian name being transposed: thus Bill Plepnpp (1915 Bungonia Police) and William Plotonoff (1926 Queensland police). All this was due to the lack of any documentation relating to Platon's identity and his lack of English-language skills.

While Gregory Piddubny commented that after a few months to a year in Australia, most Ukrainians had adopted appropriate mannerisms, dress and learned enough English to fit into Australian society,[16] this was not the case for Beloshapka. His misadventures started soon after his enlistment in March 1915 in Kiama in New South Wales, from where he was transferred to Liverpool camp in Sydney. There he overstayed his leave and was discharged with the formula 'unlikely to become an efficient soldier'. Later the commander explained that the reasons for his discharge were 'incompatibility with comrades and inability to follow military commands.' Beloshapka tried to explain that he could not understand the officers' orders and that other soldiers threatened him as they took him for a German. He left the camp to avoid persecution.

In October 1915 'Bill Plepnpp' was arrested in Bungonia, New South Wales, and brought to Goulburn by the Military Police. He had been found living in the bush without food and it was thought that he was a German escapee from the Holsworthy internment camp. He was sent to Sydney for further investigation and then to Holsworthy camp as a German. He was released in February 1916 after a visit from the Russian Consul declared him a Russian national. Failing to find work, lodgings or food, Platon returned of his own volition to the camp on two occasions, once almost being shot by the sentries. He was held at a compound outside the camp for a time for his own safety and well-being. In March 1916 he was arrested in Wollongong for wearing a military hat and boots and not having a leave pass. He was brought by the Petersham police to Victoria Barracks, Paddington, for questioning, but the officer and Platon could understand nothing of what the other was saying. He was released and allowed to keep his boots 'as any other discharged soldier'. The cycle of misadventures continued, with Platon being convicted in May 1916 in Wee Waa for stealing food and not working. He was sentenced to one month's hard labour in Narrabri Gaol. Pending his release in July 1916, the Acting Gaoler expressed his concern that 'a German subject', 'Platonff

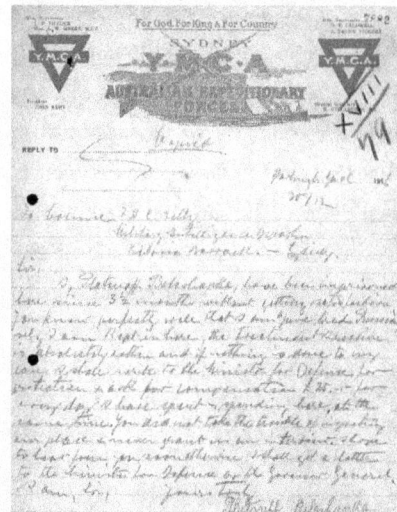

According to this 1916 letter Platon was not eager to serve and the Russian Consul was not eager to assist him in any way (NAA)

Belashapka', was 'a young strong man, and has a revolver and cartridges, and if not interned may cause trouble'. He was brought to Liverpool Camp for further investigation, and the officer noted in his file: 'probably be murdered if left in this camp', in consequence of which he was interned as a German prisoner of war in Darlinghurst Detention Barracks.

The Russian Consul-General Alexander Abaza and New South Wales Consul T.A. Welch visited him in October 1916 to establish his nationality. It was obvious to all that he was a Russian subject, and Welch informed the military authorities that 'by the agreement between Russian & British gov[ernment]s this man is due for compulsory enlistment in the AIF' and 'suggested to treat him as a military offender'. Since Beloshapka 'refused to enlist in the AIF if released', the consuls 'refused to give a certificate of nationality' and he was left in detention 'pending proof of his Russian nationality' for several more months.[17] When finally released, his troubles with the police continued: he was arrested and detained repeatedly for vagrancy and assault.

Beloshapka's story shows that although Russian subjects were never officially compelled to enlist in the AIF, pressure from the Russian consulate and the Australian authorities was ever-present. James Cochura, whom we left with fractured skull following a mining accident in May 1914, was, according to a military doctor's notes, 'in November 1914 sent to Camp by Russian Consul – discharged – sent to Civil Hospital 12 months after accident and operated on skull. Enlisted 1916 January and went to Camp – since then feels very bad on duty. – gets dizzy'.[18] Indeed, by 1916 many immigrants found themselves in a desperate situation: 'enlist or starve'. This explains a sudden rush to enlist in early 1916 by 'volunteers' clearly unfit for service – one with a hernia, others with varicose veins or a broken leg, and some lacking even basic English. The reason for this 'enthusiasm' was that everyone who was rejected received a letter stating they were unfit for service; such a letter could be produced when applying for employment and thus help allay the suspicion towards them as aliens, i.e. non-naturalised foreigners. In the meantime, the attitude to Russian subjects in Australia became more and more hostile. In April 1916, miners employed by the Mount Morgan Mining Company complained that 'a number of Russians who could not produce passports were discharged and told that they have to enlist … Our boss is distributing a letter with Russian Standart [flag] on.

This letter is demanding us to enlist.'[19] A Russian newspaper published in Brisbane reported from the area:

> Those who have been to Mt Morgan know that here, instead of work, you get an offer to enlist. Waiting for a job for several days, a man could spend his last shilling and, still no nearer getting a job, would decide to enlist to end his hunger. That's probably why Mt Morgan has provided such a high percentage of Russian volunteers.[20]

At least three Ukrainians working in the mines there were forced to enlist as a result of this pressure: Ksenofont Kozachuk, Constantine Pinkevitch, and Maxim Shular.

Technically, such victimisation was illegal, but in practice, immigrants from the Russian Empire were finding it harder and harder to find any employment. A similar story came from Friezland, where Afanasey Korniack and Egnaty Sologub enlisted. The letter signed 'One of many' published in the Brisbane Russian newspaper *Workers' Life* told of the ordeals of the immigrants there:

> One fine day while we were working at the factory in Friezland, out of foolishness but rather under the influence of Bacchus, my friend and I went to the police station and volunteered for the army. At the works office, where we went to collect our discharge papers, we enjoyed the utmost friendliness on the part of the administration and were sent off with their best wishes and a promise to re-employ us on our return from the army. When we were taken to the main camp and examined by the doctor there, my friend passed the examination, but I, having poor English and being short-sighted as well, was rejected and sent back. And what then? When I went back to the boss and asked for my job back, it was refused and I've been sitting around without work for a week already. That is the tragicomical lot which awaits our volunteers when they are discharged from the army.[21]

The Australian historian Raymond Evans comments in his book *The Red Flag Riots*:

> D'Abaza, the Imperial Russian Consul, had virtually imposed military service upon his erstwhile countrymen, without any apparent murmurs of dissent from Australian workers. In fact, the Hughes Labor Government had tacitly complied with the Czarist regime's wishes, forcing Russians in Australia 'to go into the Volunteer Armies and either enlist or get ... exemption papers in order to be allowed to look for work outside the Military enterprises; any Russian that had no such papers to show him ... unfit ... was refused employment in ... civilian life'.[22]

Indeed, the Russian consulate – and especially Alexander Abaza, the consul-general in Melbourne – played an important role in the mass enlistment of Russian subjects in the AIF. Quite apart from any considerations arising out of his duty as a career diplomat in the service of his country, Abaza probably needed something to deflect attention from his own difficulties. He feared that Australian Intelligence would discover that his wife was German[23] – a serious threat at a time when Germanophobia was engulfing Australia.

Maxim Shular's consular letter (NAA)

As early as May 1915 the Australian authorities, 'after consultations with the Russian Consul General', issued instructions 'that Russian subjects not naturalised might be enlisted'.[24] Russians turning up to enlist were normally expected to bring with them a letter from the Russian consulate to confirm their nationality. By that stage there were honorary Russian consuls in all large Australian cities, who provided such letters to Maxim Shular, Robert Nicholson, and Cemon Afendikoff, among others. But that was not enough, and Abaza continued his own campaign urging Russian subjects to join the AIF. At the end of 1915 he passed on to the Australian Ministry of Defence the Czar's order for all Russian reservists 'between ages of 21 and 38 years to immediately rejoin the colors', and those who were unable to return to Russia from abroad were 'required to join the ranks of the armies of the Allied Nations'.[25] It must be said that in the eyes of Russian officials even immigrants naturalised in Australia and their children born there were considered to be Russian subjects unless they had obtained the Czar's official consent to change their nationality.[26] Newspaper interviews with the consul in Sydney, T.A. Welch, and the Consul-General, N. Abaza, highlighted a further issue: 'Russian regulations make for imperative obedience to military commands. Shirkers are regarded as deserters, and dealt with by martial law'. Abaza further clarified that

> formerly it had been a treasonable offence for Russians to serve in a foreign army, and at the beginning of the war he was approached by many, who wished to return home and join the Russian colours, and, for lack of funds were not able to do so, and wished the Russian Government to arrange for their passages. This was out of the question, but the Consul-General cabled to Russia, and the Tsar, as a special favour, gave permission for Russians to enlist with the Australian Forces.

With the new order issued at the end of December 1915, serving in an Allied army was not considered treason; on the contrary, it was treason not to do so. The consuls also assured their subjects that 'Russians, who were living in Australia on account of political views' or 'left Russia without permission', and 'take their places in the ranks, will, after the war, be absolved from penalties'.[27]

At first sight it might seem that the Russian call-up of reservists in Australia applied only to those Russian subjects who were temporarily in Australia and planned to return home – they would not have wanted to cause problems for themselves by appearing to evade military service. One might have thought that it would not affect those who had left the Russian Empire for good. In practice, the situation was more complicated. Abaza continued his campaign to enlist subjects of the Russian Empire by attempting, in January 1916, to introduce a total ban on the departure from Australia of Russian seamen and passengers 'without written permission from the local consular authorities'.[28] Undoubtedly he would have directed into the army all potential conscripts fished out by this manoeuvre, but it lacked the support of the Australian authorities. In October 1916 Abaza appealed to the Australian Department of External Affairs to make 'it absolutely compulsory for all Russian subjects … to register themselves at the Russian consulate … and to renew registration once a year', as many who had fled Russia would naturally prefer to avoid any contact with the consulate. The Australian authorities politely denied the request[29] – after all, Australia was a bulwark of personal freedom, officially at least.

In 1916 Abaza applied his initiative in one more attempt to obtain recruits. By the outbreak of war there were thousands of emigrants from the Austro-Hungarian empire living in Australia. Many were Slavs – Poles, Czechs, Slovaks, Slovenes, Serbs, Croats, and others; a few were Ukrainians and Rusyns (Ruthenians) from the western areas of present-day Ukraine. In the eyes of Australian security officers all of them were enemy aliens and should have been interned as prisoners of war, but Abaza, understanding the ethnic nuances within the Empire, declared that Russia was happy to provide protection for these Slavs if they agreed to take Russian citizenship. His long-term aim was to ensure that the men enlisted in the AIF, as Russian citizens were required to. Abaza employed Elias Jacob Serebrennikoff – who, after being wounded at Gallipoli and repatriated to Melbourne, worked for the Russian consulate – as his agent in this endeavour. In 1916 Serebrennikoff visited the centres of Slav populations in South and Western Australia in order to provide certificates of Russian nationality to those willing, but the campaign had limited success and was soon discontinued at the request of the Australian authorities.[30] The only recruit associated with Ukraine in this wave was the Croat Joseph Rudovsky, who, when enlisting, posed as a native of Odessa and a Russian subject.

But the Australian side was not lacking in initiative either. In October 1915 the Department of External Affairs decided, as a measure to compel Russian subjects to join the army, that no Russian aged between 18 and 50 would be granted naturalisation.[31] The government had been coming under pressure from the Russian authorities, but took this action as much in its own interests as to satisfy Russia; Australia was just as keen to get Russian subjects to join up. The denial of naturalisation significantly affected these immigrants: they would not, for instance, be able to buy real estate; nor could they be given freehold rights over farmland that they had improved. More immediately, it had the effect of fostering increased suspicion of them as non-naturalised aliens. The Australian authorities must have realised that this decision rested on a dubious legal basis, as it clearly amounted to a denial of basic rights. The formal letter of refusal to applicants was diplomatically worded as 'certificates of naturalization are not being issued, at the present time, to Russians under 50 years of age'; the real reason was never revealed, but handwritten annotations ('for internal use') on correspondence concerning naturalisation made the government position obvious. One example was the note left by Atlee Hunt, the Departmental Secretary (who usually signed papers dealing with the naturalisation of Russian subjects) on correspondence concerning Theofil Volkofsky's case: 'As the only reason for refusing naturalization is to compel men who ought to fight to do so we might naturalize this man if he is unfit' – but such exceptions were very rare.[32]

Furthermore, under the Alien Registration Act of October 1916, all aliens were required to visit a police station and fill in an alien registration form; they had to repeat the procedure whenever they changed their place of residence, and failure to do so resulted in stiff fines. Many Russian subjects, not knowing English and constantly moving from place to place in search of work, were unaware that in 'free Australia' their movements had now become subject to total police control. Moreover, official surveillance of all Russian correspondence started in 1916 as well.

For the natives of Ukraine, the proportion of men who were not sent on active service after enlistment was quite similar to that of Australians as a whole (24.6 and 20 per cent respectively), but the reasons for this may have included additional ethnopolitical nuances. We have already charted the variety of troubles that stemmed from Beloshapka's lack of English. The reason for discharge, 'unlikely to become an efficient soldier', was often used in such cases, as in that of Carl Kills. A significant number, over half of all rejects, were discharged as 'medically unfit'. On the one hand this message could be an indication of their aspiration – against all odds – to join the army, as was indeed the case with Louis Brodsky, but on the other hand it may have come from a simple attempt to receive an official discharge, which could help gain the trust of potential employers. In some cases, the reasons were intertwined. Maxim Shular, for instance, enlisted in the army in Rockhampton in May 1916 in spite of a serious knee injury, which he received while working in the Mount Morgan mine. His application, where his name was recorded as Shulyar, was accompanied by the Russian consul's letter stating that he was 'a reservist of the Russian Imperial Army and has to join the Australian Expeditionary Forces owing to his inability to return to Russia'. He fulfilled his duty to Russia and received some treatment for his injury while in the army, but since the condition was chronic, he was discharged four months later as medically unfit and probably received some help with employment. We might surmise that after a while his situation became so difficult that in April 1917 he enlisted once again, this time in Townsville, as Shular, concealing his previous unsuccessful service and his troublesome knee. Soon his two identities were blended together: the knee was reassessed and he was discharged as medically unfit once again, but at least he got a few months of pension.[33]

Another reason for the service of some of our heroes being cut short was growing suspicion towards them on the part of other enlistees. While jingoism and suspicion of otherness was a characteristic feature of Australian society from well before the war, the wartime propaganda machine stirred particular hatred towards Germans and, by extension, all aliens, to new levels. As knowledge of foreigners among the public in general was quite limited, it was very easy for any non-English speaker to be perceived as a dreaded German. Suspicion

Above and below: It was not easy to record the details of a Ukrainian Anzac
Above: Stephen Provaka' application with a detailed home address (NAA)

Left: The enlisting officer heard Tkachenko's surname as 'Tkrachenro', but the word mestechko (township) is recorded correctly (NAA)
Right: Thomas Pesmany had to write his father's name and place of residence in Russian (NAA)

concerning Russian subjects increased even more after the Russian revolutions of 1917: that of February, which overthrew the Russian Emperor, and that of October, which brought the Bolsheviks to power, followed soon after by the Russian withdrawal from the war. Maxim Shular was accepted into the Army with no more than a consular letter in May 1916, but when he re-enlisted in April 1917, he had to write a special statutory declaration confirming that he and his parents were born in Russia, and he was not of 'German Austrian Bulgarian or Turkish parentage'. This is not surprising as we may remember that Platon Beloshapka was continually suspected by other soldiers and policemen of being a German, and was even detained as one in prisoner of war camps. Joseph Kleshenko, who enlisted in the AIF seven times, also complained that 'men called me German'. We may never know why Alexay Ostrinko (enlisting as Alik Osmirko), a labourer from Poltava province, deserted after two months in Liverpool Barracks in Sydney, but the suspicions of other soldiers could well have played their part.

Such suspicions were not always without grounds. There was the case of Theofil Volkofsky, a former socialist sympathiser who acquired a taste for free enterprise at Bourke; he enlisted in the AIF in June 1916 and became involved in political discussions while at Bathurst Camp. One informant reported him saying that 'he would sooner be under Germans than the present Labor government in Australia. … He also expressed an opinion that the tales about the atrocities committed by Germans was all inventions.' This was not the only occasion on which he expressed such sentiments, according to another informant. His son remembers,

> Dad did tell me that he upset some people through his political incorrectness and his honesty. They were talking about the Germans and those Australians who were there were very critical, and he said, 'German soldiers are just humans like you and I, they are just ordinary men'. That was not exactly the thing you say in times like that in certain company. So they looked on him as pro-German and he got into strife. He was not pro-German, he was definitely not. He loved Australia and he would fight against the German government.

The Bathurst Camp commandant, to give him his due, treated Volkofsky's case without prejudice: after talking to Volkofsky, he gave him a fatherly warning 'to avoid discussion of politics', and even assisted Volkofsky with his naturalisation application when he was hospitalised with pulmonary tuberculosis.[34]

Sometimes things went awry for other reasons. Huon Pollejuke, the deserter from the Russian Navy of 1901, abandoned the colours soon after enlistment, probably having found army life too hard as he was no longer a young man. Myer Levin, a tailor from Kyiv, signed his enlistment papers with a cross, as he could not write English. Later his family argued that his correct name was Morris Leneve. After several months of training at Liverpool Camp he began to suffer from rheumatism, twisted his ankle, and deserted. While Ostrinko and Pollejuke were never found by the military police and their cases were later closed, the unlucky Levin was caught six months later by Bathurst Police, court martialled and sentenced to four months of hard labour. Released from prison, he deserted once again, this time successfully.³⁵ In the case of young Samuel Trager we may never know what triggered a chain of disobedience of orders and AWLs (absence without leave) a week after his second enlistment in 1917. His mother pleaded with his commanding officer for his 'early discharge', commenting that he 'is not right in his mind, as you, Sir, know, otherwise he would not do all those silly things'. She obviously foresaw what would happen, as Samuel managed to board a ship bound for Port Darwin, was caught, charged with desertion, placed in the Darlinghurst Detention Barracks, and escaped from the guardroom.³⁶ After the war the warrant for his arrest was withdrawn and he surfaced in Brisbane.

Enlisting in the army was further complicated for Ukrainian-born immigrants by the pressure they experienced within their own communities, in which the radical Russian-Ukrainian-Jewish leaders had taken a strong anti-military stance. They saw the war as imperialist, and actively supported the anti-conscription movement, calling upon the working classes to shun the war effort. In February 1916, when the pressure of the Russian Consulate on Russian subjects to enlist was especially heavy, and those opposing enlistment were being actively dismissed from their jobs, a 'deputation representing the Russian Workers' Association, Russian Jewish organisation, and the Little Russian Association' – the latter was certainly the Ukrainian Workers' Circle – visited Brisbane Industrial Council to air their worries about such 'victimisation and persecution' fuelled by 'ignorant jingoism' in the hope that the Australian working class would support them.³⁷ At the same time the position taken by the above associations and Russian newspapers published in Australia led to the victimisation of all who supported the war effort, let alone enlisted in the army. The Ukrainian John Nesterenko (in Australia he became J. Nester) wrote in his letter to the Australia newspaper *Truth*:

> One day in February [1916] I went to the Russian Association rooms in Stanley-street, where a meeting was in progress. On my entry, one of the 'political refugees' in the room pointed to me, saying 'This man must not be allowed to attend our meetings, for I have seen his name on the list of those who are returning to Russia to serve against Germany.

The Russian newspaper *Workers' Life* rebutted these accusations.³⁸

Two socialist sympathisers, the brothers Cezar Wolkowsky and Theofil Volkofsky, probably enlisted because while in Dubbo they were out of touch with the position taken by the socialist parties; on the other hand it is quite possible that their success with the fish business was helping them to reassess their situation and to break away from the tenets of anti-capitalist doctrine. Whatever their stance, this change did not come at once and Theofil, as we have seen, got into trouble soon after enlisting. Similarly troublesome was the experience of Cezar, with which we will become acquainted further on.

The attitude of some Jews was also far from one of unconditional patriotic support for their new-found homeland. In his autobiographical story 'A Child of Wars and Revolutions',

Judah Waten, the Australian Jewish writer, tells of the experience of his family, who emigrated from Odessa to Western Australia shortly before the war:

> my mother hated the war and loathed the Czar and she hoped that he would be toppled. Mother didn't like the British of course, because they had propped up the Czar in 1905 when the Revolution threatened his rule, and also because now, as he was one of Britain's principal allies, the British and Australian war propagandists were finding nice things to say about him, making him out to be a just and virtuous ruler. She had successfully talked my father out of enlisting.[39]

As ever, ethnic and political nuances were a major factor for the diverse population of potential Ukrainian-born recruits.

Ethnic & territorial breakdown and other statistics

Before following our new Anzacs into the war, it is worth glancing at a statistical analysis of the contingent, which presents the following picture:

The total number of Australians who enlisted (416,809) represented 13 per cent of the male population; if we accept that Ukrainian-born men in Australia at that time numbered around one thousand, for the 134 Ukrainian-born men enlisting the proportion was approximately the same.

The percentage of enlisted men who served abroad was 79.6 per cent for Australians (a total of 331,781 men) and 75 per cent for Ukrainian-born (101 men).

The proportion of those who died on active service (as a percentage of men who served overseas) was 19 per cent for Australians (63,163 men in total) and 13 per cent for Ukrainian-born (13 men).

The ethnic distribution of the Ukrainian-born volunteers was not uniform across the different Australian states, as is represented in Table 2.

Table 2. Enlistment by state and ethnicity

State / Ethnicity	Ukrainians	Other Slavs, Germans, Greeks	Jews	Western Europeans	Total
Queensland	23	9	6	1	39
New South Wales	20	8	22	3	53
Victoria	3	3	7	0	13
South Australia	4	4	3	0	11
Western Australia	1	2	13	2	18
Total	51	26	51	6	134

Sources: Data from service records.

This distribution shows that New South Wales provided the majority of Ukrainian-born recruits, followed by Queensland. Ethnic Ukrainian recruits were most numerous in Queensland and New South Wales, and hardly present in other states. Jewish recruits were most numerous in New South Wales and Western Australia.

The age distribution of recruits is represented in Figure 2 on the example of two ethnic groups – Ukrainians and Jews. It indicates that for Ukrainians the peak age of enlistment was between the ages of 22 and 28, while for Jews it was 19 to 22, which can be explained by the fact that many Jews came to Australia with their parents at a young age and in that respect did not differ much from the Australian population at large – where the average age of enlistment peaked at about 20 years.

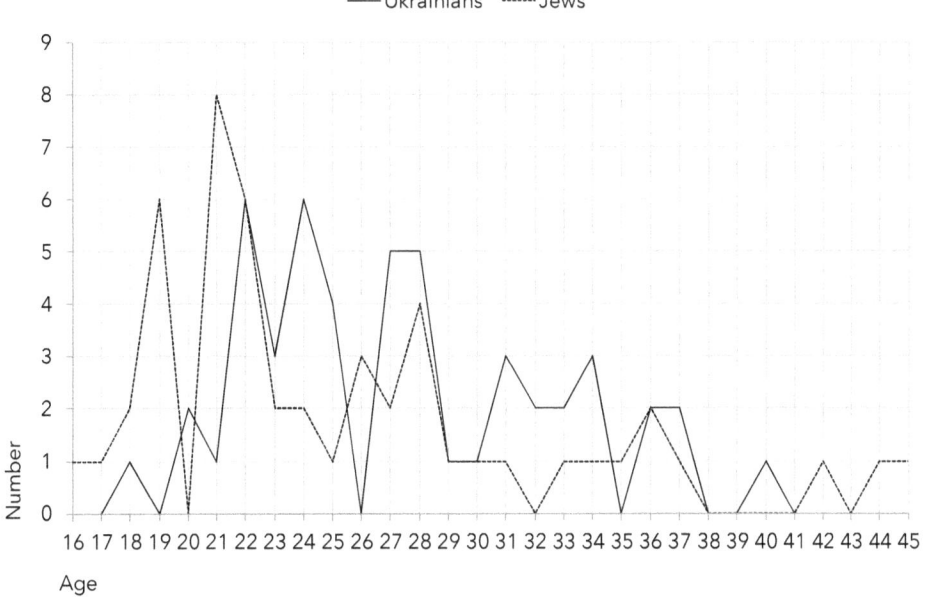

Sources: Data from service records and naturalisation files.

Gallipoli

The very first contingent of Australian troops left Australian waters in early November 1914 with two Ukrainian-born Anzacs: George Kamishansky and Alexander Sast. Between February and September 1915 they were followed by 30 more. After several months of training in Egypt, and now as part of the newly formed 1st Australian and New Zealand Army Corps, or ANZAC, 28 left for Gallipoli. They were probably unaware that the landing was being mounted, in part, to relieve Turkish pressure on Russian troops on the Transcaucasian front, but together with the Australians they were part of a legend in the making, which sprang out

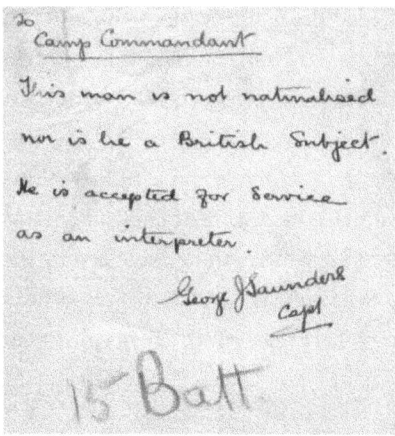

One of the first Russian subjects to enlist, Marian Pshevolodskey posed a problem to the enlisting officers (NAA)

of Anzac Cove where the first Anzacs landed on 25 April 1915.

At least three Ukrainian-born Anzacs participated in this landing: besides Kamishansky and Sast, there was Marian Pshevolodskey, an interpreter. In May 1915 they were followed by Elias Jacob Serebrennikoff, Joseph Zines, and Alexander Popow. They were to endure the hardest battles, when all regiments lost a significant proportion of their men. Alexander Sast became the first casualty among the Ukrainian Anzacs, receiving a gunshot wound in the foot on 30 April and being evacuated to a hospital in Egypt. On 8 May the 6th Battalion took part in the charge at Krithia, on the tip of the peninsula. Serebrennikoff, who had just arrived with the 3rd reinforcements to the battalion, suffered a bullet wound in the elbow in this attack. He too was evacuated to Egypt and later to Australia. At almost the same time as the battle for Krithia, on the opposite flank the 15th Battalion was attacking the Turkish trenches facing Quinn's Post. In this attack Marian Pshevolodskey was killed.

In June more Ukrainian Anzacs landed at Gallipoli: Sebastian Radetsky, Nickefor Domilovsky and Nicholas Fedorovich. The latter two had enlisted together in Cairns and sailed together from Brisbane. In July came Lamotte Alexis Sage and Wolfe Hoffman; in August, Nicholas Roomianzoff, Albert Michael Tober, Albert Krantz, Cezar Wolkowsky, Jack Vengert, and Walter Pivinski. The last two had sailed together from Australia with the 18th Battalion. Wolkowsky came with the 19th Battalion. His grandson Alyn remembers that at that time

Albert Krantz's service was commemorated in the Anzac Day anniversary edition of the Sydney Morning Herald, 2005

his English was so poor that another Russian-speaking soldier, who knew English, helped him during the training. This could be Frank Lesnie from Warsaw, who was in the same unit as Wolkowsky. The summer in Gallipoli was a trying time not only because of the constant shelling but also due to extremely poor infrastructure, which led to numerous diseases such as influenza, dysentery and rheumatism. The epidemics of dysentery were particularly severe, but being invalided away from the front with this by no means romantic ailment saved many from death during the fierce fighting of August. Among the afflicted by various diseases during these months were Radetsky, Domilovsky, Fedorovich, Hoffman, and Kamishansky. However, warfare did not

Jack Vengert, wounded at Gallipoli (SL NSW)

spare our Anzacs either. In June Alexander Popow, an engineer who came to Gallipoli with the Field Company Engineers, sustained shrapnel wounds to his arm and an ear injury. After recovering in Cairo, he returned to the Gallipoli trenches only a month later.

Frank Lesnie wrote home on 1 November: 'I can only say this; the 18th Battn. … arrived here 10 weeks ago and now 64 of the original lot remain. Most of them have gone away sick and wounded, but I don't know how many were killed. The 18th were dead unlucky, going into a charge the day following their landing.'[40] That charge was the battle for Hill 60, a fierce engagement at close range. Two Ukrainian-born soldiers from the 18th Battalion received bayonet wounds during the fighting: Jack Vengert, previously a cook, was bayoneted in the wrist; Walter Pivinski, a former sailor, 'wounded over the left eye with a bayonet', also had a shrapnel wound to the hand, a 'fracture of the skull', and was 'wounded in the back through an explosion of a shell'.[41] Both men were transported to Australia to recover, and both chose to reenlist. Cezar Wolkowsky was severely wounded in early September, only a few days after landing, and was evacuated to Egypt, but a piece of Turkish shrapnel remained lodged near his spinal cord all his life. In addition, he suffered from deafness and neurasthenia.[42] His brief, yet traumatic experience of war awakened his strong anti-militarist and socialist feelings.

Gallipoli – Archangelsk – London
Alexander Sast's story

The ordeals of Alexander Sast were particularly dramatic. A former motor mechanic from Odessa, he served in the 10th Battalion. Having recovered from his first wound, he rejoined the battalion in July 1915. Then, on 18 July – as he testified a year later before a court of enquiry – he 'was sent out in front of the trenches … to try and drop a sniper'. In the course of doing this, he was wounded in the leg by a shell. 'The wound bled freely and I was very much in pain. I shouted out to my own men but am not sure they could hear me owing to the great noise.' At night a Turk appeared and was about to bayonet him but Sast grabbed hold of the bayonet (Sast was able to produce the piece of shrapnel and show the scar on his fingers from the bayonet). As he was wounded, the Turks carried him to their trenches and finally to a hospital. When he had recovered a little, he was taken for interrogation but refused to provide any information; he was then transferred to Scutari (Üsküdar). There, he underwent torture: 'They tied my hands behind my back and hung me up to a ring on the post with my toes just clear of the floor for two hours'. Each time he fainted he was brought round and the torture continued: 'This went on for four days.' Finally he was sent to a camp, where he met several other Australians, and they worked 12 hours a day, receiving only one hot meal a day. In December, with other prisoners of war, Sast was transferred to Bulgaria, where they dug trenches under the command of a German officer.

ANZAC ESCAPES FROM TURKS.
DASH ACROSS DANUBE ICE.
AIDED BY A BULGARIAN.
ADVENTURES OF PRIVATE SAST.

ANZAC'S STRANGE STORY.
Port Pirie to London via Archangel.

BROKEN HILL SOLDIER'S ADVENTURES.
CAPTURED IN GALLIPOLI
PRISONER IN TURKEY AND BULGARIA.
ESCAPES THROUGH THE BALKANS AND RUSSIA.
SENSATIONAL STORY OF ADVENTURE.

PRISONER WHO ESCAPED
RUSSIAN ANZAC A LINGUIST.

Accounts of Alexander Sast's adventures appeared in many newspapers
(Clockwise from top left: Bendigonian, The Register, Daily Herald, Barrier Miner)

At this camp Sast befriended a Bulgarian soldier who was anxious to escape from the army. ('I understood his language for it is like Russian.') So, with the Bulgarian leading the way, together they successfully fled across the frozen Danube and were soon in Romania, where the Bulgarian joined some other Bulgarian deserters. Sast, who had several gold coins hidden on his person, changed into civilian clothes and travelled to Bucharest, where he met two other Russians. Together, they reached the River Prut and, with the help of a Jewish guide, crossed it and entered Ukraine. Sast was determined to continue his war, but the only army he wanted to fight in was the Australian army. So, avoiding contact with the Russian authorities and even his relatives, he decided to make his way to Archangelsk in the north of Russia, where British troops had landed. The journey took him right across Russia, from south to north. 'I saw the way to Archangel on the map and went by train. There I reported. I thought it was the only way I could get back to England. I was afraid to report before as the British Consul might have handed me over to the Russian Military Authorities.' Finally, in June 1916, almost a year after he'd gone out to 'drop a sniper' in the Dardanelles, the British took him to England, where he faced a court of enquiry. However incredible his adventures might appear, the 10th Battalion command was, even more incredibly, unable to confirm that Sast was with the battalion at the time of his capture! The court believed him, however, and he was shipped to join an Australian unit in France, where he served as a driver.⁴³

September saw the arrival in Gallipoli of a group of Ukrainians from Queensland: Stephen Loosgie, Joseph Rudezky, and Constantine Pinkevitch who had left Australia on the *Ascanius*, and John Kachan, Saveliy Tkachenko, Leonard Noweetsky, and William Whynsky who had sailed on the *Aeneas*. Nicholas Roomianzoff, who enlisted together with Rudezky and Noweetsky in Rockhampton, had landed in Gallipoli a month earlier. Elias Lebovitz from Western Australia joined the *Ascanius* in Perth and came to Gallipoli with the 28th Battalion. The last to arrive were Albert Morozoff and Vasily Kavitski. The toll of diseases was mounting – among those who fell sick in September-November were Loosgie, Sage, Tober, Roomianzoff, Kachan, Rudezky, Tkachenko, and Radetsky. Under constant shelling they held on until the end of December, when all surviving troops were evacuated to Egypt. Only a few endured the entire Gallipoli campaign. Albert Krantz wrote: 'I landed on Gallipoli several days after the original landing and served there until the final evacuation.'⁴⁴ Similarly Joseph Zines wrote: 'I was the only one in the co[mpan]y that served right through without being wounded or sick.'⁴⁵

Nicholas Roomianzoff landed at Gallipoli in August 1915 (QF)

From a military point of view, the Gallipoli campaign was a failure, but the legend it forged had an enormous effect on the unity of the young Australian nation. It is often said that colonial servicemen arrived at Gallipoli as New South Welshmen, South and West Australians, Queenslanders, Tasmanians or Victorians, and left as Australians. It would be tempting to extend the analogy, claiming that our heroes – Ukrainians and Jews, Russians and Poles – left Gallipoli as Australians as well. For some this was indeed the case, but the stories of many did not fit the Anzac legend and we will never know what they experienced on those barren shores so near their native land. Joseph Rudezky (26th Battalion), a former photographer, according to his daughter Violet Cotman, 'would not talk about the army. When they came back, he said, "I don't want to hear about the army". And he would not march on Anzac Day. He was fairly bitter about the army.'⁴⁶ A former railway labourer, Saveliy Tkachenko from Gusiatin in Podillia (25th Battalion), shot off the index finger of his right hand early on the morning of 4 November. By that time he had spent several months on Gallipoli and had only just returned from hospital, where he was suffering 'from nerves'. Alongside other soldiers with self-inflicted wounds, Tkachenko was court-martialled. His commanding officer characterised Tkachenko as an 'indifferent soldier', and stressed that he 'has been hard to understand, not being conversant with the English language. He is of Russian nationality.' His self-inflicted wound did not help him to get out of the army: by that stage every man was needed.[47] John Kachan, a veteran of the Russo-Japanese War, now a signaller with the 26th Battalion, became insane after several months at Gallipoli. He was evacuated to Egypt, there to lie surrounded by kind nurses in the former palace at Heliopolis, which had become No. 1 Australian General Hospital. According to his doctor, he 'wants to get away – thinks people want to kill him. Can't speak.'[48] What did he leave behind at Gallipoli? For a long time the hospital staff did not even know his name. Finally he was evacuated to Australia and died in Sydney in 1918. His name is missing from the Roll of Honour.

Among those who looked after the health of Australian troops was an Anzac from Ukraine, Reuben Rosenfield, whom we left in Melbourne after his graduation from university in 1897. During the intervening years he had made a successful career as an eye and ear specialist, got married and had two sons. When he enlisted in the AIF in July 1915, he was given the rank of major and shipped to Egypt. His skills were in high demand and he worked in No. 1 Australian General Hospital in Heliopolis, the Casualty Clearing Station in Serapeum and later in the Australian Stationary Hospital in Port Said. He wrote in his memoirs about his Heliopolis experience:

> During September, October and November of 1915 I had charge of the Eye and Ear Ward in the 1st Australian General Hospital, Heliopolis […]. It was a large ward including open air accommodation on the 'Piazza' for the less serious cases. The number of patients varied between 70 and 80 during the whole of the period. The patients were the sick and the wounded from Gallipoli […]. The eye injuries included many cases of foreign bodies – chiefly shell splinters in the eye-ball. […] There were a number of cases of Chronic Otitis Media as a result of having been buried by shell explosion.

In 1917 he returned to Australia accompanying the wounded aboard the troopship *Euripides*. After a brief stay at home he reenlisted in the AIF and worked in British Hospitals. He donated his notes about his experience as a medical officer to the Australian War Memorial.[49]

Egypt & Palestine

By the end of December 1915 all Australian troops on Gallipoli were withdrawn to Egypt, where there was much activity throughout 1915 and early 1916. During that period all new troops from Australia were also sent there for training; the sick and wounded were treated in hospital; Australian regiments regrouped after Gallipoli, and some Australian troops were engaged in operations against Ottoman Empire forces, though most of the AIF troops were transferred to the Western Front in 1916. The destinies of Ukrainian-born Anzacs intertwined with Egypt in many ways.

Several of them, sent to Egypt in 1915, did not reach Gallipoli and were soon returned to Australia. James Gretchinsky, a veteran of the Russo-Japanese war, developed varicose veins after his arrival in Egypt with the 9th Battalion, had surgery and was returned to Australia, where he was finally discharged with chronic rheumatism. For a while he received a pension, but his aspiration was to serve in the army. He attempted to enlist as a driver or work in the military censor's office, as he knew a number of languages, but to no avail.[50] The sailor Phillipp Gorbach, reaching Egypt with the 4th Battalion, was not sent to Gallipoli, but returned to Australia as an escort on the *Ceramic* in September 1915. We will learn later about the misadventures that followed. Edward Lakovsky and Alfroniza Morozoff were diagnosed with venereal disease in Egypt and returned to Australia. Australian troops were plagued with venereal infections, and in the beginning, when there was an oversupply of volunteers, the army preferred to return infected men to Australia and discharge them. It must be added that the epidemic of venereal infections, which affected many naïve servicemen, resulted in the so-called 'Battle of the Wazzir' when AIF soldiers ransacked and burned down a number of Cairo brothels which they saw as responsible for spreading venereal disease.[51] Walter Pivinski, who reenlisted after being severely wounded at Gallipoli and was returned to Egypt, suffered not only venereal disease but also severe headaches, and was returned to Australia six months later.

James Theodor Gretchinsky (QP)

Edward Lakovsky (SL SA)

The former seaman Louis Brodsky, whom we left in Sydney fighting for the rights of men with false teeth who had not been accepted into the army, won his case and reached Egypt in October 1915. He was enlisted in the AIF as an interpreter; he already had some experience in this field, having helped a group of Slav miners in the Newcastle area who were dismissed from their jobs because of eye disease in 1913.[52] Brodsky now realised that army life was not for him and sought a discharge, which was refused, so he took French leave 'and assumed the identity of a Russian refugee named David Lipschitz, whose papers he purchased'. In this guise he worked as a steward on various ships, eventually returning to Australia, where he gave himself up to the military authorities in 1918. He was not prosecuted, although he was made ineligible for all war medals.[53]

Leonard Noweetsky (QP)

The death of the second Ukrainian-born Anzac occurred in Egypt. Leonard Noweetsky, a horse driver, who enlisted in the AIF with a group of other Ukrainians in Rockhampton and survived Gallipoli, was killed at Tel-el-Kebir in an accident when a road-making roller came loose and hit his horses, causing them to bolt and drag him down the road. The Board of Inquiry found no one to blame. Noweetsky's personal effects – a phrasebook, letters, photographs, and papers – never reached his mother in Khabarovsk.[54] All that remains of him is a name on the Roll of Honour at the Australian War Memorial and a thin file with a few pages detailing his service in the AIF. Luckily his photograph, taken before his departure for the front, survived in the *Queenslander Pictorial*.

Training for the Western Front was stepped up in Egypt in the first six months of 1916. A letter written by one of our Anzacs, Wolf Dorfman, allows us a rare glimpse into their life and moods during these months.

From Rivne to Zeitoun
Wolf Dorfman's letter

When the war broke out, Wolf Dorfman, a commercial traveller who conducted business in Europe, USA and Asia, was in the Philippines. On arrival in Sydney in May 1915 he enlisted in the AIF and was allocated to the reinforcements of the 13th Battalion. It was too late for Gallipoli, but in March 1916 his battalion was shipped to Egypt for training. There Dorfman was lonely until one day he received a letter from a Broken Hill boy, R. Hooper. It was part of an Australia-wide home-front movement of writing letters to soldiers who had nobody to write to. This simple gesture meant a lot to Dorfman and on 24 April 1916 he sent a warm and sincere letter to the boy, talking about himself and his service in Egypt, which was published in the local newspaper, *Barrier Miner*:

My Dear Friend, – I was deeply touched by your kindness at writing to me, and can assure you it was deeply appreciated. It was the first letter I had received from Australia since leaving there, and it is very hard to stand by and see your friends getting letters when you are not getting any yourself. I have no relatives in Australia to get letters from, as all my people are in Russia, in a small town called Rovno.

Although it is only a small town it is strongly fortified, and has withstood a three months' bombardment by the Germans. I was born in this town, and I am feeling very anxious about my people there, as I have not had any word from them for seven or eight months. This fact worries me a great deal, as anything might have happened to them. […]

I eventually sailed from Sydney on February 16, in the s.s. *Ballarat*, and we called at Melbourne and Colombo on the run to Suez, where we disembarked and journeyed by train to a place called Zeitoun, where the camp was. This place is seven miles from Cairo, and just adjoining Heliopolis, where the big hospitals are. We stayed at Zeitoun only ten days, when we were all removed to our present camp, which is on the Arabian side of the Suez Canal, and is in close proximity to the scene of the early canal fighting against the Turks. The whole company that I came over with was transferred into the 54th Battalion.

The few days spent at Zeitoun were rather interesting, as we were allowed to visit Cairo every afternoon after 4 o'clock. I saw a fair amount of Cairo, and was impressed by its beauty. It has several fine parks, and a few fine streets; but the native quarters spoil the effect a great deal. The natives here are not too clean either as regards their places of abode or personally. Everyone there appears to be anxious to rob you if they get a chance, but the money system is very easy, as it is all piastres – worth 2½d. each. Heliopolis is also a fine city, and has some very fine buildings.

The camp we are in now is about 70 miles from Cairo, and is not as pleasant as Zeitoun. We are on the edge of the desert, and almost on the banks of the canal, which is rather fortunate, as bathing in the canal is the only means one has of washing himself here. Drinking water only is supplied. There are several thousands encamped here, and there is plenty of drill, which is very strenuous, being out on the desert all day in the broiling sun. […] We expect to go to France at any time now, and all the chaps seem anxious to get away.

I am sending you a photograph of myself, but it is not at all a good one, having been taken by an amateur. I will send you another, and I will write to you again from the trenches. I must thank you for your kindness in offering to send me cigarettes and tobacco, but I do not smoke, which is rather unusual for here, for a man not to smoke. Your kindness in sending me the books is deeply appreciated, but they have not yet arrived. They should arrive shortly, because, as you know, parcels always take longer than letters to come. I shall be very pleased to receive the photos of yourself and family, and will take the opportunity of sending one of these to a Russian paper with a request to insert it in the paper, and also point out the kindness which is being shown by Australians towards unbefriended soldiers. My right hand was hurt last week on one of the punts which cross the canal conveying the vehicular traffic. I got it jammed between a rail and a cart wheel, and it caused me great inconvenience to write, so I have got a friend to write for me as I dictate. I will look forward to seeing you on my return from the front, if I am favored by such good luck, and will hope to see you a school teacher imparting to your scholars things useful to them, and also impressing on them the many valorous deeds done by the Australian soldiers on the dark shores of Gallipoli. Kindest regards to yourself and your father, mother, sisters, and brothers. Yours very sincerely.[55]

A few weeks after sending this letter Dorfman was despatched to the Western Front.

Seven Ukrainian-born Anzacs, unlike many other servicemen, stayed in Egypt, serving in the Light Horse and Camel Corps regiments as part of the Egyptian Expeditionary Force. These units were manned by people of rural backgrounds – stockmen, drovers, and farmers – but surprisingly few Ukrainians from rural areas and Jews from agricultural colonies were chosen for these regiments. Those few who did serve came from a variety of backgrounds. James Cochura was from a village in Katerynoslav province and worked in Australia as a miner. Peter Tkachuk came from Dubno and worked as a seaman and blacksmith. Locksmith Lion Harlap grew up in Rehovot, the Jewish agricultural colony in Palestine; the family of Yur Kivovitch, a trader, also lived for a few years in Palestine. Elias Lebovitz, who grew up in Palestine and was naturalised in 1914 in Western Australia giving his occupation as a farmer, was probably the only one with suitable experience; George Ferber claimed to be a stockman in his attestation paper, as mentioned above, but probably had little knowledge of farm life. And finally, the tailor Abraham Smoishen had hardly any rural experience at all.

Although they were not practised bushmen, the Ukrainians and Jews in the Light Horse regiments and Camel Corps adapted to the hardships of camp life in the desert – the sand, dust, flies, heat, and lack of fresh food and water. Their medical problems included: gastritis and malaria (Smoishen), jaundice, conjunctivitis and malaria (Harlap), boils and varicose veins (Kivovitch), injury to elbow, pharyngitis, tonsillitis, pyrexia, diphtheria, malaria, endocarditis (Ferber), scabies and camel itch (Lebovitz). Cochura suffered more than most. His old skull injury, received in the Newcastle coal mine, caused him unbearable headaches; despite this he took part in all major battles fought by the Australian troops in Egypt.[56] Tkachuk, who served together with Cochura in the 7th Light Horse Regiment, survived his service unscathed and was transferred to the Western Front near the end of the war. Smoishen served in the Light Horse Field Ambulance. Yur Kivovitch's service was not long; in 1917 he was discharged as medically unfit, but before that he had a chance to put his languages to use in the Cairo censor's office (as mentioned above, along with European languages he also knew Arabic and Turkish).[57] Wolfe Hoffman performed similar duties at headquarters. He was evacuated to Egypt from Gallipoli in August 1915 with gastritis and injuries to the head and face. Upon recovery he was transferred to the Military Police headquarters in Tel-el-Kebir. Later he wrote that he worked for security intelligence there, but his service in this capacity was brief and in August 1916 he sailed for the Western Front.[58] Lebovitz became the first military casualty among our Egyptian Anzacs. He survived Gallipoli and sixteenth months in the Camel Corps, but in April 1917 he was severely wounded in the thigh during the battles near Gaza. He did not reach Jaffa, where his father lived, as he was repatriated to Australia following his wound.[59]

At the beginning of October 1918 the Australians had reached Damascus, and just over a month later the war ended. For Lion Harlap this was an especially happy time. His experience and knowledge of the region had been also put to good use in the army: several times he was transferred from his Light Horse Regiment to serve in the Military Police, Provost Corps, and at Headquarters. Now, with the army, he had come near Rehovot, where he grew up and where his family still lived. 'Whilst there with the Forces,' Harlap wrote, 'I was gratified to find my parents and sisters still alive though my father, who has suffered so much at the hands of our enemies, has aged considerably.' It was decided at this 'joyful' family reunion that when he received his discharge he should return directly to Palestine, to his family – and at the end of the war, he did.[60]

Western Front

By 1916 the AIF was reorganised into five divisions – each consisting of 12 infantry battalions, with artillery, newly formed pioneer battalions, tunnelling companies, engineering companies, medical and other services. In all, the number of Ukrainian-born servicemen who arrived on the Western Front between 1916 and 1918 was 67 including 16 Gallipoli veterans, and we find them in a variety of regiments. There was hardly a major battle without several Ukrainian-born Anzacs participating, and often sacrificing their lives. Gallipoli veterans were the first to be trained for elite artillery regiments: these included Kamishansky, Sage, and Sast; they were subsequently joined by Rothstein, Nicholson, Gulevich and Mackomel, who enlisted later. Alexander Popow, an electrical engineer by training, could put his knowledge to use with the Field Company Engineers. Two other Ukrainians, the engine fitter Efim Maximenko and bridge carpenter Egnaty Sologub, later joined engineering units as well. Christian Rink, an electrician trained in Odessa, served with the engineers and in another elite unit, the Australian Flying Corps. A number of Ukrainians served in tunnelling companies as tunnellers and sappers. Often the men allocated to these units had some mining experience, like Mitrofan Koropets, Joseph Rudovsky, and Stephen Surovsov, former miners who sailed together on the *Ulysses* in February 1916, followed by Joe Felipor and Peter Kusmin. Denis Papchuck, who enlisted as a farmer, also served in a tunnelling company as a sapper. Several others served in Field Ambulance regiments, collecting the wounded from the battlefield, often under heavy fire. In these regiments we meet Gallipoli veterans Constantine Pinkevitch and Wolfe Hoffman, as well as Feodot Peachenoff, Thomas Pesmany, Ivan Gorodezky and Richard Gregorenko.

Most of the Ukrainian-born Anzacs, however, served in infantry battalions. In Queensland battalions, immigrants from the Russian Empire – especially Slavs – were particularly numerous, and natives of Ukraine comprised a significant proportion of them. Five men from Ukraine served in the 9th Battalion, formed in Queensland. They were the Gallipoli veteran Nickefor Domilovsky, joined by Alexander Sank and George Malisheff, who sailed together on the *Seang Bee* in October 1915, and Nikalas Kiva and Joseph Vurhaft, both from Odessa, who sailed on the *Clan MacGillivray* in September 1916. The 25th and 26th Queensland Battalions included the Gallipoli veterans Saveliy Tkachenko, Joseph Rudezky, Stephen Loosgie, and William Whynsky, joined by the new recruits George Platonoff, Andrew Kovalevsky, and Stephen Provaka. Nicholas Roomianzoff, a Gallipoli veteran from the 9th Battalion, was transferred to the newly formed 49th Battalion where he met his fellow-countryman Andrew Snegovoy.

1916

The first AIF regiments reached the Western Front between March and April 1916. These were the old battalions which had previously fought at Gallipoli, including the 9th. They were deployed around Armentières in France. Although soldiers dubbed it a 'nursery sector' since it was supposedly quiet, many Australians experienced their baptism of fire almost as soon as they arrived there. On 20 April 1916 the farmhouse and outbuildings at Rouge de Bout, where the 9th Battalion's C Company was billeted, received a direct hit under heavy shelling, which killed and wounded many men, including several natives of Russia. Among them was Alexander Sank, severely wounded in both forearms. He enlisted in the AIF in Rockhampton in July 1915 and was too late to join his battalion at Gallipoli. After a brief period of training in Egypt he was among the first dispatched to the Western Front. Years later, in 1951, he was arrested by the KGB, who claimed that while serving in the AIF in 1916, 'he participated in the suppression of the Arab national liberation movement in Saudi Arabia'![61] Clearly the KGB officers hardly knew their history, but were proficient in formulating politically compromising accusations. But that lay in the distant future; back in 1916, after several months in English hospitals, Sank was returned to Australia and discharged as medically unfit. For him the war was over.

The battlefront experience of Wolf Dorfman was similarly brief. He probably had no chance to post his letter from the trenches to his new friend in Broken Hill, as a few days after arriving at the Western Front, he was reported missing in action during his first battle. This was the battle of the Sugarloaf salient near Fromelles in July 1916. Initially, the Australians were successful in driving the Germans out of their trenches right across the line, but at night the situation changed: lacking support from their British counterparts and with insufficient artillery cover, the Australians had to withdraw, having suffered horrific casualties, amounting to 5533 men. Among these thousands was Dorfman, taken prisoner of war. He would survive for more than two years in captivity.

Meanwhile further south, Australian troops engaged the enemy on the Somme. In the battle for Pozières and Mouquet Farm (July to September 1916) there were a number of casualties among the Ukrainian Anzacs, particularly in the 9th Battalion. On 29 July 1916 Nickefor Domilovsky was the first of them to be killed on the Western Front, and the third overall, while George Malisheff experienced severe shell shock, probably after being buried by an explosion. C.E.W. Bean, in his official war history of the AIF, describes the strain experienced by the infantry, 'who had simply to face the bombardment hour after hour in open trenches', and some never recovered from the terror they experienced there. Bean gives the example of a 'Russian' from the 9th Battalion who, 'during the bombardment ... was working like a terrier on hands and knees, whimpering the while, in desperate anxiety to scrape away the soil from comrades who had been buried. When eventually himself buried and dug out, he ran to the rear.'[62] This could have been our George Malisheff...

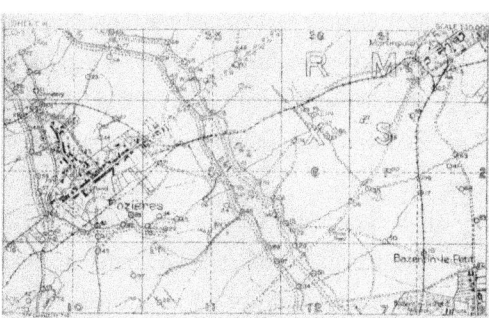

Map depicting the 9th Battalion positions during the July 1916 battle where Domilovsky was killed and Radetsky wounded (AWM)

Sebastian Radetsky, who had survived seven months at Gallipoli, was wounded here for the first time, receiving a gunshot wound in the leg. After the withdrawal from Gallipoli Radetsky went absent without leave on Lemnos; perhaps he was trying to get back to his wife in nearby Volhynia – but the war machine would not let him go. He would be wounded twice more on the Western Front, but returned to the trenches again and again. Among other casualties during this battle were more Gallipoli veterans: Joseph Rudezky (gunshot wound to the left hand) and Nicholas Roomianzoff (gunshot wound in the leg and right arm), who enlisted together in Rockhampton, Albert Morozoff, who during his first stint at Mouquet Farm experienced shell shock and was wounded several days later, and William Whynsky (gunshot wounds to back and shoulder). All but two returned to the trenches after recovery. The two 'lucky ones', for whom the war was over, were Joseph Rudezky and William Whynsky, repatriated to Australia as medically unfit. Rudezky did not know then that his experience of Gallipoli and France had left him with tuberculosis, barely treatable at that time; Whynsky did not live long either.

Young Joseph Zines volunteered with several other men from his 52nd Battalion to go into no man's land and rescue their wounded mates during the late August battle at Mouquet Farm. His commander wrote, recommending them for award,

> Some wounded men having been out in front of the Firing Line near Farm de Moquet for several days, a party under Lieut. Anderson volunteered to go up from Albert, a distance of four (4) miles and try and bring them in. This they did having to make their way for a long distance over ground and through saps that were being shelled heavily by the enemy. With much trouble in the darkness they located the men in no man's land near the enemy trenches and brought them back to safety over ground that was being swept by our own guns and then over the ground being bombarded by the enemy.[63]

Zines survived the dangerous foray only to receive a shrapnel wound to the head a few days later. Having recovered in a French hospital, he returned to his battalion the next month. The recommendation for an award fell through the cracks of the bureaucratic system and did not result in a Military Medal, but thanks to his heroism, perhaps an Australian Anzac who had probably never learnt the name of his Ukrainian rescuer was returned alive to his mother…

The tremendous strain of battle had long-lasting after-effects. Some of the men fell ill after returning from the front. The story of Viacheslav Kovalsky, who claimed to be from Moscow, was particularly tragic. His name suggests that he might have been Ukrainian or Belarusian, and, although we have no factual grounds to consider him Ukrainian and do not include him in the statistics, his story deserves to be told. Part of the wave of Russian immigration from the Far East, he came to Australia in 1912 and worked as a labourer. He was determined to join the army and, although rejected once, finally managed to enlist. After Pozières his sight began to fail rapidly; in the end he was taken to London. There, in November, nearly blind, he was discharged. Three days after Christmas he took poison: the police report stated he had 'no known friends in this country'. No friends of his were found in Australia either. He is missing from the Australian Roll of Honour. In any case, the military authorities never bothered to find out how to spell his name, recording him once as Vachalaf Kovalsky and on another occasion as Vachalar Kavolsky.[64]

After a short rest on a quieter sector of the front at Ypres, in Belgium, in late October 1916 most Australian divisions were moved back to the Somme. It was a grim return: under the autumn rains much of the battlefield turned into quagmire – the trenches filled with water and mud. Among the many casualties here was Alexander Popow, who received multiple gunshot wounds to the right shoulder, left leg and chest, and later developed gas gangrene; he was to spend nearly six months in English hospitals undergoing three operations, which left him with 63 scars on his left leg alone.[65]

Constantine Ilin sustained similarly serious wounds at Flers in December 1916. He was a sailor from Aleshki in Taurida province, who may not have been in Australia long, as he gave his address as 'c/o Russian consul in Newcastle' when he enlisted in March 1916. In November 1916 he was already on the Western Front with the 1st Pioneer Battalion. A month later he received gunshot wounds in the back and thigh. Evacuated to England, he underwent five operations and in July 1917 sailed on board a hospital ship to Australia. He was lucky, marrying an Australian girl soon after his discharge; they settled in Newtown in Sydney. Sadly, Ilin's health soon deteriorated and he died in May 1922 from complications of his wound and nephritis. The doctors considered his wife Sarah to be too vulnerable to be informed that her husband was dying, as by that time she herself was suffering from tuberculosis and neurasthenia. It was her mother, Mrs Fletcher, who stood by his deathbed. Sarah died a few months after her husband in the Waterfall sanatorium.[66] The echoes of the Western Front took a long while to fade…

Alexander Popow
(Courtesy of David Alexander)

'Bloody Russian you should be with us all in here'
Joe Felipor's story

One might suppose that by the end of 1916 the legendary mateship of the AIF would have overcome and erased differences in ethnic background. This did indeed happen, but setbacks were many, as may be seen from the court martial of Joe Felipor.

Felipor came from Odessa and had served in the Russian army during 'the Balkan war', if his statement is to be believed. Although he was a miner when he enlisted, his tattoos – a tree, a flower and a bee, a sailor on a pedestal, an anchor over a life buoy, a cross, a windmill, and a revolver – tell a story of previous adventures. Enlisting in Western Australia, he came to Belgium with a tunnelling company as a sapper. On the fateful day of 16 October 1916 he was in a party of 12, under the command of Sapper W. Monaghan, marching to Reninghelst, near Ypres, when they stopped for a drink in an estaminet. Later, under cross-examination, members of the party testified to drinking there: 'I had had about 5 glasses of beer. … I was not drunk. Sapper Monaghan had had the same amount of drink but was not drunk.' Felipor did not drink with the men, as he had no money. Finally, they came out and, as Felipor testified, Monaghan 'said "I am Officer this time, all follow me in single file." Then Sapper Monaghan suggested that they should all have another drink before moving off, but I refused and said I would go and report myself. I then started to walk away when he called out "Halt! Bloody Russian you should be with us all in here."' Monaghan ran after Felipor and hit him, trying to take his rifle off him. Felipor, who said, 'I was besides myself with pain', hit Monaghan with a bayonet, as a consequence of which he was court-martialled. Although Monaghan's mates tried to cover up what happened – 'Sapper Monaghan did not call accused any names' – and the court found Felipor guilty and sentenced him to one year's imprisonment, the sentence was not confirmed and he was returned to the battle lines.

In the final days of 1916, on 29 December, Felipor's left arm – the one with the tattoos of the flower and the bee – was severely wounded, and he was evacuated to England. When partly recovered, he deserted from the military hospital. Two months later he was captured and court-martialled again. At his hearing he argued that he had escaped in order to see the Russian consul, but to no avail: he was sentenced to 90 days' detention and only after that shipped back to Australia and discharged as medically unfit.[67]

1917

During the winter months of 1916–17 most of the Australian Divisions were holding positions near Gueudecourt, engaged in what the official history referred to as 'minor operations'. There were three further casualties among the Ukrainian-born Anzacs during this period: Woolf Zmood, who came from the same Taurida province as Constantine Ilin, was wounded in the thigh on 1 January 1917, while Albert Morozoff became a casualty for the third time – on this occasion he received a gunshot wound in the arm. George Koty, who had just arrived in France with the newly formed 3rd Division trained in England, was wounded in the neck at Armentières. All three were evacuated to England, but Morozoff was the only one to be repatriated to Australia as medically unfit. Zmood and Koty were left to continue their travails on the Western Front. Shrapnel and bullet wounds were not the only enemy in the trenches that winter – the soldiers lived for weeks in freezing, waterlogged trenches and clinging mud, many suffering from trench foot. Vasily Kavitski, who reached the Western Front in March 1916, was sent to hospital several times with trench foot until he was evacuated to Australia as medically unfit.

Meanwhile, the scraps of ground gained by the Allies on the Somme, at the cost of so many young lives, turned out to be insignificant when, at the end of February 1917, the Germans suddenly withdrew behind their newly built Hindenburg Line, some 30 kilometres east of their former po-

George Koty
(Courtesy Koty family)

Woolf Zmood (front row, 2nd from the right) with personnel of the 1st Light Trench Mortar Battery at Meteren, 1918 (AWM)

sitions. The Allies quickly started in pursuit of the retreating Germans, who put up a strong resistance. And again we find a number of Ukrainian-born Anzacs involved in these events.

One of the heroes of these days was George (Gersh) Breitman, from Chechelnyk in Podillia, where large Jewish communities still kept to their traditional way of life. A labourer in Australia, he had enlisted in Sydney and reached the Western Front with the reinforcements to the 3rd Battalion. During the pursuit of the Germans at Ligny-Thilloy on 2 March 1917, Breitman 'showed himself fearless and quick to act by rushing out from his post to assist 2nd Lieut. Boileau who had attacked four Germans in the open', as his commander wrote. 'By his prompt action this man no doubt saved his officer's life and materially assisted in the capture of the four enemy.' Twenty-year-old Breitman was awarded the Military Medal for his bravery,[68] while Lieutenant Angus Herbert Boileau, just a year older than Breitman, was awarded the Military Cross. Boileau survived the war and had a long and happy life in Australia; alas, Breitman would not be so lucky. Another hero of this advance was Michael Ankudinow, whose valour was recognised when he was mentioned in the despatches of Sir Douglas Haig. A special letter was sent to his mother at Sedanka station near Vladivostok.[69]

During the advance in late March and early April 1917 on the Lagnicourt–Noreuil line there were six Ukrainian casualties. These were the Gallipoli veteran Stephen Loosgie (wounded in the right forearm), Cemon Afendikoff (thigh), Peter Kusmin (severe shrapnel wound to the face and fractured lower jaw), Peter Komesaroff (thigh), and Andrew Snegovoy (thigh). Afendikoff alone was left in hospital near the battlefront. All the others were evacuated to England. All but Kusmin returned to the trenches after recovery. Kusmin, after his jaw was repaired, was left behind to serve at a depot in England; here his view of the war and the world order began to turn bitter. But we will hear his story later.

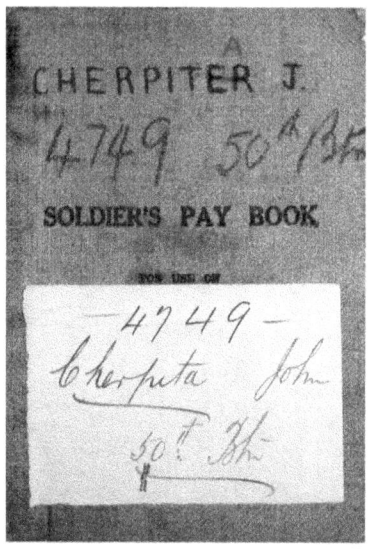

John Cherpiter's pay book (NAA)

John Cherpiter, serving with the 50th South Australian Battalion, was killed in the battle for Noreuil on 2 April 1917. Sadly, we know very little about him. A native of Kamianets-Podilskyi, he came to Australia a couple of years before the war, and worked as a bootmaker in Adelaide. Unusually among the Ukrainian Anzacs, he had a wife and daughter when enlisting. Two years after his death his wife Anastasia received his personal effects, which included '2 combs, small Australia badge, letters, Russian? official paper, shark tooth (mounted)'. She signed with a cross, which suggests she may have been illiterate.[70]

In April and early May 1917 Australian troops attacked the impregnable Hindenburg line east of Bullecourt. The first to fall among the Ukrainian Anzacs was Nikalas Kiva. While training in Brisbane, he was photographed with a group of Russians. This photo, which survived with one of his friends, Osiph Rinkevich, is now the only memento of this quiet young man. He was killed on 22 April and buried north-east of Bullecourt. His mother Mary in Odessa was never traced. During the second Bullecourt attack in early May there were four more casualties among Ukrainian-born Anzacs: a Gallipoli veteran, Sebastian Radetsky, was wounded for the second time (in the leg); Cemon Afendikoff, who had just recovered from his ordeal of March, was wounded again, this time receiving a severe gunshot wound in the arm; Ben Goffin received severe wounds to his back and both shoulders, and Frank Goldstein to the head. After recovery they all rejoined their regiments.

In the battle for Messines in June 1917 there were four more Ukrainian casualties. Ivan Rossoggsky was wounded in the shoulder and thigh, rejoined the 34th Battalion after a month, and was killed six days later, on 12 July. His previous experience as a seaman and his work at Glenrock Station near Moonan Flat, NSW, which must have improved his English, allowed him to settle well into his battalion. Unlike many Ukrainians who were destined to remain privates throughout their service, Rossoggsky was promoted to corporal while training in England. There he attended the Musketry School of Instruction and Field Battery School. Within the space of a few months at the front, he was appointed lance sergeant.[71] His connection with the Moonan Flat – Scone area also prompted Harry Willey, a local war historian, to

Nikalas Kiva (centre) with his friends Osiph Rinkevich (left) and William Averkoff (right). Averkoff, like Kiva, was killed soon after arriving at the front. (Courtesy of Rinkevich family)

collect information about him. Although his family in Bendery was never found, thanks to his connection with the local community, his name is commemorated on the rolls of honour in Moonan Flat and Scone.[72]

Efim Maximenko, an engine fitter from Sydney who reached the front with the Field Company Engineers, received severe abdominal wounds during the battle for Messines and died at a casualty clearing station. In Sydney he left a newly-wed Australian wife, Cora Peterson. Like Constantine Ilin, who was loved by his wife and his Australian mother-in-law, Efim was accepted as a son by of his wife's Australian family, who commemorated his death in the newspaper's 'In Memoriam' section.[73] The young Cora remarried only three years later.

> MAXIMENKO.—In loving memory of my dear husband, Sapper E. Maximenko, died of wounds in France, June 7, 1917. Not forgotten. Cora Maximenko.
>
> MAXIMENKO.—In loving memory of Sapper E. Maximenko, died of wounds in France, June 7, 1917. Inserted by his mother-in-law, Mrs. Peterson, and family, Double Bay.

In Memoriam in Sydney Morning Herald *placed in honour of Efim Maximenko*

Also among the casualties at Messines was Thomas Stephen Platonaff, the elder of the two brothers from Bingera plantation. He had received a bayonet wound to his right hand in May, and on returning to the 52nd Battalion, now at Messines, sustained severe gunshot wounds to both arms and was evacuated to Australia. Another casualty during this battle was John Ouchirenko (he served as Oucharenko), a tearaway who constantly got into trouble for absence without leave, bad behaviour and threatening language. While training with his battalion in England he married a local girl named Clara Lane. Ten days later he was despatched to the Western Front and gassed a month later, in July 1917.[74] His marriage to Clara would turn out to be troubled, as we shall see. Gregory Jakimov from the 35th Battalion was one more casualty of the battles of July 1917. He was severely wounded in the left arm, evacuated to a hospital in England and returned to Australia as medically unfit.

The autumn battles of 1917 in which Ukrainian-born Anzacs were involved took place on Belgian territory, just north of the earlier battles. During the fighting on Menin Road and the capture of Polygon Wood in late September 1917, Joseph Vurhaft was badly wounded. Born in Odessa, he came to Australia via the Russian Far East, landing in Cairns in 1912. He was then just nineteen and probably left Russia to avoid being drafted into the army. He worked at gardening and farming in the Rockhampton area. Having joined the AIF in January 1916, he arrived in France with the reinforcements to the 9th Battalion. The wound to his left arm that he received at Polygon Wood was so severe that the next day the arm was amputated and he was transferred to a hospital in England. But this was not the end of his ordeal. Hospital records chronicle what was diagnosed as 'shock to nervous system' and 'exhaustion psychosis':

> 19.10.1917. Queer & erratic, refused food.
> 20.10.1917. […] Worried, heard voices.
> 26.10.1917. […] Fidgety, confused and amnesic: evidently hears voices still.

In February 1918 he was repatriated to Australia to start a new life as an amputee.[75] William Kolesnikov, who, before enlisting, had settled in Sydney working as a 'hotel useful', also sustained horrific wounds at Polygon Wood: his jaw and mandible were fractured and his tongue was shot away, and he also received wounds to his left arm.

After the capture of Polygon Wood the next objective was the ridge at Broodseinde, and here on 4 October 1917 three men whom we saw during the earlier battles of 1917 became casualties: George Breitman (wounded in the hand), Michael Ankudinow (upper jaw) and John Ouchirenko (concussion). Ouchirenko's wound was not serious enough to send him to a hospital in England, where he could have been reunited with his wife. It is interesting to note that one of the fallen in the October battles was Samuel Carl Richard Stasinowsky, a son of Prussian immigrants born in South Australia, but when the Red Cross sought information from Michael Ankudinow about the circumstances of Stasinowsky's death, he described him as 'a countryman of mine and came from Odessa'.[76] It is quite probable that Stasinowsky, avoiding mention of any German family connections, preferred to be seen as a native of Odessa.

The last major battle of 1917, in October-November, was for Passchendaele and here three of our Anzacs were gassed: John Sepscak, George Platonoff (the younger of two brothers), and Stephen Loosgie. During this attack, Sepscak was also buried by a shell burst and found unconscious; his condition was so serious that he was taken to hospital and later repatriated to Australia.

The Western Front was not the only place where we find Ukrainian-born Anzacs. London and various places in Southern England were other hubs of activity where some of them stayed for extended periods. They trained in the depots there before being despatched to the front, their wounds and illnesses were treated in hospitals, and a few were employed in various sections of the AIF.

Among the latter was Nicholas Fedorovich, employed in the Administrative Headquarters in London as an interpreter. A former journalist from Odessa, he had worked for Russian and Manchurian newspapers, before settling in Queensland in 1911 and becoming a cane cutter. He landed in Gallipoli with a group of Russians and Ukrainians from the 9th Battalion in June 1915 and a few weeks later was evacuated to a hospital in Bristol with severe enteric fever. Here he obtained leave to go to Odessa to visit his sick mother. 'In his Australian uniform, he was an object of much admiration in the grain city', wrote the *Cairns Post* after the war. When he was in Petrograd on his way back to England, the paper continued,

> the interest he had created in the south grew more and more. Russia was then the most powerful of the Allies, and was driving the Germans back from the eastern frontier. He was followed around by crowds of people. When he entered cafes people rose and greeted him warmly. Groups of people listened with amazement to his stories of the great Commonwealth beyond the seas where the minimum wage for labourers was 8/– a day! The Russian military authorities decided that Fedorovich would be a valuable asset in their army, in imbuing the soldiers with fighting qualities. The news of the Anzacs' brilliant charges at Gallipoli had given them a high

opinion of the Australians as fighters, and Fedorovich found himself under orders to proceed to the eastern front. In vain he protested. He had an interview with the British Ambassador, who was unable to help him.

Only after spending several months on the Eastern Front did he manage to get back to London and rejoin the AIF. Due to various ailments he was kept in London, working in the quartermaster's store of the furlough branch, and as an interpreter at Horseferry Road. In early 1918 he was invalided to Australia as medically unfit.[77]

Wolf Dorfman, whom we left as a prisoner of war taken in July 1916 at the battle for the Sugarloaf salient near Fromelles, spent 1917 in Dulmen Camp in Westphalia, later being transferred to Sennelager in the same area. Soldiers like Dorfman, who could not get in touch with his family in Ukraine and had no relatives in Australia, felt especially isolated in the German camps. Here again Australians offered help. Miss M. E. Chomley from the Australian Red Cross in London sent regular food parcels, and cared for their other needs. People in Australia, often complete strangers, sent them messages of support. Dorfman's letter to Miss Alvina Jobs from Broken Hill shows how important this contact with people beyond the barbed wire was for him:

> Just a line or two to let you know that I am quite well. I received your two letters and also your parcel, for which I thank you. The chocolate was very nice and went down very well. We as prisoners are very limited in our writing, being allowed only one postcard each week and two letters a month, so you see how we are hampered in writing to every one we wish to. Never mind, I will write to you at every possible opportunity. I only hope that it will not stop you from writing to me at every opportunity, as I will be pleased to hear from you at any time. We have had some very cold weather lately; but it is getting warmer now. Give my kindest regards to your father and mother.[78]

Although he does not complain about the conditions of his captivity, it is known that he escaped from the camp, was recaptured and, most likely, severely punished.[79]

1918

Australian troops spent the winter of 1917–18 in the quieter Messines sector, recuperating from their losses. During this period two tunnellers, Joseph Rudovsky and Mitrofan Koropets, were gassed, but recovered.

With Russia's withdrawal from the war after the Bolshevik revolution of October 1917, Germany was able to transfer troops from the Eastern Front and build up formidable forces along the Western Front. Australian troops were brought forward, fighting this time in close collaboration with British troops and dispersed between different sectors of the front. A major German offensive started on 4 April 1918, heading towards Amiens. The fiercest fighting came the next day, with the 4th Division defending the front line near Dernancourt. The enemy broke through the Australian defences here and, although the offensive was eventually brought to a halt, the Australians suffered significant losses, which included several Ukrainian casualties. Among them were the Gallipoli veterans Nicholas Roomianzoff (wounded in the right arm) and Albert Krantz (right wrist), as well as the later arrivals George Koty (arm) and Andrew Snegovoy (right arm and face). For all but Krantz these were their second wounds. Krantz, with his injured right hand, was the only one to be repatriated to Australia. Denis Papchuck, a tunneller, was gassed a few days later.

George Koty's pay book survived all three of his casualties in his pocket (NAA)

The Germans next struck at Hazebrouck, an important railway centre, and the 1st Australian Division, sent from Messines to defend the town, occupied positions there on 12 April and held fast. George Malisheff was killed near Hazebrouck; of the seven who enlisted together at Rockhampton in August 1915, he was the last remaining at the front. Another casualty during this battle was Woolf Zmood, wounded for the second time; he would later rejoin his battalion. Australian troops were assigned the leading role in the next battle, the counter-attack at Villers-Bretonneux in April 1918. The two Ukrainian-born casualties in this battle were Morris Saffar (a gunshot wound to his right hand with the index finger shot off), and Michael Ankudinow, who was gassed. They were both taken to hospitals in England.

Throughout May–July 1918 the Australian divisions remained in the Amiens sector and kept up constant attacks on German positions. The attack on Hamel on 4 July, carried out with the support of tanks, the war's new weapon, was especially successful. In this battle Samuel Harold Krantz, an older brother of the wounded Albert Krantz, set an example of 'bravery and initiative' to his platoon, for which he was awarded the Military Medal. During the attack on Hamel, his commanding officer wrote,

> part of our line was held up by enemy Machine Gun. With the assistance of an American N.C.O. Krantz rushed the post, killed the gun crew and captured the gun. He showed an utter disregard for his personal safety as the enemy gun continued to fire until he was nearly up to it.[80]

Among the fallen during the May battles was Morris Lebovich, who received penetrating shrapnel wounds to his chest, buttocks and left leg, and died of his wounds. He had been eager to go to the front, enlisting in the AIF at the age of 20, two weeks after the death of his mother,

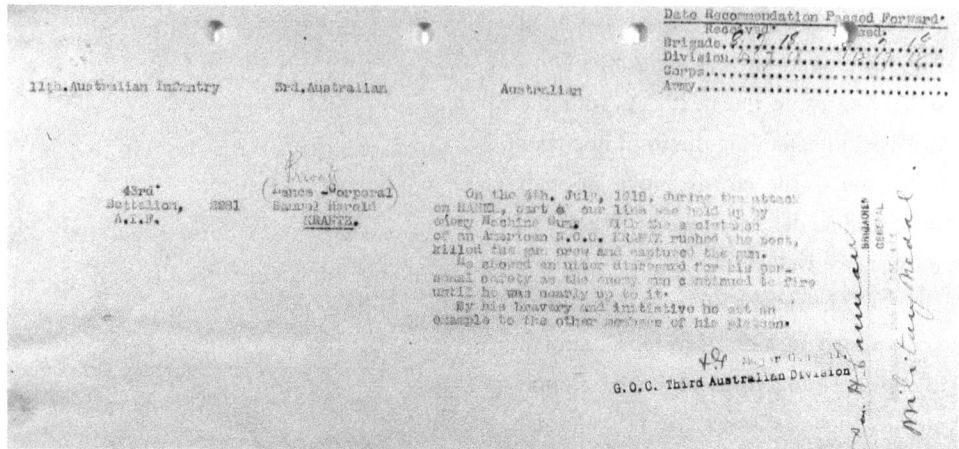

Samuel Krantz's recommendation for the Military Medal (AWM)

Morris Lebovich (NAA)

whose long illness probably prevented him from enlisting earlier. During that battle he acted as a stretcher bearer and died saving others. Also among the wounded was Frank Goldstein, a jeweller, who lost an eye; unlike young Lebovich, Goldstein was 31 and left a wife and three children in Sydney. Cemon Afendikoff and Samuel Rappeport were severely gassed during the May battles. Rappeport was repatriated to Australia, but Afendikoff, now wounded for the third time, returned to France in time for the final battles of autumn 1918. Two more of our Anzacs were wounded for the third time during the weeks to come: Stephen Loosgie received a shrapnel wound and fracture of the right arm, while George Koty suffered a gunshot wound and fracture of the leg. Both were repatriated to Australia.

'And then I fully realise what war means'
Emile Tardent's story

On 8 August 1918 the Allies – with Australian, Canadian and British corps fighting together – launched a major counter-attack south of the Somme near Amiens. Using tanks, they reached the old Amiens defensive line of 1916. The German line was broken along a 24-kilometre front and many prisoners were taken. The drive continued for several days, though the Germans began to put up determined resistance. This proved to be the finest hour of Lance-Corporal Emile Auguste Tardent, a Swiss, born in Mykolaiv, who grew up as a bushman in Queensland. He wrote about the beginning of the battle on 12 August in connection with an enquiry into the fate of his comrade E.A. Millar:

> We were on the left of the village of Proyart at the railway line between Proyart and Bray. We got down against the railway fence and bank and Millar, who was No. 1 on the Lewis Gun was firing at the Fritzies. He was hit fair through the forehead, and rolled over to the left without a word. No. 2 of Gun Harry Seaman of Yepoon, Queensland picked up the gun and just then we were ordered to advance.[81]

Later this day, Tardent's commanding officer wrote that he

> showed great skill in dealing with hostile Machine Guns. He directed the tactics of his own and adjoining sections in clearing up difficult Machine Gun posts on one occasion in order to complete an outflanking movement of another section, which he himself directed. He rushed to the post, accomplished the object, but was severely wounded.

His commanding officer concluded that 'His daring action and exemplary courage had a very inspiring effect on all personnel under his command.'[82] Tardent's own account of this episode was more personal and graphic. With an advance party of six he located the enemy machine-gun positions, and, he recounts,

> I send a man back to report. He jumps up and is immediately shot dead. There are only two of us left, and the platoon must know where those guns are. I decide to go back myself. I get ready to make a rush, and my last thoughts before I leave the shell holes is of my dear wife and kiddies. I hope I won't be killed, but if I am I want her and them to be proud of me.
>
> And now I am off. Bullets whistle everywhere, and I am still unhurt. I have now gone 50 yards, and am still unhurt. I stop in a shell hole to get my breath, and then I am off again. I am getting nearer and nearer to the platoon, which is waiting in shell holes. Only 50 yards more to go.
>
> I begin to exult. I shall make it after all. I can see the steel helmets of the platoon in the shell holes, when all at once - crash!! I crumple up. I lie still and wonder what hit me. It felt like a steam hummer. My right leg is numb and I cannot move it. I forget all about the vicious Hun and the bullets, and my one thought is to get out of my equipment and try to crawl on, and in spite of the pain, I succeed.
>
> I have hardly left my haversack when Fritz puts a burst of bullets right through it. I am jolly glad it is no longer on my back. Five yards away is a shell hole and I crawl into it. I cannot go any further. One of the men from the platoon crawls out, and comes over to me and I tell him where the guns are, and which is the best way down the hill. My work is accomplished and I try to make myself comfortable.

> I can feel hot blood slowly trickling down my leg. From the edge of the shell hole I see the platoon moving, down the hill fast, and soon get out of my sight.[83]

Tardent's heroism during this battle earned him the Military Medal. Patriotic feelings had impelled him to enlist, but he now had personal scores to settle with the German enemy: a year earlier his younger brother, 18-year-old Edward Felix Tardent, born in Australia, was killed, and his cousin Oswald Urbin Tardent was killed ten months later; now he rose up to protect his platoon. Emile's youngest brother Jules, who served in the same battalion, saw him hit by a bullet. A few days later, having been evacuated to an English hospital, Emile wrote to his father:

> Here I am in bed with a machine gun bullet in my right hip. It is a war souvenir I gathered in that great and glorious battle, which commenced on the 8th August, and is still proceeding. We got Fritz on the run on the first day, and have kept him hopping ever since. After the first day the battle developed into open warfare. The boys were just splendid, steady as a rock, fighting with determination, but throwing away no chances, and keeping wide of traps set by the crafty Hun. I candidly admit that it gave me grim satisfaction to be getting a bit of my own back on Fritz. As a fighter, I consider Fritz up to putty. [...] I met my brother Jules when I was being carried away from the firing line. He was all right and still going strong. My wound is healing well, and I hope to take part in another battle yet before the winter sets in.[84]

He did not write to his family that in fact the bullet was lodged so close to his spinal cord that it could not be removed safely. This Amiens souvenir would handicap him for the rest of the life and lead to his premature death.[85]

Brothers Jules and Emil Tardent met at the Western Front (QP)

Among the wounded during this initial Amiens advance were Sebastian Radetsky (shrapnel wound to the right arm) and Ben Goffin (severe chest wound and gas poisoning). For Radetsky, a Gallipoli veteran, this was his third wound on the Western Front; it was Goffin's second. They were both repatriated to Australia.

By the end of August the Australians had successfully advanced north and south of the Somme, continuing their movement towards Péronne. Among the casualties of this advance was Samuel Harold Krantz, the hero of Hamel, who was promoted to lance corporal on 26

August but on the same day received a wound in the mouth, at Susanne.[86] George Breitman, a hero of Ligny, was gassed, but rejoined his battalion one week before the Armistice. On 29 August the troops moved to the northern bank of the Somme in preparation for the assault on Mont St Quentin, which dominated Péronne. The sudden charge on Mont St Quentin on 31 August took the Germans by surprise, and many fled or were surrounded. But the Australians suffered many casualties too. Among the fallen was the Ukrainian-born former ship's fireman Jacob Leffow from the 34th Battalion. Sadly, we know very little about this wild and unruly man, whose service record was blotted by AWLs, venereal disease and even a court martial, and who, although having a father in 'Chanahow, Russia', made his will to the New South Wales Institution for the Deaf, Dumb and the Blind in Sydney.[87]

Ben Goffin (courtesy of Richard Goffin)

The last major Australian engagements with the enemy were south of Péronne in late September and early October, followed by an assault on the Hindenburg Line. That assault, on 18 September, was especially successful for the Australian troops, who captured 4300 prisoners. In this attack young Max (Moisey) Kotton, who had been so fearful of being returned to Russia and the Russian army, was killed. Although he had been taken in the AIF as a bugler due to his short stature, he grew into an excellent soldier: he qualified as 'very good distinguished' at the Group Lewis-gun School in England, and also trained at a gas school in France and did a German-language course there.[88] The death of the

Jacob Leffow's grave at Peronne Communal Cemetery, France (Jukka Illman)

little bugler in the fields of France made ripples that spread far beyond that place. When in December 1918 news of his death reached Naughtons Gap, NSW, where he had worked as a carter, a local newspaper wrote: 'Great regret is expressed locally at the news of his death.'[89] Moisey's parents in Harbin, learning about his death, wrote to the Union of Russian-born

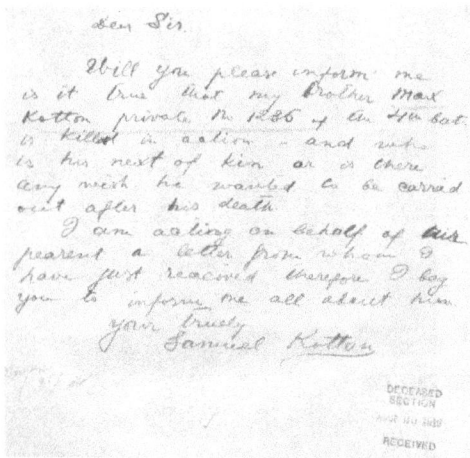

Moisey Kotton's brother Samuel also inquired into the circumstances of his death (NAA)

Workers in Brisbane: 'Doubtless you can imagine the position of their father and especially their mother. I am sure you will not refuse the parents' request to find out all the particulars about my son Moses. Surely there must be somebody who was near him when he died? There must be some record about his death, and the belongings left after him.' Ironically, this letter has been preserved because it was intercepted by the Australian Censor.[90]

On 29 September the Allies began their main assault on the Hindenburg Line itself. The Australians, whose ranks had been significantly thinned, were fighting alongside two American divisions. Attacking south of Péronne, they were to capture the well-defended German positions over the tunnelled St Quentin Canal. After hard fighting they successfully attained their objective but suffered many casualties at what was to be, for the Australian infantry, their last battle on the Western Front. On 3 October 1918, Andrew Kovalevsky was killed, the last Ukrainian Anzac to fall on the battlefront. But we will finish the story of our Anzacs' battles on a more cheerful note: on 8 November 1918, only three days before the end of war, Stephen Surovsov, who served as a sapper in 1st Tunnelling Company, attaining the rank of corporal, was mentioned in despatches.[91]

The Armistice announced on 11 November 1918 was celebrated throughout Europe and especially in the trenches of the Western Front. Some statistics may help us appreciate the scale of the slaughter. Out of 72 Ukrainian-born Anzacs who fought on the Western Front, by the time of Armistice only 22 were still there. All the rest were dead, wounded or sick and had been repatriated to England and Australia. Among those 22 who survived the ordeal, four were Gallipoli veterans: Sage, Tkachenko, Roomianzoff, and Pinkevitch. Breitman, Zmood, Afendikoff and Snegovoy had been wounded several times. A lucky few came through the war unscathed: Pinkevitch, Pesmany, and Peachenoff, who served in a field ambulance unit, Surovsov from a tunnelling company, Sologub from the Field Engineers, Lewy Cotton from the traffic control detachment, and Sage, Mackomel, Gorodezky, Rothstein, and Cooper from the artillery regiments.

George Breitman (Australian Jewry Book of Honour)

The last Ukrainian-born Anzac to die as a casualty of war was George Breitman. In spite of being gassed in August 1918, he spent the winter of 1918-1919 in the harsh conditions of the former front line, where Australian soldiers were engaged in salvage operations, reburials of the fallen and similar tasks. Breitman developed pneumonia and was transported to an English hospital, but his gas-affected lungs failed: he died on 19 April 1919.[92]

The total losses among Ukrainian Anzacs, out of 101 on active service, were 13:
- 1 killed at Gallipoli (Pshevolodskey)
- 1 killed in an accident in Egypt (Noweetsky)
- 10 killed on the Western Front (Domilovsky, Cherpiter, Kiva, Maximenko, Rossoggsky, Malisheff, Lebovich, Leffow, Kotton, and Kovalevsky)
- 1 died of illness in England (Breitman).

Blending in

Gradually all the troops were withdrawn from France and Belgium and, after a short stay in England, almost all were repatriated to Australia. Before proceeding to the Anzacs' lives in peacetime, we need to consider more closely the question of their absorption, as foreigners, into the army, and see how 'mateship', that cornerstone of the Anzac legend, applied to them.

Their blending in often began soon after they donned an army uniform. In photographs, wearing their uniforms, they appear indistinguishable from other Anzacs. Being in the Army – in a crowd of self-assured, rowdy, masculine soldiers – empowered them with extra protection, which they often lacked as civilians, especially as immigrants with poor English. As mentioned earlier, it may have been easier for hard-bitten seamen to adjust to army life. The memoirs of Alexander Brodsky, whose father, Louis, enlisted in the AIF after seafaring the globe, provide such an example:

> He was promised a commission as an officer, but was made only a sergeant! Thwarted Brodskys aren't the most companionable of people (ha ha) and Dad 'played up'. Soon at Seymour Camp, Dad was demoted to a corporal, because his leave-taking from the camp was rather 'unorthodox' (ha ha).
>
> We went to see him in his khakis one Sunday, and Issy and I, not knowing how the soldiers hated plum and apple jam, had clubbed together to buy Dad a special present. Dad swooped on us all in his enthusiastic way, arriving at the station to meet us in an army wagon. When we offered him the jam and he read the label, his face quickly darkened and he threw that tin, I reckon, about a 100 yards. He then took us to a fruit shop, to buy us something, quarrelled with the proprietor over the prices and overturned a huge barrow of the fruit, in protest! Thank goodness other soldiers were about to prevent the owner from getting at Dad.[93]

This was the behaviour of an Australian larrikin turned Anzac, seen through the eyes of a 10-year-old boy. This is followed by further tales which Louis would tell his family about his overseas 'service':

It wasn't until 1916 that Dad actually sailed for the war zones, by which time his gambling had caused him the loss of his higher rank (ha ha), though at last, he was actually pretty successful. He spent as though his money was water and on his troopship, his activities as a gambler won the unwelcome attentions of his superiors. As a result, he was thrown into 'the clink' after a court-martial, but luckily (or unluckily) he contracted acute muscular rheumatism and was destined never to have reached a battlefield. He remained at Alexandria and Cairo, and was eventually invalided back to Australia and discharged. Altogether, he served about three years (in the Army I mean, not 'the jug' ha ha); and later, much later, he was eventually granted a considerable pension when he'd run out of ideas and good health.[94]

We know that Louis' army service did not go exactly like this – upon reaching Egypt he deserted from the Army – but characteristically, when blending myth and reality about his misadventures, he obviously enjoyed portraying himself as a gambler, which was another iconic feature of an archetypical Anzac.

Another seaman, Phillipp Gorbach, on his return from Egypt found himself trapped in the training camp in Liverpool. In February 1916 he joined a protest against the poor conditions there. Riots erupted and thousands of soldiers broke out, hijacked trains and invaded Sydney, drinking the bars dry and rampaging through the streets. Gorbach was among those arrested and court martialled. In his statement he said 'that he was a Russian, and had put in eight months in Egypt, being returned sick. He came into the city on February 14, but took no part in the riots. A trooper's horse trod on his foot, he pushed the horse, and was arrested'. He was sentenced to 90 days' hard labour and discharged with ignominy.[95]

Alexander Sank, who had enlisted with a group of Russians in Rockhampton in July 1915, began his career by 'using threatening language to a superior officer', for which he was put under open arrest, but nevertheless sailed to Egypt with the 9th Battalion. Such behaviour was unthinkable for a private in the Tsarist Army, let alone a Jewish private; in the Australian Army it was less unusual. Mrs H. G. Wheeler, an Australian from Rockhampton who lived in London during the war, offered another glimpse of Sank's first steps in blending in. In a letter to a friend in June 1916 she wrote: 'Two Russians, Sholmatoff and Jank [Sank], who came from Mount Morgan, are also there [at Harefield Hospital], and they were quite excited when they heard I was from Rockhampton.'[96] This was when Sank was in hospital, having been badly wounded soon after reaching the front. Clearly he already felt that he belonged to the Anzacs and to Queensland.

Ivan Rossoggsky, who spent two years as a farm labourer in Glenrock station, maintained ties with the community there while he was at the front. He regularly wrote to a local man and 'always spoke of doing his bit for his King and good old Australia'. When he was wounded, he wrote that 'he hoped soon to be back with his battalion'. He did indeed return to his battalion, to be killed six days later. News of his death was received with 'deep regret' among 'his Glenrock friends'.⁹⁷ When Nicholas Gulevich was hospitalised with shell-shock, his friend James Young passed the news to a Rockhampton newspaper. In the case of the Jewish Thomas Pesmany, his skill at wrestling helped him to fit in.⁹⁸

A lack of English did not necessarily prevent the Anzacs from building ties of mateship, but this mateship did not come in a brochure-ready form. Peter Tilleard, a grandson of Cezar Wolkowsky, remembers:

'Ah Pesmany (Chinese wrestler)' starring in the 9th Field Ambulance Opera Company on the troop ship (The 7th F.A.B. Yandoo, 19 June 1916)

> When he joined the army he virtually had no English; he was a bit of a novelty, speaking Russian. So other soldiers gave him a nickname 'Russ', as in Russian. The soldiers had a lot of fun with 'Russ' because his English was so poor. He did not know what the swear words were. So they used to tell him some swear words and tell him to go and say them to the officers. And he did, because he did not know what he was saying. So he used to get into big trouble, because he go and swear at them. But these soldiers were not nasty, they were just having some fun.

The fact that Wolkowsky kept the nickname 'Russ' throughout all his life – 'We, grandchildren, always called him Russ, even my father would call him Russ', Peter remembers, adding that 'He was proud of it' – suggests that however rough was the beginning of his service, Wolkowsky had no ill feelings to his larrikin mates and was thus accepted into the order of Australian mateship. Who else but these very larrikins would carry him off the frontline under enemy fire when he was severely wounded soon after the landing at Gallipoli.⁹⁹

Cezar Wolkowsky proudly wore not only his returned serviceman badge but the nickname 'Russ' (Courtesy of Peter Tilleard)

Nevertheless, for many Ukrainian Anzacs the process of blending in was not easy. The alienation they felt was obvious in the case of the 'Bloody Russian' Joe Felipor, discussed above. Prominent among its causes, naturally, was their difficulty in mastering English. We find numerous references to this in their service records: '[Disease] history difficult to obtain – he is a Russian' (Kavitski), 'Does not speak English well' (Sepscak), and even 'Speaks very little English and seems stupid and useless, mentally deficient'. The latter was said about Matfeus Oleinikoff, who a couple of years earlier was characterised by the local policeman in Cordalba as 'a steady and industrious man, [who] bears an exceptionally good character'.[100]

'His High Excellency Mr Fish'
Stephen Loosgie's letter

The tragic consequence of the lack of English are obvious in the case of Stephen Loosgie. A man in his thirties from Voloskovtsy township in Chernihiv province, he served for six years in the Russian army, and, having reached Queensland from the Russian Far East only a few months before the war, had had little time to learn English. After enlisting with a group of his countrymen, he served at Gallipoli and on the Western Front, where he was wounded in March 1917. After recovery in a hospital in England, he was sent to the training depot at Perham Down to be returned to the trenches. But before risking his life once again, he had an important task to complete. He found some writing paper in the Church Army Recreation Hut and set about writing an appeal to 'His High Excellency Mr Fish'. The Mr Fish in question was obviously Mr Andrew Fisher, the former Prime Minister of Australia and now the Australian High Commissioner in London.

Stephen Loosgie (QP)

Loosgie scribbled his name and battalion number in English, but that was all he could manage in that language, so he continued in Russian, in the style of a village scribe:

I have honour to request His Excellency Mister Fish I am a Russian in Australian Army 28 months when I left Brisbane I left 3 shillings a day in Commonwealth Bank and seeing as I was always on the front couldn't never find out do I have money in bank or not.

However irrelevant Loosgie's story of his 3 shillings might seem to the duties invested in the High Commissioner, he

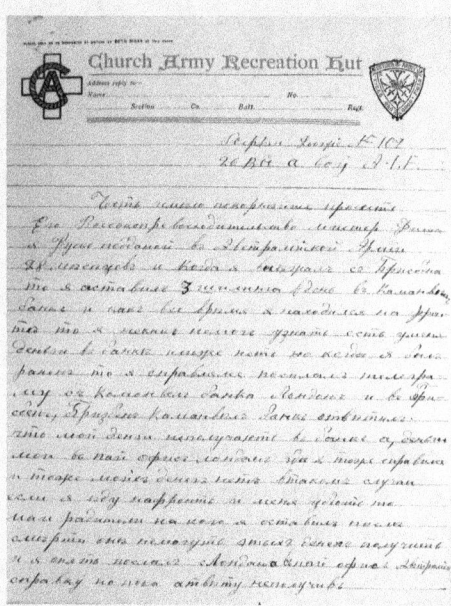

Stephen Loosgie's letter to Andrew Fisher (AWM)

had every reason to worry: from Southwark Military Hospital in London he made enquiries about the fate of the money he was deducting from his pay, and found no trace of it, either in his Australian bank, or in the pay office in London. 'In this case,' he concluded, 'if I go to the front and get killed my parents what I left my money to wont get no money.' There is no doubt that Loosgie's allotment had been properly processed, as were those of every other soldier, and the money was waiting for him somewhere, but his lack of English made for difficulties, and the many strange spellings of his surname complicated his search. In the shipping records it was spelt as Lutstschik & S. Susjic; he had signed his enlistment form as S. Loosjic, but the clerk recorded it as Loosgic, from which it progressed to Loosgie.

The concluding paragraph of his letter exhibits a stylistic and cultural struggle between the meek Ukrainian peasant and the self-assured Australian Anzac. In rough translation it reads:

> In that case I request I get possibility to stay at the camp I am at now till I get the full information where my money is and I even intend not to go before I get a full information and even I would like to get transfer to Russian army because I don't know English.
> I most humbly request to give me the answer immediately.

It appears that somebody in the Church Army Recreation Hut decided to assist Loosgie in his struggle with English, correcting the name of the addressee, 'Mr Andrew Fisher, High Commissioner for Australia' and setting out what seemed to be his main point in an extra sheet:

> Sir,
> I hereby apply for a transfer from the Australian Military Forces to the Russian Army as I have had six years service in the Russian Military Forces.
>
> Yours faithfully,
> Private S. Loosgic

Whatever Loosgie tried to explain to his editor about the 3 shillings and his parents in Ukraine was obviously not understood. His three pages – two in Russian and one in English – were passed on: the High Commissioner's Office forwarded it to the AIF Administrative Headquarters in Westminster, and a lieutenant-colonel sent instructions to the AIF depots in Tidworth: 'Will you kindly inform this man that owing to the difficulties of transport to Russia, his application for discharge is not approved.' A major at Tidworth accordingly passed the order to Perham Down Depot to inform 'the abovementioned man about the decision'.[101] Only a week had passed from the moment Loosgie wrote his appeal in Russian – which went unread – until the date when he received the response. Two weeks later, in July 1917, he was drafted to the front in France.

The case of this naïve Russian letter falling through the cracks of the bureaucratic system might seem insignificant, but for him the consequences were dramatic. In September 1917 he left his battalion, was caught four days later and court martialled as a deserter. He pleaded not guilty, explaining that his three brothers had been killed while serving in the Russian army, his elderly father needed his help and he had left his battalion in order to sort out the situation with his allotment of money, so that he could help his father. His commander testified that he was a 'good man in the line'. He was found not guilty of desertion and returned to the trenches. Only after being wounded twice more was he finally withdrawn from the front and returned to Australia – not his home in Voloskivtsi in Chernihiv province.[102]

Nicholas Gulevich (3rd row, 6th from the left) with his 8th Medium Trench Mortar Battery comrades, in March 1918, not long before he fell ill (AWM). *Inset:* Nicholas Gulevich (QP)

The wariness directed at those who did not speak like Australians was easily channelled into suspicion of a political nature. It ranged from bizarre cases like that of Platon Beloshapka, who was continually taken for a German, to less obvious ones, often with tragic outcomes. For instance Nicholas Gulevich, an educated man and a competent artilleryman, was invalided back to Australia in 1918 after suddenly developing traumatic neurasthenia at the front. His medical history has only a brief reference to its possible causes, stating that he was 'well … until April 1918 – mistaken for spy – very nervy'.[103] Soon after the Russian revolution, Christian Rink was declared 'a German, who had, at Adelaide, served a sentence of imprisonment for fraud, having been convicted under the name of Schmidt'. He was speedily shipped back to

Australia as 'undesirable' and declared to be not eligible for medals.[104] The quite successful career of the 'linguist' Yur Kivovitch, who served in the Censor's Office in Egypt, did not protect him from the suspicions of Australian Intelligence. Returned to Australia as medically unfit in 1917, he worked in the Censor's offices in Sydney, Adelaide and Perth. A letter addressed to him provoked correspondence between Intelligence Section officers, commenting that 'He left the impression in the Censor Office that he was anxious to get into the Secret Service.'[105]

The Russian revolutions of 1917 contributed to the desire of some of the Ukrainian Anzacs to terminate their service. As will be remembered, many had joined the AIF because they could not join the Russian army. Now, after the Russian withdrawal from the war, some did not feel that they should be required to serve any longer. A group of Russian subjects from the 4th Division lobbied for discharge and were finally returned to Australia in 1918 'on account of Russian nationality'.[106] The Ukrainian Richard Gregorenko, who served with the Field Ambulance on the Western Front from 1916 to 1918, was among them.

Richard Gregorenko (QP)

Andrew Snegovoy from Odessa, who enlisted as a motor driver, had also been wounded twice and returned to the trenches; he left his battalion on 12 September 1918, was accused of desertion and sentenced to five years' penal servitude. Prior to deserting he had made an unsuccessful attempt to obtain a discharge, arguing that his family in Russia needed his help.[107] Saveliy Tkachenko, who was first court martialled at Gallipoli for a self-inflicted wound, made a number of attempts to be spared further service while on the Western Front. Finally he was court martialled and sentenced to 'Penal servitude for life', although the sentence was suspended not long after and he was sent back to the trenches.[108] Having difficulties with English, he was obviously unable to explain his case.

Andrew Snegovoy (QP)

Another court martial, that of Denis Papchuck, takes us back to the matter of mateship. Born in Berezdiv in Volhynia, Papchuck landed in Western Australia as a seaman. After more than two years of exemplary service on the Western Front as a sapper with the 3rd Tunnelling Company, on 25 September 1918, he and his Australian comrade T.W. Johnson refused to get into a lorry that was to take them to the trenches without their paybooks, arguing that they were acting in accordance with company orders. They were court-martialled together and in the end given suspended sentences.[109] At the time Papchuck was worried about his mother Olga, from whom he had received no letters since the war began, and planned go to Ukraine to look after his parents after his discharge, but his act of insubordination owed more to camaraderie rather than his personal circumstances.

The turmoil caused by the Russian revolution had far-reaching implications, including social criticism of the status quo in 'Imperial' nations, and Russian and Ukrainian socialists suddenly found common ground with their British and Australian counterparts. One such 'revolutionary' was Peter Kusmin (Samuel Zadorohney) from Kyiv, whom we last saw in a depot in England after he was severely wounded in the face in April 1917. A year later the censor intercepted a letter which he sent to a relative in Siberia:

> Here in England they have a Bourgeois Government, i.e. worse than a Monarchy. The rich look down on the poor as if they were cattle. The poor are almost dying from hunger. In Russia the working people all have their own houses but in England the working classes have nothing. ... I have already asked to be sent to the Russian Army but have received no reply. They tell me I made an oath to King George V to fight to the end of the war, but I am ready to send him to the same place the Russian soldiers sent their Tzar to. I have a lot of good friends who know why the war is being continued, but they are afraid to speak, but if the war continues a year or two more the same will happen here as in Russia and the people will fight the Capitalist whom they will find is their enemy and not the Germans.

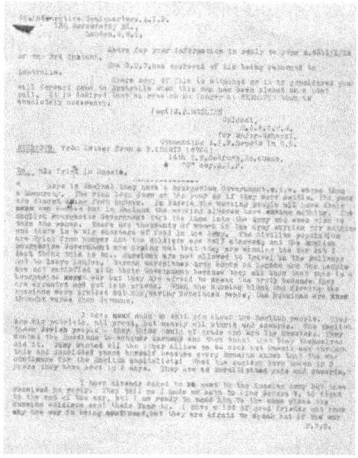

Peter Kusmin's letter intercepted by Australian security services (NAA)

There was obviously some official concern about his 'good friends' who shared these radical views, so Kusmin was embarked on the first transport back to Australia.[110] Unlike Kusmin, who wanted to obtain a transfer to the Russian Red Guards, Richard Gregorenko, after being withdrawn from the front 'on account of Russian nationality', was considering fighting against the Red Army with the British North Russia Expeditionary Force, which was then being formed, but changed his mind and was repatriated to Australia.[111]

'Ya vas lublu soldat' (Interlude)

The assimilation of our Anzacs in Australian society was facilitated not only by their comrades in the army but by women as well. A rare document from Nicholas Fedorovich, whose journey from Gallipoli to Odessa and St Petersburg we have seen above, gives us an opportunity to see the human being behind the clumsy and compressed official records, in which their words were occasionally quoted. Fedorovich's short story, *Kismet* – fate – was written in Russian, translated by Victor Marsden, the Russian correspondent of the *Morning Post*, and published after the war in a North Queensland newspaper.[112] It is emblematic that this earliest sample of Ukrainian literature in Australia was inspired by the author's experience on the battlefront.

The story starts with an advertisement placed by a soldier in a newspaper: 'Dumped down in the middle of "Nowhere," lonely Australian, badly needs cheering. What offers? Write, "Austro," 9th Inf. Bn., A.I.F.' An English woman, Esme Stuart, writes a brief to the 'Lonely Soldier Boy in the Trenches', masking her shyness under the detached irony of a girl influenced by modernity. The soldier accepts this style of mateship: 'Good luck to the modern girl, may she live long to enjoy herself. Give me the woman who can be a pal to a man, and you have the straightest, truest creation God ever made.' For a while they try to see each other as merely 'ships that pass in the night', but the war brings the reality of life very near:

> As I write, the first faint flush of dawn is tinting the skies with palest pink – the glimmering stars pale and fade away in the coming splendour of morn; far away one can just faintly hear the distant thunder of guns. God is very near in the shell-swept silent places of Flanders, and under the quiet stars a man may learn much of himself and his Maker.

The war makes both the passage of time and 'Austro' and Esme's feelings for each other develop rapidly. But when Esme is about to meet her 'dearest Boy in the world', the news come that he was killed in battle. The shrill voice of a newsboy comes to Esme from below her window: 'Extra Special! Glorious charge of the Australians. Last stand of the 9th Light Infantry A.I.F.'. The commemoration of his 9th Battalion was very important for Fedorovich, and his fallen hero is Australian, not Ukrainian or Russian, this being the world to which Fedorovich now belonged. Not often would Ukrainian writers be in a position to write 'from the inside' about the host nation where they had settled only a few years earlier. It was the war that facilitated this rapid cultural absorption.

As for the letters, it was quite common for Anzacs from Ukraine to receive letters – like those received by Wolf Dorfman – from Australian women and children, who became the bridge connecting them with the society of the country in whose army they were serving. George Malisheff, for example, 'was on terms of great friendship with [Mrs Ellen Hammersley's] family and before leaving them he said he was going to fix things so that [her daughters] would benefit in the event of his death'. They sent him parcels and letters until he was killed at Hazebrouck in 1918.[113]

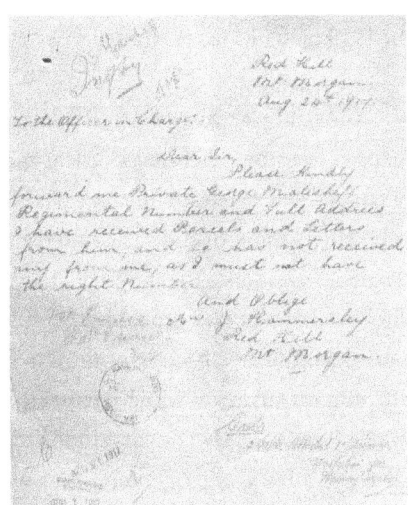

Letter from Hammersley's family inquiring about George Malisheff's address (NAA)

As in Fedorovich's story, British and Australian women, probably more readily than the fighting men, opened their hearts to strangers from distant lands, including Ukraine.

While recuperating after Gallipoli in England, Lamotte Alexis Sage, a Ukraine-born Frenchman who had been working in the Western Australian bush since the 1890s, wrote about English women in a letter:

> Am now fully recovered from my scratches and ready to take the field. The people of England are very kind to us. To give you an idea I might mention that on one occasion Queen Alexandra and the Grand Duchess George of Russia waited on us at table, and the kindness of the nurses! We are soldiers, but these women are making martyrs of themselves, the way they slave to make us comfortable. The people themselves cannot do enough for us, and in hospital I used to get letters from people I had never heard of. The other day I was waited on at breakfast by a lady who invited me to lunch with her. You cannot imagine how I looked when on my waiting friend's arriving home I found she had not less than 30 servants at her command, and was addressed as 'Your Grace'.[114]

During his brief stay in England, he met a woman called Rosa Hales, twenty years his junior; they married before he was sent to the Western Front. We learn the continuation of the story from a letter he wrote in 1917, while on leave in England:

> I, myself, am fortunate, for I am at present on leave at my temporary home at East Lis, Hants, England, and as I lift my eyes from this paper I behold a little woman of surpassing beauty – my wife. On her lap sits a little child nearly twelve months old – our war baby, born while I was on the battlefield of France, and whom I, her father, saw but for the first time on Wednesday last![115]

In 1919 he sailed for Australia on a family troopship with his wife and young daughter.

The family archive of Cezar Wolkowsky, preserved by his grandchildren, tells of another happy love story. Pictured overleaf is a hospital photo taken soon after Wolkowsky and his wounded mates left the horrors of Gallipoli behind and returned to Sydney. The young girl who enters the shot and sits comfortably on the lap of the Ukrainian soldier, our Wolkowsky, seems to symbolise the longing all of them now felt to return to love, family, and a peaceful life. Wolkowsky was probably the only one among them who had nobody to return to in Australia, nor much hope of finding someone. But miraculously, just a few weeks after returning to Australia, while recuperating in a convalescent hospital, Cezar met his girl. She was 18-year-old Gwynnyth Woodberry from a prominent Tasmanian family; she came to Sydney with a group of entertainers who would go to hospitals to cheer up the troops.[116] On the 8th of August 1916 he gave her his photograph, carefully spelling out her name in Russian, 'М-ль Гвыннетс', and adding, perhaps at the last moment, again in Russian, 'Я вас люблю'

('I love you'). Six days later he got leave and they went together to the beach at Port Jackson, where they took photos of each other. Years later these photos would meet each other in their family album, but in meantime they both carried the photo of their loved one. These faded, creased photographs (overleaf, top) must have been their dearest mementos of the day when they opened the hearts to each other, breaking all the ethnic, language, and class barriers that separated them. There is one more photograph of young Gwynnyth in the family archive, a studio portrait (overleaf, bottom), on which she wrote in English script the Russian phrase she learnt to say on that fateful day: 'Ya vas lublu soldat' ('I love you, soldier').

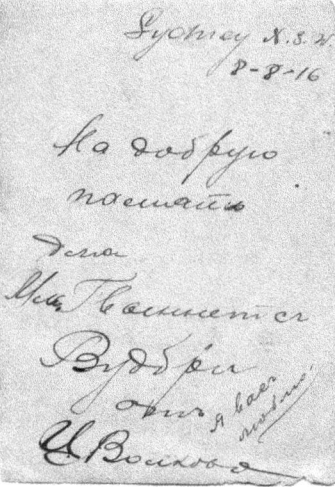

Photographs on pages 101-102: Cezar Wolkowsky and Gwynnyth Woodberry (Courtesy of Peter Tilleard)

At least ten of our Anzacs married during the war. Their brides, whom they usually met while in hospital, were often free to set off into the unknown with their soldier husbands on the army's family troopships. 18-year old Ethel Bateman, who married Joseph Kleshenko, put it simply: 'I am alone, I have nothing to remain here for.' Robert Nicholson married 16-year-old Bertha Grabert, whose father, a seaman, had already died. While recuperating in Britain, Michael Ankudinow met an Irish girl, Maggie Callaghan, and a few weeks later they married in Edinburgh. Ankudinow was discharged in London and planned to take his bride to Russia, arguing in his request to the military authorities: 'I am bred and born in Russia, and I am a Russian subject I am very stranger in Australia. War is over and I want you discharge me in England and sent me back to Russia Vladivostok.'[117] This plan did not work, and the couple sailed to Australia instead. Frank Dynowski married a French girl, Mary Hue, and chose to stay in France after the war.

In almost all such cases, both parties did their best to overcome their ethnic and cultural differences, although inevitably some of these marriages did not last. The story of John Ouchirenko's marriage, which demonstrates this tension, emerged from Ouchirenko's evidence at his court-martial, when he was charged with overstaying his leave in England. 'I was married to an English girl on 5 June 1917, with the consent of the girl's parents. Some time later the girl's parents took exception to me and when I arrived on leave refused to let me know of my wife's whereabouts.' Previously, while in France, Ouchirenko had received letters apparently

> signed by my wife stating that she did not wish to have any more to do with me. These letters affected me so much tat I attempted to commit suicide but was stopped by my C.O. who especially gave me leave to come over and investigate [the] matter. … I was so distracted by the way I was treated by my wife's people … that I really did not know what I was doing.

He suspected that his Ukrainian origin was the reason for such treatment. He was in hospital when his wife Clara found him and it turned out that the letters had been forged by her family. The court, like Ouchirenko's commanding officer in France, was very lenient with him and merely forfeited a fortnight's pay. The story did not have a happy ending, however. Clara had a daughter, Ruby, but did not go with him to Australia, and later cancelled a free passage to Australia that Ouchirenko had organised through the military authorities.[118] Luckily, he subsequently married an Australian girl, with whom he had a large family.

The stories of failed marriages can be continued. Peter Kusmin, while recovering from his wounds in England, married a widow with two children, Mabel Kneller. When he was returned to Australia at short notice, he left her with a child of his own as well.[119] Jack Vengert, wounded at Gallipoli, upon his return to Australia worked as a railway watchman at Dora Creek Bridge near Newcastle. There he met Emma Adeline Gudshus, a fisherman's daughter. They married and had a baby, but the marriage did not work; they separated, and Jack enlisted in the AIF once again. He sailed to England in July 1918 but arrived on the Western Front only after the armistice. When he returned to Australia, his life did not go right, but as in many cases, this was part of the tapestry that our heroes were to weave in their postwar life.

Personal Description.

Height 5 ft. 10 in. Colour of eyes Brown

Colour of hair ~~Fair~~ Dark Build Medium

Notable marks Scar on right forearm and instep of right leg. Small scar on cheek under left

Remarks

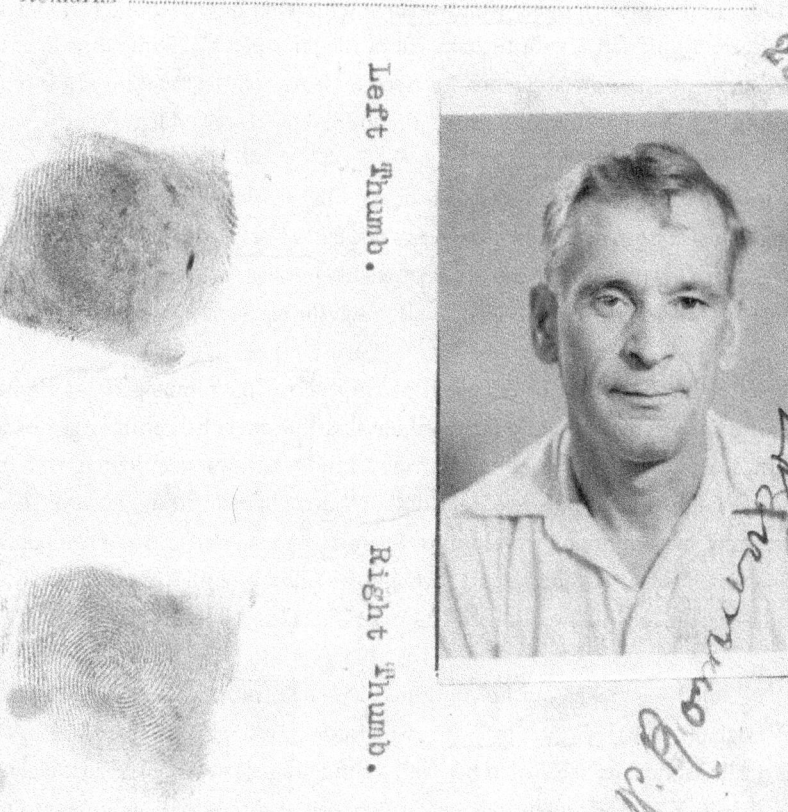

Left Thumb.

Right Thumb.

25 SEP 1939

THREE

LIFE

Nicholas Roomianzoff's Second World War alien registration document. Roomianzoff fought at Gallipoli and on the Western Front but when he returned he never settled and naturalised just before his death, remaining subject to the dictates of the Alien Act. (NAA)

The Bolshevik shadow in Australia

The return to peaceful Australia was long awaited by many AIF soldiers. A few of our Anzacs had families to return to, but the majority were single, or their loved ones were far away in war-torn Ukraine, where civil war was raging. Now they had a chance to make a new home in Australia, but the process of settling down was often far from easy.

Although they were war heroes, they were now also associated with Red Russia, detested for the Bolshevik October Revolution of 1917 and its withdrawal from the war. Australian restrictions aimed at Russian subjects were mounting. The denial of naturalisation, introduced as an incentive to enlist in the AIF in 1915, continued after the war. Alien registration, introduced during the war, remained in force until 1921; if aliens failed to register or notify the police about a change of address, severe fines would follow. 1918 brought a new restriction: Russian subjects were prohibited from leaving Australia, due to fears that they would join the dreaded Bolsheviks in Soviet Russia. At the same time, in many cases they were denied employment and experienced xenophobia from the population at large.

Tensions grew and the culmination came during the Red Flag Riots in Brisbane. On 23 March 1919, several hundred Russian subjects, together with various left-wing radicals, held a rally under the prohibited red flag to demand repatriation for Russians who wanted to return to Russia, the repeal of the War Precautions Act, and an end to Allied intervention in Russia. As a result, 'loyalist' groups, mostly ex-servicemen, took revenge and the following day attacked the lodgings and businesses in Merivale Street, South Brisbane, in the heart of the Russian-Ukrainian-Jewish community. These events were followed by the arrest, conviction and deportation of some of the participants in the rally, along with an Australia-wide targeting of Russian subjects – sackings, evictions, boycotts of their businesses, physical abuse and other humiliations.[1]

After the events in Brisbane, public opinion throughout Australia not only made little effort to distinguish between the community of émigrés from Russia and the organisers of the Bolshevik coup, but became increasingly xenophobic. In April 1919, a month after the Red Flag Riots, when a Brisbane policeman checked 'Russian aliens' in his district, he discovered a boarding house in West End, a Brisbane suburb, with five tenants who had all served in the AIF. One of the five was Ukrainian Constantin Pinkevitch. The landlady, Mrs Bogie, assured the policeman that 'all of them are quiet well behaved men, and they are always in early at night, about eight o'clock playing cards among themselves. No other Russians visit them'. And of course they all reported to the local police station to register under the Alien Registration Act. Nevertheless, said Mrs Bogie, 'the military have already raided the place twice, and searched the effects of these men'.[2] Being 'Russian' was now fraught with risk.

Formally speaking, Ukrainian-born Anzacs enjoyed more privileges than their civilian countrymen. They could be naturalised free of charge, but if not naturalised, they and their British or Australian-born wives had to undergo the humiliating procedure of alien registration at the police station. The oath of allegiance to the King that they took when enlisting in the AIF, let alone their service to the Empire on the battlefields, now counted for nothing. Moreover, service in the AIF was not, in itself, sufficient proof of a man's loyalty in the eyes of the Australian security services; in some cases, quite the opposite. Thus in 1919 AIF Base Records prepared a special report for the director of the Investigation branch, Major Harold Jones, on the service of a number of Russian-born returned soldiers, including the Ukrainians Wolkowsky, Kleshenko, and Kusmin.[3] An Investigation Branch inspector noted, 'for internal use': 'The fact that so many Russians are returned soldiers of the A.I.F. is, in the main, due to the fact that many of them enlisted in our forces to avoid being conscripted by the Russian Government at the time, which demanded of its subjects one of these courses.'[4]

The biggest hurdle for foreign-born Anzacs wishing to settle in post-war Australia was the inequality that they experienced in respect of employment. In October 1919 Cezar Wolkowsky, 'a Russian, who served with the A.I.F., informed the Minister in Sydney that he and about a dozen other Russians, returned A.I.F. men, had been refused work on the wharves by the Shipping Companies, ostensibly because the Companies' policy was to give preference to Australians', according to a Repatriation Department memorandum. In November that year Joseph Kleshenko appealed directly to W.M. Hughes, the Prime Minister, about the same matter:

> Dear Sir,
>
> I was speaking to you on the wagon at Sussex St and you asked me to write my case. I am a British subject born in Russia. Eleven other Russians and myself – all who are discharged soldiers who have fought with the A.I.F.
>
> We had a disc at the Returned Soldiers Bureau and had them taken from us at a moment's notice without the slightest reason.
>
> We tried to find out why it was that we should have the bread and butter [taken] from us, but could get no satisfaction. We were told that so many Australians were out of work and we were taking the work from them.
>
> The majority of us are married men [with] the Australian wives and children, and is it fair to us who have fought for England's King and Country just the same as any Australian man and we carry the scars of battle just the same as any Australian to be put out of work because we are born in Russia.
>
> Our Australian wives have to suffer, also our children. There is nothing else for the wives to do but go to work and keep the home going the best she can.

I would [like] you to do something for us. We can get no one to listen to us. Because we are Russians. But Mr W. Hughes has never been known to turn the diggers down. So we feel sure you will try and help us. [...]

I remain Yours
Faithfully
Joseph Kleshenko

The Repatriation Department Deputy Comptroller investigating the case provided the following explanation: 'The Russians are reported to me by the Secretary of the Shipping Labour Bureau as being distinctly undesirable, and the cause of considerable trouble through their Bolshevik tendencies which are continually canvassed amongst the wharf labourers.' Clearly, employers were taking advantage of the jingoistic attitudes of some Australian workers when, in order to rid themselves of any threat of a 'Red menace', they singled out 'Russians' for dismissal on the pretext that they were taking jobs from Australians. There is some suggestion that the Repatriation Department may have then contemplated offering the Russian subjects free passage back to Soviet Russia and that at least some of them were sounded out over the idea, but nothing came of it.[5] When the Bolshevik scare settled, some of our heroes returned to the waterfront; others moved elsewhere.

The Ukrainian-born Anzacs were returning to Australia in the midst of turmoil brought about by the Russian Revolution and radical ideas in general; as a result, ideological confrontations split the Russian-Ukrainian communities in Australia. In Brisbane, for example, Ukrainian-born Matfeus Oleinikoff and Nicholas Fedorovich were among those who signed a collective letter in response to the anti-war sentiments of a Russian, Walter Kalasnikoff (Kalashnikoff), declaring that they would 'fight the so-called Bolsheviks to the bitter end'. Kalasnikoff returned from the war severely wounded and nearly blind and died in the arms of his Ukrainian wife Mary Rudovsky; a denunciation received by the police stated that 'the wife is well known for her Bolshevik views, and that Kalashnikoff is led by his wife'.[6]

Others, on the contrary, came under the influence of Bolshevism and aimed to defend their own rights with the help of Bolshevik ideas. Thus John Ouchirenko was heavily fined for 'exhibiting a Red Flag at Yarra Bank' (Flinders Park, Melbourne) on 16 March 1919. His trial took place only the next year 'on account of Oucherenko being a patient for some months in the Mont Park Military Hospital'. He was fined £2, with £3/5/6 costs, which equalled a month's wages.[7] It did not deter him from taking part in the Melbourne riots of 1923, which followed a police strike, when crowds poured into central Melbourne, smashing

John Ouchirenko (Victoria Police Gazette, 1924)

shop windows, looting, and overturning trams.[8] The dock worker Joseph Kleshenko was, according to police records, 'known to write to newspapers on Bolshevism'.[9] So did Cezar Wolkowsky, who was considered 'to be of Bolshevik tendencies' because he 'contributed articles to papers of that type, advocating Bolshevik principles'.[10] These newspaper articles show that his ideas at that time were a combination of Bolshevik slogans, some very sound reasoning, and naivety. Giving 'an idea of how Sydney would live under Bolshevik rule', he predicted:

> Once under control, the State would be divided into districts and counties, according to a population basis. Each area would elect a Soviet, which would govern. [...] To best illustrate how the Bolsheviks would control business, let me take the case of a big city house as an example. The first thing we would do would be to reorganise the working conditions. There would not be a four-hour day for one section of the workers and a longer stretch for others. All would do an equal amount of work. Wages would be equal. In general there would be no reason for the factory system to exist, and the existing conditions would disappear.
>
> The Bolsheviks claim that they can destroy what they consider one of the world's greatest curses; that is, profiteering. Having accomplished that, we consider the workers would engage in industry with a harmony hitherto unknown.
>
> By free love is meant a system of permitting men and women to make their own choice in the matter of a partner. It means that, with women emancipated from the servitude of factory and shop-life, they will be able to choose such partners as they desire, without looking out for an escape from the drudgery of the slavish work behind a counter, or in front of a machine. Free love, arising from economic freedom, would abolish prostitution, and the evils concomitant with it.[11]

But while the opportunity to govern Australia with Soviets remained slim, our heroes had to find their place in the real life of post-war Australia. Cezar Wolkowsky started a family with his newfound love Gwynnyth, and became a tram conductor in Sydney; this reduced his involvement in pro-Bolshevik circles, but we will return to his story later.

On land and sea

Miners and seafarers

Despite the fact that a number of Ukrainian Anzacs were discharged on medical grounds or spent time recuperating in hospitals, many took on difficult and dangerous work in mines and on ships. Ksenofont Kozachuk, who was discharged from the AIF in 1916 as medically unfit, was healthy enough to spend four years cane-cutting in the north, near Cairns, and as a trimmer on a ship; in 1922, after his marriage, he found permanent employment in the Collinsville coal mine near Bowen. When rumours about gold in New Guinea reached Australia in 1926, Kozachuk, with a group of Australian gold-seekers, went to Salamaua Bay and Edie Creek, in the mountains. Apparently he did not make his fortune, as he returned to the Collinsville mine. In 1941 he suffered 'a fractured skull and severe shock caused by a heavy fall of coal' while working there.[12] Richard Gregorenko found work at a steelworks in Newcastle upon his discharge from the army.[13]

After the war, Robert Nicholson was seafaring from the UK (UK National Archives)

Ouchirenko, a mechanic by trade, spent 1919 in the Repatriation Hospital, and then found work for a short time at a workshop in Melbourne, then went to sea. In 1919 he worked as a fireman on the *Dimboola* and the *Bombala* sailing from Melbourne to Sydney; in 1922 he was a member of the crew of the SS *Australbrook*; in 1923-1926 he served as a fireman on the *Koonda* and other ships. It was only health problems and marriage that made him leave the sea and settle in the country.[14] For the educated James Gretchinsky, an electrical engineer, seafaring was an option to which he had to resort when all else failed. Discharged from the AIF as medically unfit in 1915, he could not find work as a driver or as an interpreter in the censor's office; he was reduced to the duties of an engine-room rating on ships. In 1917 we meet him as a greaser on the *Borda*; in 1923, a greaser on the *Makura*; in 1924, a wiper on the *Niagara*. Only after several restless years did he manage to find employment as an electrician and settle in Sydney. As time went by, some of our labourers and seamen became waterside workers. Denis Papchuck, a former seaman, worked as a painter and docker in Fremantle, while Nicholas Roomianzoff, a labourer, became a docker in Mackay in 1939.

Swagmen

Australia offered other options for those who were not ready or not able to settle. Alien registration, which tracked every movement of non-naturalised foreigners, helps us to see the patterns of their migrations across the land. After months in hospital, Joseph Rudezky, a Gallipoli veteran who was severely wounded in the left arm at Pozières in August 1916, was demobilised in Australia in August 1917. At first he had enough money from his war service to stay at the Soldiers Residential Club in Brisbane, but by November 1917 he had set off to the north in search of work, which he found at the Macknade Sugar Mill on the Herbert River near Halifax. In January 1918 he moved to Townsville and in February 1918 was back in Brisbane. In June of that year, probably running out of money again, he set off back to the Macknade Sugar Mill, then to Ingham and Townsville. In November 1918 he was back in South Brisbane for the Christmas holidays, when his countrymen from all over Queensland would congregate in the Russian-Ukrainian-Jewish enclave there. In February 1919, during the influenza pandemic, he was at Wallangarra Quarantine Camp, on the border with New South Wales; three months later he was back in Brisbane, staying in different boarding houses including 'Kiev' in Woolloongabba.[15] By that time he had abandoned his cane-cutting excursions to the north, as his health was rapidly deteriorating with the onset of tuberculosis.

Joseph Rudezky (QP)

Nicholas Roomianzoff enlisted in the AIF with Rudezky, fought at Gallipoli and was severely wounded at Mouquet Farm soon after his mate. He returned to the trenches only to be wounded once again, but was on the Western Front at the time of the November Armistice in 1918. Discharged in Brisbane in July 1919, he set off to Mackay, another centre of the sugar cane industry. In April 1920 he found a job at Haggy Rock Railway Construction. Six months later he migrated back to Mackay. By that time alien registration had been abolished, but he continued his nomadic lifestyle in the following years. Maxim Shular, who twice tried to enlist in the AIF, made similar movements between three places: Brisbane, where he would stay at the 'Moscow' boarding house; Townsville; and Mount Morgan, a mining centre.[16]

For some, like Platon Beloshapka, the classical Australian patterns of 'swagmanship' tended to evolve into destitution bordering on vagrancy, perhaps inspired by a naïve philosophy of class struggle. Unable to find and retain jobs, he would wander the streets and scavenge for food in rubbish bins. His behaviour sometimes seemed to border on insanity, but the occasional Bolshevik slogans which he uttered when arrested, his 'unkempt black beard' and obvious 'Russianness' turned sympathies away from him. In 1924 he was arrested while 'scantily clad and without boots chasing fowls' near Glen Innes; standing in the dock he declared: 'I am a Bolshevik', while 'the court visibly shuddered to think the real thing was so near'.[17] Later that year, when he was jailed again in Inverell, New South Wales, for vagrancy, the police investigation discovered that 'his convictions in order were at the Central Court, Sydney, Wee Waa, Liverpool, four in Queensland, then back again at the Central, then Gunnedah, Glen Innes, and finally … for the ninth time, at Inverell'. A journalist attending the court hearings tried to present a socio-psychological portrait of the vagabond:

> His clothes were green with age, and when the weather was cold he wore an overcoat that was in tatters, so that people turned to look at him. […] He was frankly a vagrant, yet he wore his rags with an air. Well set up, about twelve stone in weight, with the square shoulders and upright bearing of the man who has seen military training, he looked the whole world in the face.

The 'Russian' origin of the vagrant clearly matched contemporary stereotypes, and the 'military training' imagined by the journalist was part of the same image of dreaded 'Russians'.

Moreover, the journalist managed to see in Beloshapka's Ukrainian face 'the broad flatness of the Kalmuk with the Tartar infusion' (it went without saying that all 'Russians' were Asiatic!) The fact that he spoke English produced a new conclusion: this 'shows that he has originally some education, a remarkable thing in Russia, where only the nobles and higher classes are literate'. Ordered to leave the town at once, Beloshapka, 'horribly alone but unruffled, shouldered his dirty bluey and strode along Otho Street with an air of a king in disguise. He still looked the whole world in face, with a certain amount of philosophic interest.' 'There may be a story behind Platonoff's fall, or he may be just continually lazy, but he is certainly unconventional,' concluded the journalist.[18] In the late 1920s, when Beloshapka left for America, he disappears from police records, but in 1930, back in Queensland, he was arrested again for vagrancy, then for attempting to commit a serious offence on a girl under 17. After his release from jail in March 1935, he was arrested in the same month for vagrancy and again for the same offence in June 1935.[19]

Left: Platon Beloshapka in Tamworth Gaol (State Archives, NSW)

Right: The Armidale Express and New England General Advertiser, 1924

Michael Ankudinow, who did not succeed in travelling to Russia from London, returned to Australia with his young Irish wife, and here his life began to fall apart. His police record has a long list of crimes, from drunkenness to larceny, and his wife too had problems with the police. She returned to Britain a decade later, while he became a rolling stone — 'shifting', as he said, from camp to camp, from state to state. In 1940 while living in the Old Men's House at Mount Royal Park, Victoria, he applied to be naturalised. His police report stated, 'He is somewhat of a wanderer, neglects himself and consequently suffers from lack of suitable food.' Nevertheless, his faultless military service outweighed other considerations and he was naturalised in 1941.[20]

ADVISED TO LEAVE PORT PIRIE

RUSSIAN & WIFE SENT TO GAOL

On Saturday Constables V. V. Kennedy and F. W. Ferguson arrested Michael and Maggie Ankudinow, aged 29 and 21 years respectively, for having insufficient means of support, and being deemed to be idle and disorderly. They later appeared before Mr. D. C. Scott, S.M., at the Police Court, and both pleaded guilty.

MICHAEL ANKUDINOW, *alias* GEORGE WILSON, native of Russia, farmer, born 1891, 5ft. 10in. high, medium build, dark complexion, dark-brown hair, blue eyes, ordinary nose, mouth and chin, scar on left side of face, woman holding flag on left forearm, snake and bird outside right forearm. Tried at Port Adelaide on October 15th, 1934, as idle and disorderly; 14 days.

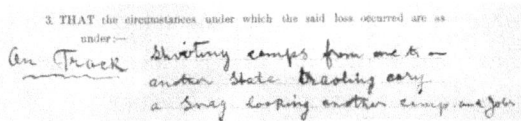

Clockwise from left: Barrier Miner, *27 April 1921;* The South Australian Police Gazette, *1934; Michael Ankudinow's statutory declaration, 1938 (NAA)*

A few continued to lead a nomadic life even after marriage, like Albert Michael Tober, the seaman. Invalided back to Australia after Gallipoli, in 1917 Tober married an Australian girl, Lily Teresa Lawler, and had four children, settling in Cecil Park, west of Sydney, but would still go wandering from time to time, working on various construction projects – he was also a skilled blacksmith, driver, mechanic and carpenter. According to his granddaughter Janice: 'He was versatile and worked at engineering (at the Wyangala Dam project), carpentry (cedar panelling at Parliament House, Canberra) and farming (innovative heated market-garden for early tomatoes) amongst other things.' She remembers that 'all the polish work in Old Canberra [Parliament] House' was done by him. 'He was there when it was built, they lived in a tent and dad was a little toddler and Uncle Pat. Every time grandma was pregnant to have a baby no matter where he was working she always went back to Sydney to have the baby at the Women's hospital in Sydney.' Her grandfather, she added, was

Albert Michael Tober (SL SA)

> a man who could put up a tent, do anything, and could do very good cooking. Dad spent a lot of time with his father – his mother and father sort of separated; pop went his way, a tent in the bush, you know, and he took dad with him, and dad was 14 or 15. And dad learnt a lot of the ways of grandfather.[21]

Documentary records confirm that in February 1925 'Mr. A. M. Tober, Perth Avenue, Canberra', was commissioned to erect a telephone line 'between Canberra and Westlake (Perth Avenue)'. Perth Avenue, in the heart of the national capital, which at that time existed only on the map, must have been where he pitched his family tent. In September the same year he was fined 'for allowing stock to stray on Federal Territory lands'.[22] In February 1927, when the Federal Parliament in Canberra had just opened in the middle of a sheep paddock, Tober sailed to Darwin in the Northern Territory, to return five months later. In 1929 he applied for construction work in Komungla, south of Goulburn, and in Cardiff and Sandgate near Newcastle. More than many conventionally married Australian men, he seemed at home anywhere in Australia.

Settlers

Along with carrying the swag, farming was another classical trope of the Australian cultural narrative throughout the nineteenth and early twentieth centuries. Some of our Anzacs became part of the last Australian generation who toiled the legendary outback. The dream of land ownership was always a part of the Ukrainian psyche, and Australia, with its vast expanses of land, seemingly allowed it to come true. The returning servicemen were entitled to receive a block of land, with a long-term loan on favourable conditions. A number of soldiers' settlements were established all over Australia for this purpose. In 1916 James Gretchinsky applied for a block in Wyalong in remote New South Wales, north of Wagga Wagga; his application was not granted and he, as we have seen, left for the sea.[23] Trooper James Cochura was more successful: in 1919 he took up a block of 458 acres on a soldiers' settlement at Temora, in the same area. Nicholas Fedorovich became a soldier-selector at Glenlyon, southwest of Stanthorpe in 1919: when applying for naturalisation, he wrote, 'I live 45 miles from the railway, only getting mail twice weekly.'[24] His occupation was recorded as a grazier, but by the mid-1920s, when he married, he moved to Brisbane and occasionally worked as a translator. Albert Michael Tober applied for a block of land in the Breeza-Gunnedah area in 1919 as a soldier-settler but, although his loan was approved, he never settled on the land.[25] John Sepscak settled in Bilboa near Kingaroy (Queensland) under the soldiers' settlement scheme; he was also recorded as a grazier. Unlike some others, he stayed on the land until his death in 1946.

Ben Goffin, a young Jewish man from Tulchyn in Podillia, moved to a soldiers' settlement in Walpole near Albany in Western Australia after his marriage in the early 1920s. The couple had three young children, and, as the local newspaper reported, Goffin 'was a typical settler under the Walpole Scheme, hard working, industrious, and most optimistic as to future prospects'. In 1931 he was fencing his block when tragedy struck: as he was carting a load of fencing posts towards his house, the dray overturned and the falling posts crushed him in front of his wife.[26]

A number of Anzacs tried their hand at farming outside the soldier settlement scheme. In many cases they failed and we have very scant information about the hardships they endured.

Albert Morozoff, a seaman, wounded three times on the Western Front, tried to settle on the land in 1918 at Mypolonga irrigation farm, in South Australia, but soon returned to the sea, moving first to Cardiff in Wales, then to California. Joe Felipor, who was court martialled in 1916 as a 'bloody Russian', made an attempt to settle on the land: in 1923 we meet him as a farmer in Bruce Rock in Western Australia, but again he got into a fight with local farmers and his agricultural endeavours probably did not last long.[27] Those who were more persistent achieved success. Agricultural work was Gregory Jakimov's main occupation; having arrived in Australia in 1911, he worked for two years on Momba station, in the remote north-west of NSW. After the war, recovering from his wound, he settled closer to Sydney, in Smithfield, working as a farm manager and then as a 'rural worker'.[28] Joseph Rudezky, fighting tuberculosis, had to move to the dry climate of Dalby, and farming was the only way to feed his large family (by that time he was married and had four daughters). His daughter Violet remembers that when they moved to Dalby 'he built us up a home. We got 3 acres of land from the Catholic church. He worked very hard on the farm. We had goats and horses, he grew all kinds of vegetables and fruits, and he used to send these to the markets'.[29]

Elias Jacob Serebrennikoff's farming career began promisingly. He had worked for a while as a clerk and military attaché in the Russian consulate in Melbourne, but fell out with the consul Alexander Abaza, who accused him of unlawful financial dealings. His entrepreneurial spirit then took a new direction. In early 1917 he married Alice Swanson, who was six years older than he was, and probably had some capital; they farmed in the Templestowe area to the north-east of Melbourne. The rich River Yarra flats of the area provided good land for intensive dairying, which supplied Melbourne with fresh milk. Serebrennikoff's education as a botanist provided him with some agricultural knowledge and in 1922 a Melbourne newspaper published an account of his successful application of advanced farming methods. On his 80-acre farm, Comely Bank, he kept a herd of 42 pedigree cows and even planned to establish a stud. His milking sheds were kept scrupulously clean and the cows were rugged at night to keep them warm. Their balanced diet, which included special home-grown fodder crops, produced splendid results. 'A cow must show a profit on her upkeep, or she is no use to me,' he explained to the reporter. To make delivery easier, Serebrennikoff built a suspension bridge over the Yarra, which provided him with a direct route to Heidelberg and Melbourne, where milk was delivered by motor-lorry.[30] In spite of all their success the Serebrennikoffs did not stay long on the farm; in 1924 it was put to auction, and Jacob travelled to Elko Island in the Northern Territory, where he became involved in exploring oil deposits. In 1927 he died, probably of a tropical disease.[31]

In Queensland, Slavs from the former Russian Empire often farmed in the same areas, which allowed them to maintain community ties. A few sugar cane farmers who started farming before the war in the Booyal area continued working there. The brothers Thomas Platonoff (who served as Platonaff) and George Platonoff returned to Booyal, where they had grown sugar cane with their parents before the war. Thomas, the elder son, severely wounded in the hand, was the first to return in January 1918 and was warmly greeted at a residents' gathering and presented with a gold medal by the chairman of the Booyal Patriotic League. At his request, wrote the local newspaper, 'the returned hero's mother, who was accompanied by her husband, Mr Stephan Platonoff, pinned the medal on her son's breast.'[32] George was discharged in 1919 but returned too late to be reunited with his father: Stephan Platonoff died in December 1918. Their mother, Tatiana Odarchinko, a simple Ukrainian woman whose sacrifice and pride were so publicly recognised, would live for twenty more years, earning the respect of the community, and her passing would be commemorated in the local paper. Soon after demobilisation, Thomas married Vera Kurtish, a girl from a Belarusian family engaged in growing sugar cane. At first they all lived in Booyal, but in the late 1920s Thomas and his family moved further north, to the Mackay area. There they settled in Wundaru and continued sugar cane growing, employing a number of compatriots in the cutting season. George, who never married, stayed in the Booyal area. A friend of their father, Feodot Peachenoff, demobilised in 1919, also returned to Booyal, but worked at cane-cutting as a labourer rather than a farmer; during the Second World War he moved to Sydney. Their third friend Matfeus Oleinikoff moved to Brisbane after demobilisation.

Some Anzacs migrated in the opposite direction, from the city to the country. Richard Gregorenko, who was suffering from tuberculosis, married an Australian girl, Vera Scriven, in 1920, and after five years at a Newcastle steelworks moved with his young family to Brisbane. When his marriage broke up, he decided to make a fresh start, and moved to the Callide Valley, south of Rockhampton, in 1929, taking with him his two young sons, Leonard and George. They took up a selection at Lawgi, where he had to first clear the thick scrub before gradually building a small house from bush timber with cement-rendered bag-walls and a packed earth floor. Scrub wallabies, brush turkeys, damper and rice were the main components of their diet.[33] His Ukrainian farming experience – he grew up in Karapishy near Kyiv – may have helped him to master the Australian bush. Although life was hard, there was one significant compensation for being there: Callide Valley had become the centre of a community of 'White Russians' who had fled the Revolution and now played an important role in pioneering the area. In the early 1930s about a hundred of these families lived along the Valley, including General Tolstoff with his Cossacks. They established the Russian Club at Tangool with a library and organised Russian concerts and dances, which attracted the interest of many local Australians. Russian children accounted for nearly half of all pupils in the local schools. Although this community is known as 'Russian', Ukrainians comprised a significant proportion among the settlers, so Gregorenko must have met a number of his countrymen. For instance, the families of Pavel Dudarko, Semen Gniliak, and Samuel Demchenko were from Kyiv province; Vlas Bessmertny was from Kharkiv, Ivan Makagon from Kherson, and Nikolai Babkoff from Pereslavl in Poltava province.[34] The Gregorenkos became an integral part of this community, and the boys are still remembered by local old-timers.

Remembering Ukrainian Olya near Cobar
Theofil Volkofsky's story

Theofil Volkofsky from Lypky in Kyiv province was probably the most successful of the Ukrainian-born farmers. We last saw him in the army camp at Bathurst, where his outspokenness got him into trouble and he was accused of pro-German sympathies; he was discharged from the army shortly afterwards with tuberculosis. He returned to the outback, but this time did not go quite as far inland as Bourke, where he and his brother Cezar had run their successful fishing business before they enlisted. First, he leased a government water tank at Booroomugga, east of Cobar, where 'there was an abundance of water and good soil', says his son Tom. 'Dad was a wonderful gardener and he grew beautiful vegetables there. He was interested in beehives; there was a photograph of his beehives, "Skyscrapers in Australian desert", in an American magazine. He used to take honey, fresh vegetables and eggs on drays to the Canbelego mining camp, a township southeast of Cobar.'

Theofil Volkofsky (Courtesy Thomas Volkofsky)

Although Volkofsky was ineligible for soldiers' settlement concessions, that did not deter him from the settling on the land. Tom continues the story:

> There were lots of properties coming up for ballot. He was successful in getting a 21,300 acre property on the western side of Cobar (it was a portion of the Amphitheatre station). ... He had saved a fair bit of money by that time. He then bought a second-hand house at Cobar and he had it demolished and loaded on drays and taken out to the property. He built the house on the hill overlooking the beautiful dam there ... He named the station Olino – it's a Russian girl's name, some girl-friend he had once in Russia.

Married men usually do not name their properties after a girlfriend, so perhaps Olya was the name of that fair-haired Ukrainian girl whom Theofil had been unable to protect from the powerful priest, and the memory of whose tears became the touchstone for the rest of his life. His son goes on:

> He then established very nice fruit trees and gardens around the house. You wouldn't believe the cabbages and cauliflowers and fruit we had! We took a

> trailer and went down to the creeks and shovelled up all the leaves washed by water that were rotting there; we took that up and dug it into the soil, and sheep manure from the shearing shed. He was brought up on a farm and had seen it done as a boy. ... Dad improved the property, had good merino sheep; he became a wool classer. He selected his own rams – he was very proud of his sheep.

Then came the depression, which was 'a disaster', as Tom says.

> Everything was going beautifully. Dad bought some more of Amphitheatre station on terms and he sold a mob of sheep at a very good price and he told the man, 'Right-oh, you take them now and I'll pick up the money at Cobar next week', but the depression hit so quickly that the man returned the sheep and dad had a terrible time with the owner of Amphitheatre. He had a very difficult time during the depression. He battled through and he got through it OK.

In 1941 there was another disaster – he lost the house in a fire. But he survived this too, and moved on again later, as Tom relates:

> We bought Curraweena station in 1950 (50,000 acres approximately). It was very well-known between Bourke and Cobar. It had been a property established in 1870, with about 40,000 sheep, a magnificent woolshed built out of stones, 32 shearers working at the woolshed originally. The homestead was built by an architect. Soon after he bought it the wool prices skyrocketed; Russia was starting to buy wool. So there was a very prosperous time for sheep-farmers.[35]

Although such large projects as Volkofsky's were not in the remit of many of our heroes, many, finding themselves on the land, nevertheless found ways to demonstrate their love for their exotic adopted country. At the intersection of South Creek Road and Campbell Avenue in the Sydney suburb of Dee Why, a traveller can still see a cluster of old trees surrounding a 'small timber cottage which is […] now a heritage item because it is "an intact example of inter-war housing"'. This house was built by Stephen Surovsov in the early 1920s. Surovsov became the gardener for the owner of the estate, Smyth King, and it was by his work that the grove of figs, pines, camphor laurels, turpentines, willows, brush box, coral trees, and eucalyptus grew here, becoming known as a local botanical garden.[36]

City life

City life seemed to be an easier option for those not willing or able to test themselves on the land, but without a profession, often suffering from wounds or gas poisoning, it was as hard to find a city job as to make ends meet on a farm. Some Australian newspapers would have a special column with advertisements for work for returned soldiers. Here we meet George Didenko, a fireman, who was returned to Australia as medically unfit due to an old wrist fracture; in 1918 he was looking for work as a watchman, and in 1920 as a light labourer. Vasily Kavitsky, a sailor, demobilised as medically unfit, was looking for work on ships in 1919. Sebastian Radetsky, once a leader of the Russian Workers Group in Port Pirie, wounded three times on the Western Front, sought work as a printer, and Cezar Wolkowsky, who returned from Gallipoli with gunshot wounds, looked for work as a motor driver in 1918.

As they settled down, the Anzacs managed to find a place of their own in the variety of trades and professions available in the cities. Afanasey Korniack, a mechanic and fitter by trade, had started his life in Australia as a miner and was not accepted for active service as he was medically unfit. He settled in Brisbane after the war, working as an engine driver and mechanic; later he found employment as a freezer at a meatworks. Another Afanasy, Nesterenko, who also tried to enlist in the AIF in 1916 but was rejected, began his working career in Australia in spectacular style. In 1916 a Sydney newspaper reported his technical inventions which could save the Railway Department £20,000 a year.[37] He opened a machinery shop on Goulburn Street, but in October 1917, the shop caught fire and the subsequent police investigation found Nesterenko guilty of arson. He was put on trial and sentenced to two years' hard labour in Goulburn Gaol.[38] In 1923 he was arrested and jailed once again for three years, this time for theft.[39] He does not appear in the police records after that, and seems to have turned his back on crime.

Constantine Pinkevitch, who served throughout the war in the Field Ambulance, returned to the North after being discharged. After spending some time in Brisbane, he moved to the Mount Morgan area, working as a turner in the mine; in the early 1920s he moved with his young family to Newcastle where he secured permanent employment at the Government Railway Workshops in Honeysuckle. Albert Krantz, wounded in the right wrist on the Western Front in 1918 and evacuated to Australia, had to abandon his former trade of carpenter, but he received vocational training in the new field of electroplating and worked in this capacity in Sydney. Similarly, Frank Goldstein, a working jeweller, who lost his right eye on the Western Front, had to change his profession, becoming an ice-cream vendor in Kogarah, a southern suburb of Sydney. John Ouchirenko, who also had to abandon his work as a ship mechanic due to ill health, moved with his young family to Ballarat after marrying, and found permanent employment as a mechanic. Young Wolfe Greenstein, who managed to enlist in the AIF at the very end of the war, returned to his parents in Sydney and worked as a printer and compositor for the Consolidated Press.

Other Anzacs who settled in the cities worked in the service sector. Alexay Ostrinko, who enlisted as Osmirko but deserted soon afterwards, changed his name to Ostrin and mastered the art of photography. In about 1923

Alexay Ostrinko's 'Ostrin Studios' logo (Rootsweb, A.M.R. Smallwood)

he opened his own business 'Ostrin Studios' in the main street of Ayr in North Queensland. The Ayr community saw him as 'our local artist' and his photographs of important North Queensland events often appeared in Australian newspapers.[40] Even when he was compelled by ill health to sell the studio in 1938, its name was preserved. Saul Haiff, who started his career as a tailor in Perth, continued to work as a tailor when he settled in Sydney after the war. Roland Arthur Cooper, an Englishman born in Mariupol, who had some technical education and was a draughtsman, chose the modest occupation of a newsagent, taking over his father's business.

Lewy Cotton, Prince of head waiters. Portrait by Dan Russell, 1967 (SL SA)

Lewy or Louis Cotton, who served on the Western Front as Lewy Cotten, is one of the few natives of Ukraine to be honoured with an entry in the *Australian Dictionary of Biography*. Leaving Odessa in his youth, he spent some time in France and England, where he received training as a waiter. Coming to Australia in 1914, he worked in Perth and Adelaide in this capacity, but became a celebrity after his return from the front, when he was appointed head waiter in the South Australian hotel on North Terrace in Adelaide. According to Cotton's biographer Suzanne Edgar:

> The establishment was patronized by snobs, the rich and the famous. Cotton went to an excellent tailor and wore a morning suit, then white tie and tails at night. Patrons savoured his European background and counted his smile or nod an accolade. Lewy's manner was discreet, his bearing lofty; he reputedly gained substantial tips, though was apparently never wealthy. His supervision of the gilded dining-room, where drunks never disturbed his aplomb, ensured that his and the hotel's reputation remained untarnished. This 'Prince of Head Waiters' relished meeting the great, among them Pavlova.[41]

Several men attained success in business. Their beginnings might be as humble as those of Abraham Smoishen, a tailor, who returned to Sydney after two and a half years in Egypt. According to a police report he would 'drive a grey horse attached to a cart with the name Abraham Smoishen thereon, hawking doorstoppers'.[42] Woolf Zmood, who survived for over two years on the Western Front, continued his business as a draper upon his return, first in Shepparton and Wangaratta, then in Melbourne. In 1921 he and his cousin Peter Komesaroff applied for permission to use the letters 'A.I.F.' after their trading name 'Zmood and Co', stating that 'At present time we have shops in Albury, Cootamundra, Hay, Tumut, Leeton, Young, Narrandera and Wagga Wagga, N.S.W., and Daylsford, Vic.'[43] Later on Peter Komesaroff worked as a travelling optician. Israel Heselev first worked as a musician, but in the late 1920s, when he married, he became a manufacturing furrier and then a fur merchant. His shop, trading in fox furs, was on Swanston Street in the centre of Melbourne.[44] Wolfe Hoffman, who started his life in Australia as a millhand at the timber mills in remote south-western Australia, settled in Melbourne after the war and opened a knitting factory in Brunswick. In 1927 he could proudly write that he was employing '11 girls'. Later his business was known as 'Hoffman's blouses'.[45]

Having spent over two years as a prisoner of war in Germany, Wolf Dorfman settled in Melbourne and was engaged in trade with China. In the mid-1920s he lived for a time in Shanghai. In 1924 an Australian newspaper published an article about him noting that 'Geographically the East is the market for Australian products, and Mr. Wolf Dorfman […] believes that boundless opportunities exist there for trade. The time is opportune to grasp them, he says.' Dorfman argued for China and Japan as potential markets for Australian goods and shared his knowledge of successful trade there. The correspondent observed that at that time Dorfman spoke 'five languages and the principal Chinese dialects'.[46] On his return to Australia, he became a hotel keeper in Victoria. David Lakovsky also achieved success overseas. According to his niece, 'David Lake went to America, and became interested in movies, and he started Metro-Goldwyn-Mayer Pictures in Australia. He was the one in the depression who kept all the family going.'[47] By 1941 he was general sales manager of Metro-Goldwyn-Mayer Pictures.

Left: Wolf Dorfman (News, Adelaide, 28 June 1924)
Right: In his later years (courtesy of Dorfman family)

For some others, however, the business route led only into the wretchedness of city life. After the war, Jack Vengert spent several turbulent years in Sydney running a 'gyx-shop', allegedly selling sly grog and being implicated in court cases involving prostitutes. Eventually he left for Brisbane where he opened a fruit shop on Stanley Street, the core of the Russian-Ukrainian-Jewish community, but later he returned to Sydney to make a living as a flat proprietor.[48] Christian Rink, although an electrician by trade, after the war became a licensee of the Premier Hotel in Albany, but was heavily fined for interfering with its electricity meter. He left for New Zealand in 1931, but a year later was convicted for false pretences and assaulting the police. After serving his sentence he married and worked as an electrician and, briefly, as a wine agent in New Zealand.[49] For others, like Samuel Mackomel, business brought only bankruptcy and endless court cases.[50] The story of Samuel Trager, a young recruit who deserted from the army, ended in crime. Although he started his career as a 'boot clicker', cutting out shapes for shoes, he later chose a life of petty crime, working with a gang of pickpockets in Brisbane and Sydney.[51]

A few Anzacs who managed to gain qualifications and experience made successful professional careers in Australia. George Kamishansky, whose health was shattered after Gallipoli, studied electrical engineering at Sydney Technical College. He found work first as a telephone mechanic, studied accountancy and, after passing his exams, was finally taken on by the Customs Department in Sydney, where 'he found scope for his linguistic ability'.[52]

*Alexander Barr Winning
(http://www.architecture.com.au)*

Alexander Winning, a British subject born in Kharkiv, remained in Glasgow after the war and received an education and professional training in the field of architecture. On his return to Perth, he was involved in designing numerous of the city's new buildings.[53] Alexander Popow, after six months in British hospitals, was discharged from the AIF in London in June 1917 as medically unfit. Two years later he landed in New York. The only evidence of his life during those two years is a note in a passenger list stating that his last residence was Blagoveshchensk in Siberia, which probably indicates involvement in the anti-Bolshevik movement, which was strong in that area during the Civil War in Russia. On his arrival in the USA, he settled near Boston, where his training as an electrical engineer at the University of Liège in Belgium helped him gain work in electrometallurgy research; in 1933 he defended his doctoral thesis 'The preparation of pure chromium' and filed a number of patents.[54] The success of another electrical engineer, James Gretchinsky, was less spectacular, but he too deserves recognition. In 1940 a local correspondent wrote from Stuart Town, New South Wales: 'The electric lighting in our village is now progressing satisfactorily, and Mr. Gretchinsky, of Sydney, late A.I.F., a licensed electrician, who has now completed several installations, seems to be giving every satisfaction wherever he is employed.'[55]

A few found cultural occupations. While serving in the Australian Light Horse, David Borszcer, a musician, developed pulmonary tuberculosis, which was probably aggravated playing the cornet. He was discharged from the army in 1917, but after recuperating he resumed his patriotic musical endeavours as conductor of the Chatswood Orchestral Society in aid of the Red Cross.[56] After the war he stayed in Sydney, continuing to work as a musician, but spent the last years of his life in provincial New South Wales, dying in Tumut in 1939. Emile Auguste Tardent, a member of a cultured Swiss family from Mykolaiv, worked in the

Repatriation Department in Ipswich, but later 'took up regular journalism', working for the *Truth* newspaper. He also served as an alderman on Wynnum Town Council.[57]

The Depression

The Great Depression hit many Anzacs hard. Theofil Volkofsky did manage to get through it with his business relatively intact, but others were not so lucky. James Cochura, whom we left working his land at Temora, had to leave his block of land in 1933. He suffered from headaches after his skull was fractured in a mining accident in 1914; his condition was most probably aggravated by his army service in Egypt, where he spent several months in hospitals. He also suffered from back pains, but all his applications for a war veteran's pension fell on deaf ears at the Repatriation Department. He had to move to Sydney, and then to Brisbane, where he took 'casual work as a wharf labourer'.[58]

The story of the financial ruin of Vera and Thomas Platonoff's family, who by the time of the crisis had several young children, was especially dramatic: between 1928 and 1929 two of their babies died one after another, but this was not the last of their woes. Although they worked hard on their sugar cane farm, in 1929 they were unable to pay their workers. Borrowing money in lieu of the next crop, and in debt to the sugar mill and local businesses, Thomas had to declare insolvency and they were evicted from their home in Wundaru. This involved numerous court hearings, which were chronicled in the local newspapers. Scenes in which Vera, stick in hand, fought the people evicting them from their property might have served as valuable material for an anti-capitalist novel of the 1930s.[59] After that Thomas had to work as a labourer to support his family. In 1937 he worked at Mount Isa, camping on the football grounds.[60] During the Second World War the family moved to Rockhampton and then to Brisbane, where Thomas, in spite of his age and wounds, worked as a wharf labourer and waterside worker, dying in an accident. 'A wharf labourer died a few minutes after falling and striking his head in the hold of a ship last night,' a local newspaper reported in 1954.[61] Thomas and Vera's two sons became seamen. Thomas' brother George also had his share of hardships. During the Depression he had to leave his mother and go to the North, working as a labourer in a soldiers' settlement called El Arish. Later on he moved to Innisfail and worked in a sawmill. He never married.

We meet Denis (known as Daniel or Dan) Papchuck in 1930 among a group of unemployed men who, driven to despair, marched through the streets of Perth to Parliament to make their voices heard. Instead they were arrested by the police and fined. Working as a labourer, wharfie and lumper, Papchuck struggled to survive even in the better years before the Depression. While in England during the war, he married an English girl, Edith Agnes Fletcher; their first child was born at sea as they were sailing to Western Australia in 1920.[62] They had two more children and lived in Geraldton, Kalgoorlie, Busselton and Churchman's Brook, where they camped in a tent. In 1926 his wife left him for his boss. Several years later Papchuck married Annie Mabel Hannan and started a new family. Tragically, she died in

1943, leaving him with six young children. The same year he was knocked off his bicycle by an army truck and left severely injured. The next time we hear about his misadventures is from a newspaper article, 'Lumper steals chocolate', in 1944. While working on a ship he pilfered several bars of chocolate worth 7 shillings for his children. Papchuck admitted the theft and was fined 15 pounds plus 11 shillings costs.[63]

Daniel Papchuck in the 1940s, photographed for WWII alien registration (NAA)

Life cut short

For some of the Anzacs, life was tragically cut short. War traumas both physical and mental, hostile attitudes, unemployment, and economic depression all had their adverse effects, with which some could simply not cope.

'Fed up with life altogether'
The mystery of Mitrofan Koropets

DOMAIN MYSTERY

KOROPET'S DEATH

BELIEVED TO BE SUICIDE

The finding of the body of a Russian, Matrofan Koropets, aged 32, in the Domain on Thursday morning, with a bullet wound in the head, has received the close attention of the police.

Report about Koropets' death in Sydney Sun, *1920*

On 1 April 1920 a gardener making his rounds in Sydney's Domain park saw 'a well-dressed figure lying under a tree', who turned out to be a young man with a bullet wound to the left side of his head. Today this area is a part of the Botanical Gardens, a beautiful spot facing Government House, near the modern Palm Grove Centre. The deceased man was Mitrofan Koropets from Dobrotove in Chernihiv province, who worked in Australia as a miner and then served as a sapper in the 1st Tunnelling Company on the Western Front. After discharge in September 1919 he lived on Liverpool Street in Surry Hills.

While the first newspaper reports stated that 'everything points to murder', Police inspector Robinson, conducting the investigation, inclined to the opinion that it was suicide. In support of the former theory was the fact that Koropets' body was lying some distance from the pool of blood which marked the place where he had clearly been shot, and the revolver was missing. The bullet entered 'above and behind the left ear', 'in an unusual position to be self-inflicted', according to the doctor conducting the examination. This also posed questions, as to inflict such a wound the man had to be left-handed. Inspector Robinson, insisting on suicide, suggested that Koropets 'could have walked some distance after firing the shot, and the revolver might have been picked up by somebody passing'. If it was murder, however, the police had little hope of solving the crime, 'so little being known of the man, and less of the night's occurrence'.

But some details about Koropets' life did emerge at the coroner's inquest from the evidence of Herbert John Everitt, who served with Koropets in the tunnelling company. He said that Koropets was his friend and they 'knocked about together'. According to Everitt, he was always saying 'I won't work for the capitalists any longer'. 'He was low-spirited, and in ill-health,' Everitt added. He recalled how freely his friend was spending money, saying 'I don't want it. … I am on my last lap.' And indeed Koropets' bankbooks showed that he had spent all his savings (265 pounds) during the last year. Everitt also mentioned that Koropets had a girl somewhere on the South Coast, but when they were talking about his marrying her, he said, 'I am no good for her. I am fed up with life altogether. I am not fit to live.' Everitt's evidence, and the fact that a policeman, searching Koropets' belongings, found 'a box of cartridges of the same calibre as that found in his head' and an empty revolver case, persuaded the coroner that his death was suicide. His verdict was that 'Koropets died from a bullet wound in the skull, probably self-inflicted'.[64]

Mitrofan Koropets choose to end his life on Holy Thursday, when Australia was preparing for Easter celebrations, while he had no hope of seeing his family in Dobrotove in war-torn Ukraine. Obviously, even having an Australian mate did not make Mitrofan feel at home in Australia. Although he was buried in an unmarked grave in the Methodist section of Rookwood Cemetery, his death certificate provides evidence that two Ukrainians took him on his last journey: Joseph Kleshenko, an Anzac, and Theodor Bjelonoshka.[65]

Mitrofan Koropets' forgotten grave (marked by flowers) at Rookwood Cemetery (Photo: Oksana Hull)

Similarly mysterious was the end of William Kolesnikov, a single man in his forties. He returned from the Western Front with horrific wounds: his face was disfigured and his tongue had been shot off. In January 1923 his coat and hat were found near Brown's Rock, a secluded spot in Botany Bay, near La Perouse. The police found his military discharge in the pocket of the coat and worked out that the last time he withdrew his war pension was a few days before

Christmas 1922.⁶⁶ His body was never found and it is most likely that he drowned deliberately rather than accidentally, as no other items of clothing were found. His disappearance was not noticed by the communities of his countrymen or ex-servicemen in Sydney – neither the newspapers nor the *Police Gazette* reported anyone who knew and missed him.

Brown's Rocks where William Kolesnikov ended his life (photo by Dusan Berjanovic)

William Whynsky, who was severely wounded at Pozières, ended his life in broad daylight, with witnesses, jumping from a bridge in Brisbane. Since his arrival in Australia in about 1910 he had worked as a stone dresser in Helidon near Toowoomba in Queensland; not long before Christmas 1920 he came to Brisbane. The incident occurred on Victoria Bridge, connecting Central Brisbane with South Brisbane, in the heart of the Russian-Ukrainian-Jewish community. A woman, Mrs Blanch, was crossing the bridge on Saturday evening when she

> was accosted by a man who was wearing a returned soldier's badge. He was dejected and had an utterly down and out appearance, and explained to her that he had been drinking heavily and had gone through some £40 or £50. He then remarked: 'Tomorrow is Sunday, and I will suffer. I might as well end it all. I will throw myself in the river.'

Although the woman tried to dissuade him, imploring him to think about his family, he climbed over the rails and jumped to his death.⁶⁷ Sadly the case might have been that he had no family left, and his grave at Toowong Cemetery was forgotten for many years.

Jack Steinberg, a cabinet-maker, born either in Odessa or Brest, was not accepted for overseas service in 1917 because of his depression and suicidal inclinations (he had previously tried to hang himself). In 1923 a Perth newspaper reported that 'a middle-aged Russian Jew', 'wearied of life by years of ill-health' tried to commit suicide but was rescued; in 1944 he finally succeeded, putting his head in the oven and turning on the gas.[68]

Alexander Spisbah lost his battle with life during the Depression. A former Russian officer, he came to Western Australia in 1911 with a young family. While working as a miner in Boulder, he enlisted in the AIF, but became sick while training, losing the sight of his right eye, and was discharged from the army as medically unfit. To feed his family he worked at the sawmill in Mornington, but, as the local newspaper wrote, 'when this mill closed down in 1931, he was thrown out of work, and he had been unemployed ever since.' Another newspaper added that he 'had been unemployed some considerable time and was greatly depressed'. In April 1934, when his wife left the house for a walk, he shot himself with a rifle, using his old violin bow to release the trigger. The violin must have been all that was left from his former comfortable life in Imperial Russia.[69]

The life of some of our Anzacs was cut short by sickness. We have already told the tragic story of Constantine Ilin, who succumbed to illness and died in 1922 in Sydney. Another Ukrainian, Peter Tkachuk, who served in Egypt, was placed in the Mental Hospital in Gladesville near Sydney in 1922; he died there in 1926. John Mamchin, about whom we know only that he was not accepted for overseas service because of rheumatism acquired on railway construction in Queensland, and then was twice rejected because of defective vision, died aboard a ship in Lyttelton in New Zealand in 1921. Alexander Sast, whom we left in France after his daring escape from Turkish captivity and journey across Russia to return to the AIF, had several peaceful years upon returning to Australia, but soon he went blind and in 1928 died in Sydney of heart failure, leaving a wife and three stepchildren.[70]

Joseph Rudezky, although ill, received help. By 1921 he had developed tuberculosis, probably contracted at the front – he 'had a cough ever since' serving in France – and although it was rapidly progressing, he had to keep working as long as he could because his tuberculosis was not officially recognised as a war injury, and he was therefore ineligible for treatment as a veteran. However, like some other immigrants, he was fortunate enough to come across compassionate Australians and one, Dr Melville, a medical officer, took a personal interest in his case. Melville wrote: 'If his statements are true, and I have no reason to doubt them, being very much impressed by the man's appearance and the way he made the statements, I consider that his T.B. is the result of his exposure in Gallipoli and France, and recommend that he be given the benefit of the doubt.' Owing to Melville's support, Rudezky received better treatment and was placed in the sanatorium in Stanthorpe.[71]

Leaving for good

Some among the Ukrainian-born Anzacs in Australia left the country and never returned again. Many aspired to be reunited with their families in Ukraine or Russia, but this was far from easy. Postal communication during the war was suspended, and barely functioned dur-

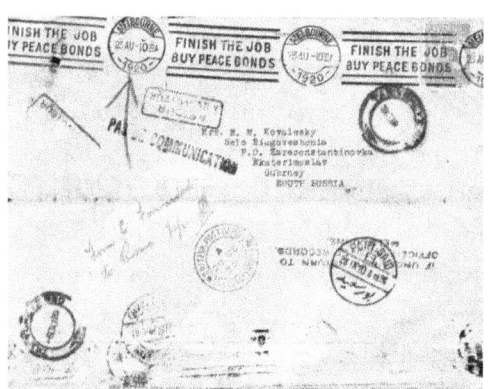

A letter to Ukraine for the mother of Andrew Kovalevsky, fallen on the Western Front, was returned in 1920, marked 'No communication'. (NAA)

ing the Civil War as it swept over Ukraine. After the October 1917 Revolution the Australian authorities, as noted above, banned nationals of revolutionary Russia – whether or not they identified with the new government – from returning there, out of fear that they would contribute to the Red forces opposing the imperialist war.

The ban remained in force for some time after the war, and Peter Simonoff, who acted as the unrecognised Soviet consul in Australia in 1918-1921, made numerous representations for repatriation on behalf of former subjects of the Russian Empire. A significant proportion of the people who appeared in his lists expressing a desire to return home were Ukrainians, including a number of our Anzacs. In his 1921 list, Vasily Kavitski, Thomas Platonoff, Andrew Snegovoy, Stephen Loosgie, Egnaty Sologub, and Saveliy Tkachenko all appear.[72] At least two of them – Kavitski, whose mother was in Ukraine, and Sologub, whose wife and two children were living in Spasskoe in the Maritime province in the Russian Far East – did get a permit from the Australian authorities and left the country in 1920-1921.[73] Loosgie and Snegovoy left Australia in 1924 but did not manage to travel further than Harbin and finally returned to Australia. We have seen the misadventures of Loosgie during the war when he tried to help his father; Snegovoy's attempts to help his family in Odessa also started while he was on the Western Front. He did not give up hope and in 1928, after naturalisation, he made a new attempt to visit the Soviet Union to see his people. Tkachenko, who probably also attempted to reach his family while in the army, and Platonoff, who like Tkachenko was on Simonoff's list, stayed in Australia. Jack Vengert, who was unemployed in Sydney in 1919 and wanted to be repatriated, stayed in Australia too,[74] but two Jewish men, Alexander Sank and Sam Clesner, did manage to get permits and returned to Soviet Russia. One more Ukrainian, George Didenko, who disappears from Australian records after the war, most likely returned to his motherland as well.

Egnaty Sologub (QP)

Stephen Loosgie (NAA)

The adventures of Alexander Belfort, whose AIF depot service was short, as he tried to enlist in the AIF with an old fracture to the right forearm, took him all over the world. In 1919 he sailed from Australia to New Zealand, then to Hawaii and Vancouver. During the following years he made numerous trips between Mexico, Peru, Spain, Turkey and the USA. In 1926, when his American ship visited Black Sea ports in the Soviet Union, he deserted the ship in Odessa. We still do not know how his life and the lives of other repatriates in Ukraine or Russia turned out, but as their archives begin to open to the public, we will one day be able to uncover their stories.

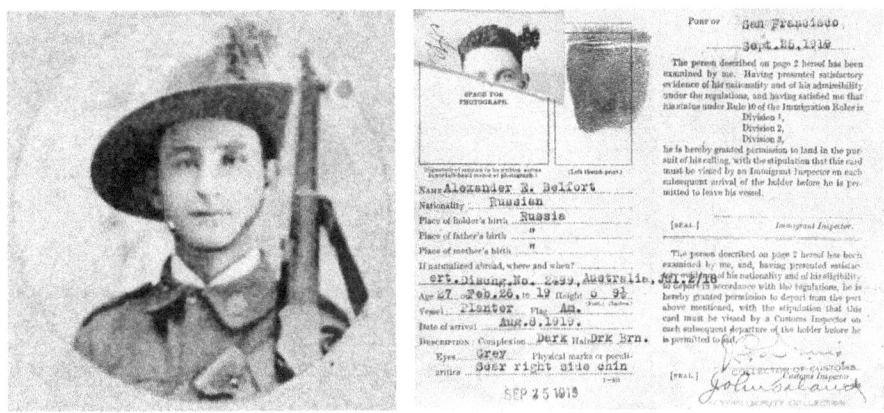

Left: Alexander Belfort, the last Ukrainian-born Anzac to enlist in the AIF (QP)
Right: Belfort's application for a seaman's protection certificate,
USA, 1919 (Washington, D.C. National Archives)

One of the few families about which information has surfaced is that of Egnaty Sologub. After three years in the AIF on the Western Front, he left Australia and sailed to Russia's Maritime province, to be reunited with his family who had remained there. In 1938 a Stepan Ignatevich Sologub, born in Sosnovka in the Maritime province in 1901, was put on trial before the Soviet High Court; this was most likely Egnaty's son. Under Article 58, the well-known political tool of the Soviet regime, Stepan was charged with six offences from 'betrayal of the motherland' to 'terrorist acts against representatives of Soviet power' and executed on the day of the trial. In 1957 he was posthumously cleared of all charges, but we do not know if his father lived long enough to see justice restored.[75]

Louis Brodsky's visit to 'Russia' (it was most likely Ukraine) was primarily for political reasons. By 1923 he was a secretary of the Australia–Russia trade committee and in 1924 left for the Soviet Union via London. He spent eighteen months there and later said that he was very impressed with its workers' clubs. He clearly got into trouble with the Soviet authorities, as all his papers were confiscated, but he was able to return safely to Australia. In 1928 he opened the Marine Workers' Communist Club (also known as the Transport Workers' Club) in Sydney, inspired by his Soviet experience. The building was at the corner of Druitt and Kent streets and the financing of this project provoked a lot of interest from the press, but Brodsky denied receiving any money from the Soviets. What he admitted was that his new name Marlen, which he assumed 'for psychological reasons', was a combination of the names of Marx and Lenin. In 1948 he developed a more practical project to explore goldfields in Queensland, but it seems that he never lost his fascination with the social experiment that was underway in his motherland and until his death he continued to dream of moving to the Soviet Union with his family.[76]

George Ferber (courtesy of Ferber family)

Some Anzacs headed to other destinations. Dermy (Demetry) Morozoff from Kharkiv, after an unsuccessful attempt to enlist in the AIF, left for Harbin where his mother lived; in 1938 he emigrated to California. Joseph Vurhaft, who lost his arm at the battle for Polygon Wood in September 1917, made a similar journey, but moved from Hong Kong to San Francisco earlier, in 1924; he worked in the USA as a clerk. George Ferber, a draper, who served as a trooper in Egypt, did not stay long in Australia either: a few months after his discharge he left for America, where he settled in California, married and worked as a salesman.[77] The USA was the largest recipient of our Anzacs departing Australia between the two world wars. Walter Pivinski, after two enlistments in the AIF, went to America and enlisted in the US Army, serving in Manila in the Philippines. He later married and lived in Tacoma, Washington, serving as a ward master in the US Army Medical Corps.[78] Several other seamen who came to Australia not long before the war similarly moved to America without difficulty. Among them were Phillipp Gorbach, who took part in the soldiers' riots in Sydney in 1916 and was subsequently discharged from the AIF, and Victor Neborotchko, who was not accepted for overseas service. George Koty, who was wounded three times on the Western Front, after discharge joined his relatives in New York; there he married and worked in dyeing and cleaning.

It was not only seamen who found their way to America and other countries. Thomas Pesmany, who served on the Western Front in the field ambulance, left for San Francisco in 1920; his trail is lost after that, but he might have changed his name and worked as a photographer. Abraham Smoishen, who was hawking on Australian roads, separated from his wife and three children and left Australia for good in the late 1920s, settling in London. Ivan Gorodezky, demobilised in London after the war, married and lived in France. Even the wanderer Platon Beloshapka was tempted by America in the late 1920s. In 1927 he appears in New Kensington, Pennsylvania, in the city directory listed as a labourer and living with his wife, Nellie.[79] Evidently he was unable to mend his ways and soon returned to his vagabond life in Australia.

Clockwise from top left: Phillipp Gorbach (Washington, D.C. National Archives), Victor Neborotchko (UK National Archives), George and Lilian Koty's wedding (Courtesy of Koty family), Ivan Gorodezky, France, circa 1936 (NAA), Albert Nickalay Morozoff (UK National Archives)

Becoming Australian

The Australian spirit of multiculturalism which began to develop in the 1980s, and the strong pro-Ukrainian feelings that dominated among Ukrainian émigrés after the Second World War, when thousands came to Australia from war-torn Europe, has made it an axiom that the preservation of native language, religion, culture and communal ethnic life are the cornerstones of a viable ethnic community. Within the writings of the Ukrainian and Russian communities in Australia it is often apparent that the preservation of ethnic identity is seen as a positive process, while assimilation, coupled with the abandonment of native language and communal involvement, is a negative process. From this point of view, the processes that took place among the Anzacs from Ukraine, be they Ukrainian or Polish, Russian or Jewish, can be labelled as rapid assimilation and, in many cases, as a loss of ethnic identity. It therefore comes as no surprise that when Ukrainians came here in their thousands after the Second World War, they hardly noticed any Ukrainian presence dating back to before the First World War. But to understand the complex processes which occurred in these early communities from Ukraine, we need to see them within their historical, social and political context.

Pressures to assimilate

Ukrainian-born Anzacs, especially those among them who had spent years at the front or in barracks in the midst of Australians, seemed to be the perfect material for assimilation. And indeed many of these men participated willingly in this process, which often started with a change of name and culminated with the choice to use English as the only language of communication in their families.

In respect of their names the list is long. First names would usually be replaced by their English equivalents almost immediately upon landing in Australia or even earlier, at sea. Thus Andrei/Ondriy would become Andrew (e.g. Snegovoy and Kovalevsky), Yuri and Girsh – George (Kamishansky and Breitman), Ivan – Jack or John (Vengert and Ouchirenko), Stepan – Stephen (Loosgie, Surovsov, and Provaka). Names that did not have a ready equivalent in English tended to be replaced with a similar-sounding equivalent: Afanasey Korniack turned into Alfred, Erofei Gregorenko into Richard, while Boris Poselnikoff's name changed from Boris to Bob, then to Robert, while he was serving on ships.

Surnames underwent various degrees of transformation, but usually the imprint of the original surname remained. Alfroniza Morozoff and Ivan Poleshchuk, the two seamen-deserters of 1901, became Jack Morris and Jack Pollock. Joseph Kleshenko was known as Klesh, William Kolesnikov as Koles, Carl Kiles as Kills, Afanasey Korniack or Korneiuk as Corren, Stepan Proiavka was naturalised as Stephen Provaka, David Lakovsky became Lake, Alik Osmirko/Ostrinko became Ostrin, and Frayam Yacker Zwillen Horstain – Frank Goldstein. Samuel Mukomel (his original name) tried to Anglicise his surname when he joined the AIF as Samuel Mack, but the entry was corrected to Muchomel. However, after the war he amended his surname to the more English-looking Mackomel. The names of a few underwent radical changes which were often connected with business or professional careers. Thus Judah Myer Kivovitch already used the name Yur by the time of his enlistment, but later on he changed his name by deed poll to the completely anglicised Victor Michael Carmichael; Samuel Harold Krantz changed his surname to Grant in 1919 immediately after discharge. Sometimes transformations were quite intricate. Alexander Popow, on settling in the USA, became Peter Popow Alexander, incorporating into this new name his former names in reverse order. This allowed him in the professional world to appear as the neutral Peter P. Alexander, but still preserve the memory of his glorious father-general Aleksandr Popov.

Some, on the other hand, preserved their original names throughout their lives in Australia. This however did not preclude their Australian neighbours and friends from giving them nicknames or Western versions of their names. For instance, Ksenofont Kozachuk and Feodot Peachenoff would stick to their unusual names in official documents, but Feodot, as his English-speaking relatives remember, 'was always referred to as Fred'.[80]

The next milestone of assimilation was the switch to English. Those who could hardly communicate in English when they joined the army were numerous, but those who survived the battlefront and returned to Australia were enriched with a new skill – to speak (and swear) as dinkum Aussies did. 'He learned more naughty words while in France than during the rest of his life', complained Matfeus Oleinikoff's wife.[81] This natural language, learnt not from textbooks but from real life, opened a door to the process of rapid postwar blending into Australian society. The work that they had to do as wharfies and labourers, as commercial travellers and miners, often involved active communication with mates and customers. Even the marginalized Platon Beloshapka, who in 1915 could not communicate with his commanding officers because of a total lack of English, in 1924, as we have seen, could speak some English. This process was similar for all our heroes, be they Ukrainian, Russian or Yiddish speakers. The acquisition and mastering of English was something that these Anzacs were proud of, as can be seen in the stories of Theofil Volkofsky and Reuben Rosenfield. Tom Volkofsky tells: 'Dad would not teach us Russian; I know just a half dozen Russian words. He said that Russian would never be any good to you, you don't want to know it. He said, you are Australians, you be Australians: he was very definite this way.'[82]

In many cases, Ukrainian-born immigrants who mastered English, and so were able to better communicate with Australians, saw a decline in the use of their native languages, coupled, in a way, with a fading sense of their Ukrainian identity. In some cases marriage to a Ukrainian or Russian woman, as well as communal life and contacts with relatives in the motherland, may have helped preserve Ukrainian identity, but this turned out to be all but impossible after the Russian Revolution.

The emerging Ukrainian communal life, with its Ukrainian Workers' Circle established in Brisbane in 1915, was short-lived, as some of its organisers left for Ukraine after the revolution. A number of Ukrainian-language newspapers published abroad, such as *Svoboda* and *Haydamaky*, to which the Circle subscribed, were prohibited in Australia during the war, and the fate of the Circle's tiny library is unknown.[83] Australia's major Russian organisation, the Union of Russian-born Workers (known as the Russian Association), which aimed to be inclusive of all Russian-born émigrés, had been undermined by unending factional splits. The final blow came with its involvement in the Red Flag March in 1919 and the diggers' attack on its headquarters. It never again regained the mass character it had before the war, when it had united hundreds of émigrés all over Queensland and laid claim to the role of an all-Australian community centre. Each of the organisations that grew out of its ruins – the Communist Party of Australia, the Society of Technical Aid to Soviet Russia and the Union of Russian Worker-Communists – had its own narrow ideological focus.

Even though Australia did not prohibit ethnic-based societies, at that time involvement with such groups might still put an émigré on the blacklist: for evidence of this, one needs look no further than the naturalisation files. When Ukrainian-born émigrés applied for naturalisation the local police would investigate their contacts with ethnopolitical organisations and add these to their files. It goes without saying that a lack of contact with such 'suspicious' organisations and therefore with the communities they represented was seen in the applicant's favour. Thus, Kills' application was accompanied by the comment: 'Has completely lost interest in his native land', while Afanasey Korniack was attested in 1924 as a 'Member of a society which will preclude him from the privileges of naturalisation'; he also was suspected of being a member of the Communist Party of Australia. This debarred him from naturalisation for six years, until in 1930 he denied that he was 'ever connected with any organisation other than the Russian library'.[84]

A common trend among pre-revolutionary Slav émigrés from the Russian Empire was to call themselves 'White Russians' irrespective of their ethnic origin. The stepson of Helen Peachenoff, a daughter of the Ukrainian Anzac Feodot Peachenoff, for example, remembers her 'saying that she was related to White Russians'.[85] White Russians, who opposed the Russian Revolution, were admitted to Australia in thousands between the wars and after the Second World War, mostly from China. Their strong anti-communist stance helped to improve the image of 'Russians' in Australia, which had previously been synonymous with Bolshevism. This hybrid ethnopolitical identity had become their protection in the hostile and suspicious environment of Australia of the time, where any Eastern Slav easily could be labelled a 'Red Russian'. For many of our Anzacs, the time was clearly not right to complicate the situation with the nuances of their Ukrainian identities and political beliefs.

Between the wars a number of objective factors – a small population, a nomadic lifestyle or life in remote areas, material hardships – were coupled with the suspicion of the Australian authorities towards all natives of the former Russian Empire as 'Bolsheviks', and general resentment towards 'aliens', who looked different and spoke English with an accent. The combination of these complex factors drove many of our heroes to recast their ethnic and social identity, their wives and children often forming the first step towards assimilation.

Families and the role of women

While it became impossible to maintain one's original identity through communal organisations between the wars, it was also increasingly difficult to maintain it through family ties. Correspondence with the Soviet Union was restricted after the October Revolution and all mail in both directions was censored. When in the 1920s the censorship was lifted, the Stalinist regime made it dangerous for the relatives of our Anzacs to have any contact with the West. Tom Volkofsky remembers: 'Dad sent money to his people, too, back in Bolshevik times and it did a lot of harm to his people, I believe.'⁸⁶ George Kamishansky, applying for his sister's admission to Australia in 1925, wrote: 'I have not seen any of my relations since I left my native land in April 1913 and was not able even to correspond with them from 1917 until just recently. ... A very strong bond of affection exists between us and I am very anxious to see once more the dear friend of my childhood.'⁸⁷

Seven years of torture
The story of Morris Saffar's family

Morris Saffar reunited with his family (The North Queensland Register, *15 January 1923*)

Among those whose families were stranded back in Ukraine, Morris Saffar was the only one who managed to locate and bring to Australia his wife and children after 10 years of separation. Morris came to Australia in 1914, on the eve of war, planning to prepare a home for his wife Sarah and three children, whom he had left behind in Goldingen (Kuldiga), on the Baltic Sea. When war broke out they lost contact, and while Morris was fighting on the Western Front, his family underwent their own sufferings. 'A woman's story of seven years of tortured life in Russia was told in a neat little cottage at Brighton-le-Sands', Australian newspapers reported in December 1922, providing the full account of the story:

> Came the invading German hordes, and the population were herded like sheep in trucks and carriages, and despatched they knew not whither, toward the centre of Russia. Mrs. Saffar carried a baby in her arms, and her two other children clung to her skirts.
>
> At Riga they were fed and housed for a while, and then were sent off to Brodijansk [probably Berdiansk], a village in the Crimea. There they struggled along as best they could.
>
> When the revolution came, the village was the sport of the contending forces. One day it would be pillaged by the Bolsheviks, and another by the anti-Bolsheviks. Soon the barren shelter in which the family lodged had no glass windows; they had been shattered by shot and shell, and replaced by bullet-holed boards.
>
> Relatives, neighbors, and friends succumbed under the onslaughts of marauding bands. One day Mrs. Saffar's mother was killed. At last her baby boy died of starvation. For the sake of the other two children the grief-stricken mother struggled on. [...]

> Horses' flesh was eagerly sought by human beings. Once Mrs. Saffar begged two beans, and boiled them in water, so that her children might live. Some days not even beans could be got, and the little ones lay down, crying of hunger. Death was taking toll in hundreds.
>
> All the while not a word had come to Mrs. Saffar of her husband. One day she received a document from the British Embassy which showed that he was alive and seeking her, but this knowledge was turned into an instrument of torture when she found she was unable to get away. Two years later she set out for Smolensk, which she reached after travelling for four months, sometimes afoot, sometimes in a cattle truck, often on the verge of starvation and despair.
>
> At Smolensk she found shelter in a disused railway carriage, and made up cigarettes, which the little girls sold to passers by. At last, aided by a kindly traveller, and then by the British Consul, she and her children got away to London; where her passage was booked for Australia.

Now the elder girl, Ella, was 12 and Freda was 10. For the newspaper journalists this seemed to be the ideal material for a happy ending:

> Mr. M. Saffar, the husband, considered that Australia, in which he was building his fortunes, was worth fighting for, and he bears in his body the wounds he received during three years' fighting in the A.I.F. He appeared a happy man with his family round him yesterday. Of course, they have to start at the bottom rung again; but husband and wife will start together, and in a free country.[88]

Within a year their third daughter, Millie, was born in Perth, where they made their home. But probably nothing could replace their baby son Aaron who starved to death in Ukraine, and nothing could fully repair their family life and erase the memories of war, the horrors of which they could not share. There was no happy ending: a few years later they divorced and Sarah struggled to raise the three girls in her new country alone. Morris moved to Melbourne and when the next war came, he enlisted in the AIF once again.

Marriage to a woman of similar ethnic background sometimes helped maintain the ethnic identity of our Anzacs, but in most cases this proved impossible. Only a few had a Slavic wife and a network of Russian-born contacts, as can be seen from the lives of three families – the Platonoffs, the Peachenoffs, and the Oleinikoffs – who settled before the war in Booyal, a cane-growing area which attracted a number of their compatriots. As mentioned earlier, Thomas Platonoff married his Belarusian neighbour Vera Kurtish, and they then employed other Slavs for cane-cutting at their farm. It might be assumed that their assimilation was slower than that of others, but it is likely that their children grew up completely assimilated; their first names, Stanley and Thomas, did not distinguish them from other Australian children.

Feodot Peachenoff, who came to Australia with his wife Maria and daughter Nina, returned from the war to Booyal. He and Maria then had a son Victor, but it seems that their family fell apart because of Maria's unshakeable homesickness for her native land. In May 1921 Maria, Nina, and baby Victor took ship for Europe, with the clear intention of returning to Ukraine, but something obviously prompted Maria to give up her plan: three months later, they all boarded a ship in Port Said bound for Australia. They settled in Sydney, where she died of tuberculosis in 1926. In the meantime, Feodot had found a new partner, Akelina (Akulina) née Neeshita, who was born in Stavropol in Southern Russia and came to Queensland in 1911 with her parents, settling in Booyal. Her first husband was Peter Maximenko, a Ukrainian.[89] Feodot and Akulina had two children, Helen and Valentine, and probably managed to maintain their Ukrainian and South Russian identities. Valentine, who became a doctor, married a Slavic woman, Anne Josephine Wojeszlovszky, while Helen, as mentioned before, told her Australian relatives that 'she was related to White Russians'.[90]

Feodot Peachenoff (Courtesy of Barbara Scott)

The Oleinikoff family had eight children, of whom the four youngest were born in Australia. They lived in the suburbs of south Brisbane, where they had opportunities for close Russian-Ukrainian contacts. In 1922, when people in Russia and Ukraine were dying of famine, Matfeus Oleinikoff became the secretary of the Russian relief committee, and, as a Brisbane newspaper reported:

> Received £22 14s, the amount collected at a recent meeting of Russians, £13 14s 1½d, proceeds of benefit concert held in the Stone's Corner Hall on April 15, and £1 4s from a dancing party at Gold Creek.[91]

However, the names of their children appear more and more often in Brisbane newspapers in connection with their academic and sporting achievements, reflecting their successful integration into Australian society and acceptance of its values.

Klavdia and Zacharias Pieven just married in Harbin in 1909 (Courtesy of Piven-Large family)

Zacharias Pieven (or Piven), a mechanic, was another Ukrainian living in Australia with his Russian wife, but their story was a tragic one. He came to Brisbane via the Russian Far East in 1911 and worked first in Dalby and Maryborough foundry as a machinist. When he was joined by his young wife Klavdia and baby daughter Nadia (Nida), they moved to Sydney, where in 1913 they had their second child, Harold. In 1914 his wife died from a self-administered abortion. Their situation was probably so unstable that she did not think they would be able to support another child. In Sydney she would have been isolated and unable to find proper medical help. When in October 1915 Zacharias applied for naturalisation, the children were living with a 'Mrs Gamble' in the township of Wellington in New South Wales. He was refused naturalisation as the Australian government had by then stopped naturalising Russian subjects. He may have believed that he needed naturalisation to join the army, as his family archive has a letter indicating that soon afterwards, in January 1916, he applied for release from his job as a fitter at the NSW Government Railway Workshops in Eveleigh, but the authorities decided to retain his services 'owing to the shortage of mechanics in the iron trade, and the fact that the manufacture of munitions of war will shortly be undertaken'. In April 1916 he married a German-born woman, probably hoping that she would become a mother to his orphaned children. A few months later he enlisted in the AIF but was discharged on medical grounds. In April 1917 he died of heart failure in Sydney.

Zacharias' papers, preserved by his grandson, allow us to better understand the troubles plaguing this unfortunate man. A few months before his death Zacharias inscribed a photo on behalf of his son as a memento to a friend, in which 'Harold Zacharovich' asks 'not to forget me, a citizen of free Australia'. And indeed in the photo the 3-year-old Harold, holding a tennis racket and ball, looks like a real Australian boy. In a letter to his children written on his deathbed, Zacharias wrote: 'My past misfortunes and my homesickness have broken my health.' These two enigmatic comments suggest that his emigration was probably politically motivated. Klavdia and Zacharias intentionally chose the name Harold for their baby, wanting him to become part of a free country, but their hopes of assimilation went hand in hand with homesickness. The last words of Zacharias to his children were quintessentially Ukrainian in spirit: 'I hope you will think well of me, and that kind people will take you into their tender care and look after your future.' Luckily, the family of the witness named in his death certificate, William J. Large, took in Zacharias' children after his death.[92] His son Harold Piven-Large became an engineer in the steps of his father, and their descendants now run successful companies in Sydney. Zacharias was clearly unable to pass on his Ukrainian heritage to his children, but the fact that Harold and his descendants preserved the surname Piven and kept his papers suggests that they treasure their histories.

Nicholas Fedorovich, the journalist from Odessa who wrote the beautiful wartime love story *Kismet*, found his happiness with a Russian girl, Eraida Nezhintseva (Nejinzeva), making a perilous journey to Moscow in 1924 to marry her. When Eraida managed to join him in 1925, they settled in Brisbane.[93] Although Fedorovich was very much open to Australian culture and had farmed in a soldiers' settlement in the outback, this marriage reinforced his attachment

Harold Zacharovich Piven, a citizen of free Australia (courtesy of Piven-Large family)

to the Russian community and the newly established Russian Orthodox Church on Vulture Street in South Brisbane. One of the clauses of his will was a bequest for the Church to provide hostel accommodation for the old, sick and destitute; he also wanted to cover university fees and maintenance for two Russian children in poor circumstances.[94] When he died in 1946, he was one of the few Ukrainian Slavs buried with a funeral service in the Russian Orthodox Church. His death was also noted in a local newspaper by the Gallipoli Legion of Anzacs, who must have been his second family.[95]

Untangling identities
The story of John Cherpiter's family

In 1932 Melbourne Police Inspector Roland S. Browne summoned Marjory Maneeken, a young Australian typist at Customs House, for an interview at the station. She confirmed that her father, John Cherpiter, had valiantly fallen on the Western Front in April 1917, while her Ukrainian stepfather, Paul Koslick, had recently left for the Soviet Union. It was Koslick's misadventures there which had drawn the attention of the Investigation Branch to the widow and daughter of John Cherpiter. The results of Inspector Browne's investigation gave cause for concern. He discovered that John Cherpiter was not her father at all, while her real father, Vasily Maneeken, a Russian, was living quietly somewhere in Queensland. Neither, from the point of view of the law, was Mr Koslick the lawful husband of her mother. Browne also justly inquired how it had happened that nobody at Marjory's government department had paid attention to the fact that her surname was different from her father's, and that she was an unnaturalised Russian alien![96]

Inspector Browne's investigation had cracked open the case of John Cherpiter from the middle, but we are able to start at the beginning of the story. Nadya Manikina, born in 1910 in Siberia, arrived in Melbourne from the Russian Far East in May 1914 with her parents Vasily and Anastasia. They moved to Port Pirie, where the parents soon split up, and her mother, whose English was limited to a few words, set off for the bright lights of Adelaide. There she met John Cherpiter, a fellow-countryman, and they started to live as husband and wife. Australian divorce legislation was quite complex at that time and immigrants obviously did not care or did not know how to use it. Anastasia simply assumed a new identity as Mrs Cherpiter. While Vasily Maneekeen never inquired as to what happened to his wife and daughter, John Cherpiter did care about his de facto wife and her little daughter, who also assumed an Australian name, Lucy. When a year later he left for the war, he recorded Anastasia as his wife. After his death on the Western Front they received his pension, which amounted to £3 a fortnight, but they could hardly make ends meet and Anastasia decided to move from Adelaide to Melbourne, where the community of émigrés from the Russian Empire numbered several hundred. To survive, she went to work in a clothing factory, renting accommodation on Tope Street. She also provided rooms and board for single émigré men, usually seamen. The Charity Organisation Society enquired after her circumstances in 1919, and wrote to the Department of Repatriation in 1919:

> Mrs. Cherpiter is a Russian, and the only reference she could give us was another Russian whom we found living with quite a colony of Russians in South Melbourne. As in the case of Mrs. Cherpiter most of them professed to know very little English but they all agree that Mrs. Cherpiter is a respectable and deserving woman.[97]

But obviously not everyone in the Russian community was of this opinion: the military pension that she received became the subject of envy, and in 1922 an anonymous denunciation was sent to the police stating that she was not the widow of Cherpiter and that her husband lived in Queensland. Brought to the police station and interviewed through an interpreter, Anastasia honestly told her story. Although she was not legally the widow of an Anzac, the authorities decided not to deprive her and her child of the pension, a decision which was not forgotten: 'It is incredible that this woman should have received such great benefits, amounting to about £1000, and including war gratuity,' commented Inspector Browne in 1933.⁹⁸

While in Melbourne, Nadezhda/Lucy changed her name to Marjory, and Anastasia was recorded in the alien registration document as Anastasia Maneekena and in the Melbourne city directory as Annie Maneekeena. However, when she married one of her boarders, the Ukrainian seaman Paul Koslick, in 1925, she had no means of legalising their relationship but to marry him as the widow Anastasia Cherpiter. They settled in Port Melbourne, mortgaging a house on Graham Street, and Anastasia supplemented their income with boarders. In 1926 Melbourne newspapers reported a 'Foreigners' Brawl':

> The scene of the fight was a house in Graham Street, occupied by Paul Koslick and his wife, who are Russians. A number of countrymen had been spending the evening at the house, and the argument concerning money is alleged to have arisen between Paul Mahovsky [...] and Stanley Maklossak, a Pole. [...] Koslick and his wife were both severely gashed.⁹⁹

The communal networks of countrymen, be they Russian, Ukrainian, or Polish, remained an important feature of Melbourne life in the 1920s and later, and the Koslicks were an integral part of these communities. Even in 1932, when interviewed by the police, Anastasia spoke 'hardly any English' and 'an interpreter was necessary'.¹⁰⁰

Having heard favourable reports about working conditions in the Soviet Union, Paul Koslick decided to return there in 1931, at the time of the Great Depression. By that time he was a naturalised British subject, but as soon as he arrived the Soviet authorities seized his Australian passport and declared him a Soviet citizen, banning him from leaving the country; as the mail was under surveillance, he could not even inform Anastasia of his plight. The more Paul saw the reality of the Soviet Union, the stronger became his desire to escape.

Reaching Leningrad, penniless and devastated, he asked the British consul there, R.W. Bullard, to help him to return to Australia. The consul seemed to be willing to intervene in the case unofficially, especially as Koslick stated that he had a wife and a daughter in Australia. Bullard duly wrote to the Australian Prime Minister, who forwarded his letter to the Investigation Branch, enquiring whether Mrs Koslick would be able to pay her husband's passage. Anastasia and Marjory were then interviewed; the Investigation Branch brought all their names together and discovered that Koslick did not have an Australian daughter and that his marriage to Anastasia was bigamous. Now the only way for him to escape the Soviet Union, the British consul informed Anastasia, was to obtain an Intourist passport and tickets from Leningrad to London and then to Australia, amounting to the vast sum of £250. Anastasia, whose only income was board from a couple of tenants, told Inspector Browne that she was unable to rescue Koslick.[101] What became of him remains unknown.

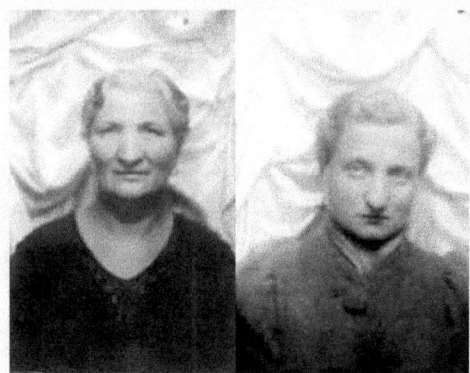

WWII alien registration of Anastasia Koslick (left) and Nadezhda Maneekeena (NAA)

In the meantime, Marjory had to make her own decisions about her identity. In the 1930s, when she was in her twenties and still lived with her mother, working as a typist and stenographer at the Myer Emporium, she registered in the electoral rolls as Marjory Maneekeena. In 1941, however, she married under the name of Nadezhda and subsequently kept that name. Her husband was an Irish Australian Anzac twenty-five years her senior. These many changes of name suggest that while Anastasia was at home in the Russian milieu, her daughter was at ease in a new world, but did not abandon her Russian/Ukrainian heritage. Anastasia lived a long life, finally paying off the mortgage on her house.

The contradictions of assimilation are interesting to see in the example of George Marion Tchorzewski. He came to Australia with his parents as a young child, born, according to his service records, in 'Russian Poland', and a Roman Catholic. On reaching England with the AIF, at well over the age of forty, he suffered from rheumatism and was returned to Australia. While English must have been George's main language and his family seemed to be exemplary immigrants, their life on a secluded sugar cane farm probably allowed George to maintain his Slavic and English identities alongside each other. In 1924 he married a newly arrived emigrant from Harbin, Polly Guilko (Hilko), whose maiden name was Sakaranko. She and her first husband Roman Guilko were Ukrainians and her son Sergius was born in Harbin in 1912. Most likely this marriage reinforced George's identification with the land of Ukraine: in the land purchase deeds of 1941 he revealed for the first time that he was born in 'Ukraine Poland' and recorded his name in the Polish way, as Marian Georgius.[102]

It might be supposed that when our Anzacs married British or Australian women, assimilation proceeded rapidly. In such families English was the only language of communication, even if the husband at first had a rudimentary command of the language. 'His wife taught him English,' Albert Michael Tober's family remembers.[103] Wives and children became the bridge that facilitated the Anzacs' integration into local communities and social life, including sporting events. As in England, developing a friendship with a local girl or a nurse while in hospital was a familiar pattern for these men, and often led to marriage. These women were prepared to marry these homeless strangers and build a home with them: they learned to heal not only physical wounds, but spiritual ones as well. George Kamishansky 'spent the greater part of his time up to 1921 in hospitals and convalescent homes'; at the end of his recovery he married an AIF nursing sister, Jean Smith. John Ouchirenko, who was obviously deeply traumatised by his first marriage in England, which failed because of the xenophobia of his wife's family, found his happiness in Australia. His son recalls that he served in the merchant navy and was then 'admitted to Heidelberg Repatriation Hospital through war illness. There he met Doris Robertson who was to become his wife.'[104] Joseph Rudezky met Agnes Annie Burns, who had an illegitimate son, when he was in Brisbane suffering from tuberculosis and seeking medical support. In spite of his ailment she decided to share his life. She followed him to the sanatorium in Stanthorpe, where they

Lily Lawler, Albert Tober's wife (Ancestry.com)

took up residence in the soldiers' settlement. They later moved further north to Dalby, for its dry climate, which prolonged Rudezky's life for a few more years and allowed him to bring up his four elder daughters and his wife's son before he died in 1931.[105]

The families of Jewish Anzacs from Ukraine often managed to hold onto their ethnic traditions longer than the Slavs, marrying Jewish girls, although the level of assimilation was increasing among them too. Their spouses often came from families who had left the Russian Empire earlier than they had, or had come from England, and were assimilated to a much greater degree. Yiddish, Russian and Ukrainian, which some of these Jewish Anzacs would use in the early years, were now replaced by English. Peter Komesaroff, who kept up his involvement in Jewish community affairs throughout his life, spoke English at home with his Ukrainian-born wife Sarah Isaacman. According to their daughter Thelma, 'My mother was educated here, completely. My father came here when he was [a boy] and he was very determined to learn English.'[106]

There was clearly a direct correlation between the mastering of English, involvement in local communal life and loss of original identity. But it seems not to have been quite an entirely straightforward process. Without detailed memoirs and first-hand accounts of these changes we can reconstruct them only through circumstantial evidence, which nevertheless sheds some light on the phenomenon.

For the purposes of highlighting these complexities, we can consider two families: Matfeus Oleinikoff and his Ukrainian wife Daria, and Joseph Rudezky and his Australian wife Agnes. After the war the Oleinikoffs moved from the cane-growing area of Booyal to Brisbane and settled in Woolloongabba, an area with a large Russian-Ukrainian-Jewish community. The naming pattern of their eight children suggests that in spite of being Ukrainian they underwent rapid and voluntary integration. They came to Australia in 1912 with four young children – Pavel, Vera, 'Nedechola' (probably Nadezhda or Nadeja), and Petr. The names of the boys were easily converted into their English equivalents Paul and Peter; Vera retained her name; Nadezhda (born in 1909) chose the English name Ida. Their first child born in Australia in 1912 was named Lubov (completing the triad Vera-Nadezhda-Lubov – Faith-Hope-Charity), but very soon this name was replaced by Lucy. After that the new children received English-sounding names: George, Harry, and Eva Jean. Oleinikoff's wife Daria used the name Dorrie by 1915 and settled on Doris in the 1920s.

The family of Rudezky, who first lived in Stanthorpe and then in Dalby, where they had hardly any Ukrainian contacts, gave their five daughters a mixture of names popular with English speakers and Slavs: Lilly, Violet, Tanya, Doris, and Tamara. Violet remembers how in 1930 her father's health deteriorated and he was sent to the 'repatriation hospital for servicemen. There were floods all over and my mother could not get there and he died down there in 1930. The last child born was Tamara and he asked my mother before he left, if it is a girl, call her Tamara, because we had Australian names except Tanya. Tamara was born in 1930.'[107]

A similar mixture of English and Slavonic names may be seen in several other Ukrainian-Australian families. The daughters of Cezar and Gwynnyth Wolkowsky had the unusual names of Marea Victusya and Sonia Mae. John and Doris Ouchirenko named their children Ivan, David, Alexander, Stepanida, and Ann. The choice of 'Ivan' is notable as his father recorded his own name consistently as John, the English equivalent of Ivan. Ksenofont and Bessie Kozachuk had children named Sybil, Ksenofont William, and Hilda May. Here it is clear that Bessie's influence had an effect. Similarly, Albert Michael Tober had three children with English names and a daughter Olga.

'Russian romance crashes'
Kozachuk's and Olenikoff's stories

Several of our Anzacs' marriages did not survive the trials of family life. In a number of cases the reason for the breakdown of marriage, separation, and divorce was domestic violence. This was a complex phenomenon where traditional Russian-Ukrainian attitudes to the position of the woman in the home, unrecognised mental trauma caused by war, and the strain caused by ethnic and cultural differences came into the conflict with modern Australian attitudes towards the equality of women. Ksenofont Kozachuk's story is one example. In 1928 his wife Bessie lodged a complaint in court that after an altercation between them she was 'badly knocked about' and had to leave her husband and earn money to support their three children. Ksenofont was confined to jail for one month and fined. They had a temporary peace, but new beatings followed until they finally divorced in 1948.[108] The abuse experienced by Bessie was lodged in her mind so firmly that decades later the children and grandchildren of Ksenofont would have nothing to do with a man who had 'bashed a woman'.

Ksenofont Kozachuk's family, 1925 (courtesy of Kozachuk family)

The case of the Oleinikoffs, where both parents were Ukrainian, provides some further insights into the evolving dynamics of the woman's position even in an ethnically homogeneous home. In 1925 their family discords, leading to Doris and the children leaving her husband, came to the attention of the Australian tabloid newspaper *Truth*. As we remember, in Australia Daria Oleinikoff became Doris and was evidently well on the way towards cultural emancipation. The family's move from Booyal to Brisbane, and exposure to the children's English learnt at school, allowed her to pick up some English herself. This was the general pattern, as Solomon Stedman describes in his impressions of Brisbane at the time: 'The children attended public schools and their daily speech was English. The mothers continued to address their offspring in Russian or in Yiddish and received answers in English. This served a double purpose, the children did not forget the language of their parents and their mother learnt English'.[109] The borderline-racist newspaper reporter characterized Mrs Oleinikoff's speech as 'a jargon of pidgin English, amply interspersed with typical gesticulations'. He nevertheless had to admit that 'Mrs Oleinikoff bears her 23 years of married life very well. She is still

The Oleinikoffs, as seen by the Truth tabloid artist (1925)

a prepossessing woman.' Indeed, she was depicted in the newspaper ostentatiously dressed and wearing a fashionable hat.

The conflict that caused the family crisis reflected changing familial roles. Matthew came home from the meatworks 'after a hard day's work, and found there was no tea, and that his wife was at the movies'. This was not the first time that Doris' behaviour had departed from traditional norms: 'He frequently felt that she needed correction. She says that Matthew was for ever abusing her and knocking about. Matt reckons she could do her share, too,' wrote the reporter. Notably, Doris complained about the effect of AIF service on Matthew: 'The wife reckons the war had a corrupting effect on Matthew's morals. He learnt more naughty words while in France than during the rest of his life and he took delight in treating her to his choicest samples.' Perhaps he had also picked up far heavier mental baggage during his war service. The participation of their daughter Ida, who was brought to Australia as a baby, in the court hearings provides further insight into the changing roles. She was, according to the reporter, 'a smart, attractive girl, and a dead sticker for her ma. She reckoned that Matthew was frequently abusing and hurting her mother', and she obviously had the courage to stand up to her father's abusive behaviour.[110] Ida's position was similar to that of Kozachuk's children: they all adopted the new trends developing in Australian society. As for Matthew, he was obliged, according to the court order, to pay 20/- per week for the maintenance of his estranged wife and children.

A Ukrainian imprint

Of course, in many other cases, the families managed to go through their trials together, be these war wounds, cultural differences or the community's hostile attitude. For instance, Stephen Provaka's marriage to a British girl, Bertha Finnimore, seems to have been happy: for several years after his death, on the day of his passing his wife would place commemorative notices in the newspapers in memory of her 'Steve, dear'. As mentioned earlier, not long before his marriage Stephen had changed his distinctly Slavonic-sounding name Stepan Proiavka to the more cosmopolitan Stephen Provaka. His daughter Joyce may not have had much trouble with her surname at Holland Park School in multinational Bris-

'In Memoriam' placed by Stephen Provaka's wife and daughter in a Brisbane newspaper

bane,[111] but in the outback the attitudes to children with Ukrainian names were different. Joseph Rudezky's story tells of the courage that children in such families sometimes needed just to bear a Ukrainian name. His daughter, Violet, more than 70 years later, still has not forgotten:

> When we went to school at Dalby, the kids used to throw stones at us, and met us after school and told us to go home to Russia, to Red Russia, and stay there. 'We don't want you in this country, it is our country' … It must have come from the parents because the kids would not have known. It was a terrible time in our lives.

Theofil Volkofsky's children had similar problems:

> During the war, some of the nastier sort of kids at the school [would say], 'You are a Russian wog!' There was always a backlash there somewhere in the community. Some people just did not appreciate people from Russia or other countries. It was very much a British colony in those days and foreigners were not popular.

The fathers had to find ways of countering such treatment. Volkofsky's solution was to tell his children to be Australian. Rudezky, his daughter says, 'used to come and meet us from the school and he used to teach us a little bit of Russian, but I only remember a few words of it. He was a beautiful cook, he used to make *borshch* and *pirozhkis* – oh, beautiful.' He used to tell his children that one day he would take them to Ukraine, though he must have known he would never see it again, as he was terminally ill with the tuberculosis he had contracted in the army. As we remember, his last wish was to give his newborn daughter a name popular among Slavs at the time – Tamara. Carol Gregorenko, a granddaughter of Richard Gregorenko, once asked her father why she had such a strange surname, and her father told her: 'You have a Russian surname and you should be proud of it.'[112] All they could do was leave to their children and grandchildren a drop of their love for their motherland, which was unfortunately associated at that time with 'Red Russia' and the Soviet Union.

Nevertheless, this connection with their native land of Ukraine left a hardly visible imprint. Janice, a granddaughter of Albert Tober, tells: 'I never knew grandfather, I was about 14 or 15 when he died and I never ever met him but I always had it in my mind that I would have loved to have met him and just spoken to him, because I always had the idea that he could tell some tales.' Yet a little of her grandfather's heritage did reach her. Of her childhood she says, 'We lived in the West of Queensland, and my father used to go down to Brisbane and he come back with yoghurt culture and black pudding, special cheeses. You could never buy them in the shops. And dad and I got dishes our grandfather used to cook.'[113]

George Kamishansky, who successfully joined the Australian middle class, with an Australian wife who was the president of the Nurses' sub-branch of the R.S.L., named their house on Barton Road in Artamon 'Kertch', after his birthplace. Similarly, the family of Wolfe Greenstein from Odessa, who were well assimilated having spent 13 years in England before finally settling in Australia, named their mansion on Jeffrey Street in Canterbury in Sydney 'Odessa', after the city they had had to leave forever, but which still lived in their memories.

John Ouchirenko, Alik (Alexay) Ostrinko, Saveliy Tkachenko, and Denis Papchuck, in their applications for naturalisation, specified that they were born in Ukraine 'in the country of Russia'. Ostrinko even used 'Ukrainia', in an approximation of its Ukrainian pronunciation, and stated that his mother and father were of Ukrainian nationality in the section where applicants were supposed to write 'Russian', since, as far as the Australian authorities were concerned, this was the nationality of Russian subjects.

Elias Jacob Serebrennikoff's expression of his connection with his native land was subtler, but equally significant for him. Engaged in farming and business enterprises, he was adapting perfectly to Australian society. He had shortened his surname to Serennikoff and sometimes used the name V. Dennis. Yet when he married an Australian woman in 1922, they made their vows in the Greek Orthodox Church in Melbourne. By the time Joseph Rudezky died of tuberculosis in a Brisbane hospital in 1931, a Russian Orthodox Church had been established in the city. His wife could not join him at his deathbed because the railway line to Dalby was cut by flooding, so he was probably given his last rites by the Russian Orthodox priest. 'The interment took place in the South Brisbane cemetery on Sunday, according to the rites of the Greek Church, of which he was a member,' a local newspaper reported.[114]

In some cases, integration into Australian society went hand in hand with the amendment of political views. In his youth Theofil Volkofsky had been inspired by radical social ideals, as a result of which he later came under suspicion during his army service. After he settled in outback Australia his views underwent a telling transformation. His son Tom relates that he

> very quickly became disillusioned when he hit Cobar, when he saw the union men there and what they were doing, how they behaved. He was an idealist. He became a great patriot of the king, he brought us kids up to be great patriots. He always voted Liberal. Dad would always write in the paper about things like kangaroo problems, always writing to a minister for this and to a minister for that. He started an organisation called the Western Settlers Association. He fought very hard to get a high school at Cobar and he succeeded in getting that and he fought for a school hostel so that kids from the land could come and stay at the hostel. That succeeded too.

Kangaroo problems and a hostel for schoolchildren in an outback town seem quintessentially Australian, but were they? To the Ukrainian or Russian eye, it is obvious that these are the actions of a pre-revolutionary *narodnik* who finds himself in the countryside. These were the cultural and social values that Theofil acquired during his Ukrainian youth in the teachers' college, which set him apart and were noticed by his son:

> Dad did not drink, and he did not gamble. That was probably something that made him stand a little bit aside from the rest of the community. If you want to get along in some of those country towns you have to go to a pub or a club, and bet on the race horses. And it just was the last thing he was interested in. I think Cezar would fit in better. He would gamble too, and spent a lot of time with his mates.'[115]

The brother, Cezar Wolkowsky, in spite of his own disillusionment with Bolshevism, did not sever all connections with his Russian-Ukrainian past. His nephew Tom remembers, 'Cezar was a member of Russian Club in Sydney, that was part of his Russian connections.' However, he adds, 'He was an easy going chap and drove taxis in Sydney for ages. […] I think he became a businessman in his own right with his own taxi and I think this changed his attitude.' Cezar's children grew up cherishing their Slavic identity.

Cezar Wolkowsky with daughters Sonia (left) and Marea and grandson Alyn (Courtesy of Thomas Volkofsky)

The elder, Marea Victusya, a famous soprano opera singer, changed her name to Maria Prerauer after marrying Curt Prerauer, the philharmonic orchestra conductor, but used her distinctly Slavonic maiden name Marea Wolkowsky in her children's books. Among the children of our Anzacs she was probably the first who tried to visit the long-forbidden land of their fathers. According to Tom's memories, in her work as a soprano, 'She went to Covent Garden, to Europe, she ended up in Russia behind the iron curtain, they wouldn't let her back out because she was of Russian descent.' It is quite likely that Maria in fact did not manage to go further than Eastern Germany, but at least she tried.[116] Among Maria and Curt Prerauer's papers in the National Library of Australia there is Maria's translation of a Russian play, *Sputnik 293*, which suggests that she may have known Russian, but it is most likely that her father helped her.[117]

Naturalisation and the Anzac spirit

Along with Ukrainian, Slavic, or Yiddish identities, which were not easy to maintain in Australia at that time, new identities were taking shape among our Anzacs – a belonging to Australia, the land for which they had fought and which was becoming their homeland. These tendencies can be labelled as assimilation, which in modern studies of émigrés is often seen as a negative process, but was in fact a complex, multifaceted process, of which our émigrés were rightfully proud.

Naturalisation was one of the manifestations of this transformation. While it had a direct and practical dimension – it was, for instance, impossible to buy real estate or to obtain a passport to travel overseas without naturalisation – it was also an emotional process. The graph of Ukrainian-born Anzacs' naturalisation (below), which corresponds with wider trends of Russian-born naturalisation, shows an upsurge between 1914 and 1915. It is quite probable that many of those being naturalised during this period did so on the eve of enlistment, aspiring to serve in the AIF as British (or Australian) rather than Russian subjects. The second surge was between 1918-1925 when they returned, aiming to become British subjects. It is also noteworthy that out of the 33 Anzacs who survived the war and were not naturalised in Australia, 20 died early or didn't naturalise because they had moved to live in another country.

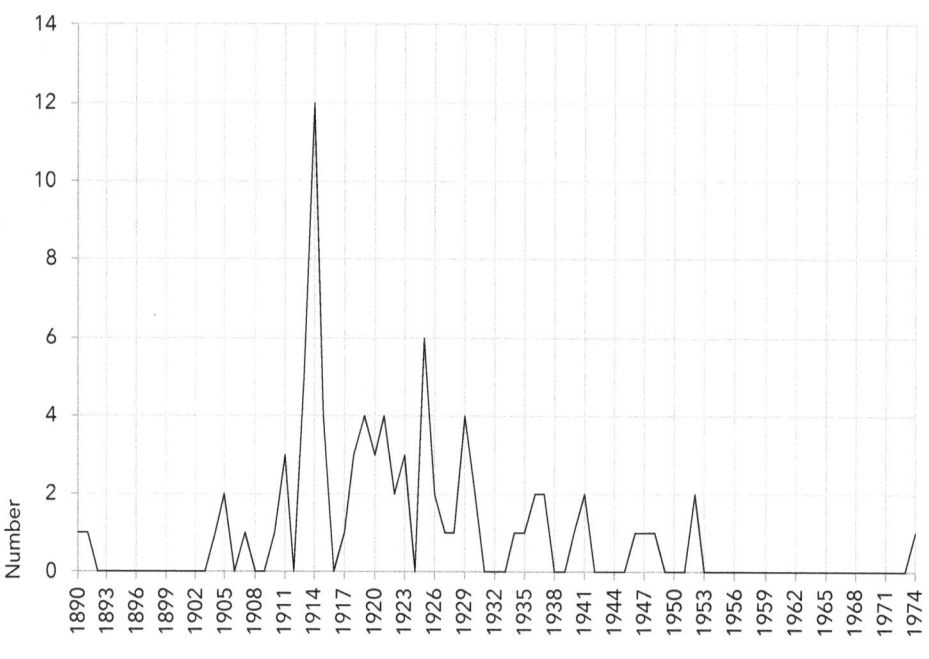

Figure 3. Naturalisation of Ukrainian-born Anzacs, 1890-1974

Sources: Data from naturalisation files.

Naturalisation might have been seen by those who were on active service as an act secondary to their oath of allegiance to the British Crown, which they made when enlisting in the AIF and of which they proved themselves worthy on the battlefields. For them an added dimension was their feeling of having now earned their right to be sons of Australia – this place where many had originally landed only by chance. Yur Kivovitch, for example, having been invalided out of the army and seeking to be naturalised, wrote in 1918: 'my desire for naturalisation is so that I would be able to execute duties such as a citizen should – It struck me rather hard when I found that I am not able to vote after fighting for King and Country.'[118] Joseph Vurhaft applied for his naturalisation from hospital in 1918; on being requested to submit his

Russian birth certificate, he exploded: 'I lost everything I had when wounded at the front. ... I gave my service freely for the country, and am suffering from shock to the nervous system besides losing an arm. I fail to see any reason why there should be any delay in this matter, or to be worried any further.'[119] Denis Papchuck, one of the last among the Ukrainian Anzacs to take out naturalisation papers, was reported as expressing similar sentiments: 'Having served with the A.I.F. in France and Egypt for three and a half years and been gassed and wounded, ... said he had regarded his honourable discharge as sufficient proof of naturalisation.'[120] Similarly, a policeman interviewing Joseph Rudovsky (Mikulicic-Rodd) for naturalisation recorded that he 'has always considered himself to be an Australian and desires to be officially recognised as a British Subject'; Peter Komesaroff also believed that his naturalisation 'had been conferred by service in the A.I.F.'[121]

At the same time naturalisation had become an effective weapon in the hands of the authorities in their dealings with potential dissidents. Even those who acted within the bounds of democratic institutions, exercising their right of free speech and not breaking the law, were often victimised. Thus, on the Investigation Branch's recommendation, Cezar Wolkowsky's naturalisation was rejected several times, which meant that he would lose his block of land (non-naturalised persons could not own land). But what worried him even more was that this decision had turned his Australian wife and their newborn daughter into alien subjects as well. Finally, he appealed to Senator Pearce, minister for Home and Territories:

> My military record is good and I am married to an Australian girl. I left for Gallipoli in 1915 willing to lay down my life, if needs be for the British Empire. I was very badly wounded in shoulder and was in receipt of pension for some considerable time. I was not refused permission to fight for the Empire and think now I should at least be allowed the privilege of living as an Australian with British Freedom.

Suspecting what had caused his rejection, he went on:

> During the Russian Chaos I being young and ignorant, was influenced by older Russians and was naturally at first in sympathy with the Bolsheviks, until I began to read and think for myself ... I then saw the mistake I had made and repented my folly in thinking the Bolsheviks good, and I assure you there are no more loyal subjects than my wife and I today.

It was this repentance, rather than his excellent military record, that helped: those words in his letter were underlined by an official. Wolkowsky was finally granted naturalisation in 1923.[122] John Ouchirenko, who was heavily fined for displaying a Red Flag in Melbourne in 1919, also regretted his involvement with the radicals. In his case the police inspector recommended his naturalisation: 'I do not think that he is an undesirable. He had 1300 days active service.'[123] Joseph Kleshenko was finally naturalised too, even though police records showed that he had a period of fascination with Bolshevik ideas as well.[124] At the same time Peter Komesaroff, an outspoken fighter for justice, received quite a balanced character reference from the policeman interviewing him for naturalisation: 'he holds advanced views but not incompatible with good citizenship and is not a member of the Communist Party'. His daughter Thelma considers that her father 'was not a communist, but he was a socialist', and adds: 'I think Stalin cured him.'[125] Nevertheless, the Australian Security Intelligence Organisation (ASIO) assembled a dossier on him.[126]

Sometimes the officials dealing with the naturalisation applications were pedantic to the point of absurdity. Ben Goffin had enlisted in the army on the day he landed at Melbourne, and on the Western Front was severely wounded twice and gassed once. He was refused naturalisation because he could not write, even though during the war the army had been happy enough to enlist illiterate foreigners who could only sign their papers with a cross. The Returned Sailors' and Soldiers' Imperial League of Australia (RSSILA) appealed on his behalf, but it was another two years before he was naturalised, and only when a policeman had ascertained that he could write.[127]

Anzac values were another manifestation of the bond built between our heroes and Australian society. In the thick of the battles of 1917 on the Western Front, Lamotte Sage wrote a letter of love to Perth, at the same time giving vent to his hatred for the Germans:

> Dear, dear old Perth, I greet you from beyond the seas! I envy them all who are now treading thy beloved pavements; oft I wonder what changes these three long years have brought to thee. I wonder if the German pest is allowed to pollute still thy fair name, or art thou free? [...] Thy warriors will deliver thee from the masters of *kultur*, for I know their temper, I know their steel, and if I do not then who should, for have I not followed their fortunes in Gallipoli, on the Somme, at Bullecourt, Messines and Ypres?[128]

Sometimes we learn about these feelings not from lofty declarations, but from police reports, as in Alexander Sank's case. It is obvious that for him, his AIF discharge certificate took on a spiritual significance. 'I'm, justly, highly proud in possession [of it],' he wrote, seeking its speedy return from officials. This again was in connection with a naturalisation application, which Sank was making as he was in trouble with the police in Sydney for not registering as an alien: 'His excuse was that being a returned soldier, even though Russian, he did not think it necessary.' The police dealt with many other such cases leniently, but not Sank's. Major Jones, Director of the Investigation Branch, wrote: 'A perusal of the police file showed that despite warnings, this man, then a tram conductor, took no notice, and failed to register, treating the police generally, both by word and deed, most insolently, and they were most desirous of processing against him.' With two years of army service, Sank clearly considered the demand to register as an alien to be an insult to his Anzac pride. He was prosecuted and fined 10 shillings.[129]

Indeed, the discharge certificate or returned serviceman badge was the visual proof of the Ukrainian Anzacs' belonging to the Anzac brotherhood. Cemon Afendikoff, three times wounded on the Western Front, carried his swag all over Australia, from Nimmitabel in the Snowy Mountains to Gordonvale in North Queensland. In 1935, applying for a copy of his discharge certificate, he explained that he needed one because of the 'wear and tear of constantly carrying it on my person in all weather'. He evidently kept up his membership in local RSSILA branches, as after his lonely death in 1939 in Gordonvale, it was the RSSILA which looked after his grave.[130] Abraham Smoishen, who saw three years of service as a trooper in Egypt and Palestine, wore his returned soldier badge while hawking with his cart along Australian roads.[131] Carl Kills, who was discharged from the AIF before sailing to the front, tried to use his short AIF experience to promote his business, posting the sign 'C.S. Kills, late A.I.F.' at his woodyard in Ripponlea, and got into trouble with the police for false advertising.[132]

A sense of belonging to the Anzacs facilitated the emigrants' involvement in Australian political and social life. As early as 1918 we meet the name of Stephen Surovsov among the tunnellers who signed a petition in support of the policies of the Labour Premier T.J. Ryan.[133] The social involvement of Constantine Pinkevitch was more gradual. After several years of a wandering life in the north, Pinkevitch finally married and settled in the Newcastle area, where he joined the management committee of the Hamilton sub-branch of the RSL.[134] He and his son Leo competed in the Newcastle and Maitland District Rifle Club.[135] Joseph Rudezky, according to his daughter, 'was fairly bitter about the army', but in Dalby he became 'an enthusiastic member of the Dalby District Diggers' Association'.[136] Emile Tardent, an outspoken journalist of Swiss origin born in Mykolaiv, founded and presided over the 42nd Battalion Reunion Committee. He also inaugurated the RSSILA sub-branch at Wynnum, where he settled after the war.[137]

The Anzac spirit was cherished by the children of our Anzacs as well. In January 1939, when the clouds of war were once again gathering over faraway Europe, 16-year-old Marea Wolkowsky, the Anzac's daughter, wrote a poem:

On the Battlefield

Is it a dream?

Mists are rising,

Voices are singing

Out of the west,

Songs of the blest.

Poppies are falling,

Voices are calling,

Shadows are closing.

Angels are bringing me – rest.[138]

Marea Wolkowsky, aged 15 (NLA)

Eight months later the new war broke out.

The Second World War

The Second World War was the major proof of the bonds forged between our Anzacs and their adopted country. Their involvement in the military effort varied, but its main manifestation was their enlistment in the 2nd AIF.

According to the database of the Australian Second World War nominal roll,[139] only six people enlisted in the 2nd AIF as natives of Ukraine, but further study of the place of birth of servicemen provides quite different statistics. It can be estimated that about 1400 people born on the territory of the former Russian Empire and neighbouring connected territories enlisted in the 2nd AIF. In the neighbouring territories we include the section of the Austro-Hungarian Empire which was occupied by Poland between the First and Second World War and in 1939-1940 joined to the USSR as a result of the Molotov-Ribbentrop pact, and which now forms part of Ukraine. Other neighbouring territories which we include in our statistics are Bessarabia-Moldova and Harbin in China, the Russian city built on Chinese territory during the construction of the Chinese Eastern Railway. Among these recruits, men born on the territory of present-day Ukraine numbered nearly 200. They were to become the new generation of Ukrainian and Ukrainian-born Anzacs, whose story is yet to be told. The recruits of 1939-1945 included fourteen First World War Ukrainian-born Anzacs, a considerable number, bearing in mind that by this time some had left Australia for good, some had died, and others were sick or too old to be accepted.

Age seemed to present no major obstacle to enlistment, however: some of the men simply 'adjusted' their birthdates, and the authorities regularly failed to insist on documentary proof. Michael Ankudinow enlisted twice in the 2nd AIF, each time changing his year of birth (which for enlistment in the 1st AIF he had stated was 1886), to 1896 and then 1901. Isaac Chain shed almost a decade between 1878 and 1886, while Wolfe Greenstein took off just two years, changing his year of birth from 1899 to 1901. Stephen Surovsov, on the other hand, changed his age in the opposite direction: when he joined the 1st AIF he gave his year of birth as 1891, but now he claimed to be born in 1882, which was probably true.

Now, after nearly three decades in Australia, sharing both good and bad times with its people, the Ukrainian-born Anzacs had become part of this nation and quite naturally held patriotic feelings for their adopted country. Louis Brodsky, despite having taken 'French leave' from the 1st AIF, had a strong desire to defend Australia in July 1940: 'although I am 58 years of age I am still capable to serve in the Home defence force in any capacity, I am anxious to serve in the present crisis'.[140] The desire to enlist may also have been due to a wish to relive a sense of camaraderie remembered fondly – or in rosy hues – since their earlier service.

'Marshal Timoshenko's nephew'
Michael Ankudinow's story

Michael Ankudinow, whose life in post-war Australia was punctuated by vagrancy, larceny, drunken brawls (once his face was slashed with a razor and once he was severely beaten on suspicion of being a scab), enlisted in the 2nd AIF twice, in 1939 and 1940. When, despite manipulating his age, he was finally discharged as medically unfit, he joined the Civil Construction Corps (CCC), which did building work for the Army. This may have been his attempt to relive the best years of his life, his time in the 1st AIF, when he was mentioned in despatches for bravery and was trusted to serve in the Australian Provost Corps. Alas, like many other Anzacs from Ukraine, Ankudinow left no memoirs, so we can only piece together his world from the documentary records. These include a court case in 1943, when he was discharged from the CCC and arrested in Melbourne because he 'had annoyed people in Spring Street when he was drunk by stopping them, holding out his hand, and muttering something'. It had been some time since he had been in trouble with the law and now, in court, he used his trump card to defend his honour. Asked if he had anything to say, he answered, 'Yes, Your Worship. I am of Cossack descent. Both my parents were true Cossacks. Tom Timoshenko is my uncle.' He further 'claimed that his brother, General George Ankudinow, at present was serving with the Red Army at Kharkiv under his "uncle"'. Although the famed Soviet Marshal Semen Timoshenko came from Furmanivka, not far from Odessa where Ankudinow was born, it is highly doubtful they were related. As for his brother 'General George', Michael Ankudinow did have a little brother George, but he died in 1915, aged four, in Sedanka. This white lie betrays Ankudinow's aspiration to be associated with the war effort in Ukraine. He added that he himself 'when a lad' 'served with the Lancers in the Russo-Japanese war', and while serving in the AIF he was twice mentioned in despatches and received the Military Medal.[141] The only element of truth here was that he had indeed been mentioned in despatches, but only once. Yet this is not the story of a petty liar, but of a man aiming, by all possible means, to belong in Australian society, let down by alcoholism, an unruly temperament and his ethnic background… He died in 1951 in the Repatriation Hospital in Heidelberg, Victoria. There was no one near him to add the names of his parents to his death certificate.

Michael Ankudinow, 1940 (NAA)

As for other Ukrainian veterans who enlisted in the 2nd AIF, some may have been motivated by feelings as quotidian as loneliness. Stephen Surovsov, when he enlisted in 1941, had only recently divorced his wife and was working as a gardener in Dee Why. Isaac Chain from Sydney had also become separated from his family, and James Cochura had never married. Others may have been tempted by readily available employment in the auxiliary services, but this applied more to veterans with professional skills.

James Cochura, 1939 (NAA)

A number of our veterans served in Garrison Battalions (GB) organised for coastal defence. James Cochura served six years in the 1st GB in Mount Gravatt in Queensland; Surovsov and Chain were in the 7th GB (Internal Security) in the Collaroy – Dee Why area in Sydney. George Platonoff and Robert Nicholson were in the 15th GB; the latter, discharged from the AIF as medically unfit, served the last part of the war on US vessels.[142] Alex, a son of John Ouchirenko, remembers that 'in 1941 we moved to Queenscliff, Victoria, where Dad served in the Home Guard until the end of WWII'.[143] Aaron Lemish worked in the 21st Supply Depot Company, Max Perlman from Perth in the Australian cooking school, and Morris Saffar, a mechanic, in ordnance workshops in Victoria. Wolfe Hoffman, a successful businessman, served in the Attestation Office in Caulfield.

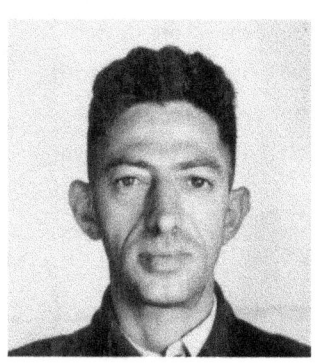

Wolfe Greenstein enlisting in the AIF in WWII (NAA)

Only one of our veterans, Wolfe Greenstein, managed to see active service with the 2nd AIF abroad. Born in Odessa and brought up in England, he was eager to serve the Empire. Having arrived with his family in Sydney in 1913 at the age of fourteen, he received military training in the Cadets. He tried to enlist in the 1st AIF throughout the war, but was rejected for having a small chest measurement, while his height was just five feet two. He was finally accepted in June 1918 on reaching the age of eighteen. He arrived in London with the infantry reinforcements three days after the armistice was declared, and although he did serve in France, in clean-up operations at battle sites, he felt that he had missed his chance. Now, when the Second World War broke out, he enlisted again, although he was a married man aged over forty with two children. He was physically fit, having been a famous footballer in the 1930s, playing for a Jewish sporting club.[144] By taking two years from his actual age, he succeeded in enrolling in the 1st Infantry Battalion, which was sent to Egypt in September 1940; there he was promoted to lance corporal. In March 1941 his unit was despatched to Crete where he was captured and taken to Salonika. According to the memoirs of Keith Hooper, published by P.D. Monteath, Greenstein came to the attention of the Germans at the waterfront there. The men were lined up, standing to attention, as a German officer came along. The officer said, 'Any Jews, step forward'. ... The men stepped forward, but on seeing the relatively modest figure of Greenstein, the officer said he could step back.¹⁴⁵

Samuel Rappeport served in the 10th Garrison Battalion in WWII (NAA)

From a newspaper report it transpires that he survived, spent some time in hospital in Germany, and was repatriated to Egypt in late 1943.¹⁴⁶ His daughter Esther joined the AIF in 1943, when Wolf was still a prisoner of war, and served in the Accounts office in Sydney.

Although all the other Ukrainian Anzacs were too old to be sent overseas, their names are still represented at all major battles of the Second World War, because their children carried on the tradition. It is no exaggeration to say that the majority of them who were of age volunteered for the Australian Army, the Air Force (RAAF) or the Navy. The enthusiastic response to the call to arms by these boys and girls, born in Australia with unusual names, was one of the greatest achievements of those Anzacs from Ukraine who, decades before, had come to this country as aliens.

In a number of cases, several members of one family enlisted during the war. Not only Aaron Lemish served, but his two sons enlisted in the AIF: Myer served in New Britain and Lazarus in Australia. Leon Rothman, who at the time of the First World War was underage and was discharged from the army at the request of his parents, now had two sons of his own, Aaron and Samuel, serving in the AIF, while his daughter Rose Ray served in the RAAF; his son Samuel served in Papua and Dutch New Guinea in the Signal Corps. Edward Dryen served in the depot of the Ordnance Corps in Sydney, while his son Ronald Gordon served in the coastal artillery in Sydney, Newcastle and Lae in New Guinea, attaining the rank of major. Both sons of Constantine Pinkevitch served in Australia as well. His younger son Leo Carson, a mechanic by trade, wrote about his service: 'We were sent by troop train to Alice Springs, where I joined the 146th AGT mainly as a driver and in numerous convoys carried stores, fuel and bombs and ammunition of all types quite often into the Darwin area.'¹⁴⁷ Ksenofont Kozachuk's son, Ksenofont William, was in the Service Police, while his daughter Hilda served at an RAAF wireless station in Queensland. Two of Albert Michael Tober's sons and a daughter were in the army as well; the eldest, Albert Jr., served in the Middle East, Greece, and Syria, and 'when he came back here then he went up to New Guinea', his relatives remember.¹⁴⁸ Two of Louis Brodsky's sons, now both medical practitioners, served through the war in Australia and New Guinea. Morris Leneve's son Maurice served as a gunner and in 1946 was posted to New Britain. Alexander Spisbah's son George served in the Northern Territory and in Lae in New Guinea. Feodot Peachenoff's son Victor served as a signaller and gunner in New Guinea and the Solomon Islands from 1943 to 1946. Alexander Barr Winning's son Ian served in the RAAF in Australia.

Continuing their fathers' tradition
Children of Ukrainian Anzacs in WWII

Isadore Brodsky (NAA)   *Alexander Brodsky (NAA)*   *Esther Greenstein (NAA)*   *Leonard Gregorenko (NAA)*

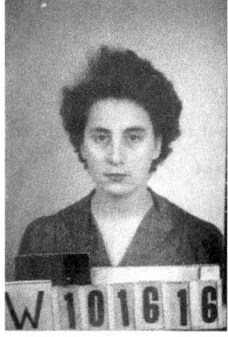   

Hilda Kozachuk (NAA)   *Myer Lemish (NAA)*   *Maurice Leneve (NAA)*   *Victor Peachenoff (Courtesy of Barbara Scott)*

Samuel Rothman (NAA)   *George Spisbah (NAA)*   *Mary Tober (NAA)*   *Albert Tober (NAA)*

Among the servicemen were both of Gregorenko's boys, who had grown up on a farm in Lawgi. Lexie Boon, also from this area, 'recalls the District giving the two boys a send off in the Regent Picture Theatre, wishing them well and a safe return'.[149] They also left the mark of their Ukrainian names at the major theatres of war: the eldest, Leonard, served in the Middle East and Tobruk ('I did a number of patrols at Tobruk for which I volunteered,' he would later tell), while George was in New Guinea, Borneo and Bougainville. But their service did not go smoothly: they were both court-martialled. The trouble started in 1939 on the eve of the war, when their father Richard Gregorenko, already gravely sick with tuberculosis, initiated the transfer of the farm to the boys. Leonard was in Cairns at the time. Later he would tell of this time at the court-martial hearings:

> I have been most of my life on a farm – ever since a kid. Since I have grown up I have been working on the farm – that is the only work I know. When I got a bit older I went to Cairns. I wanted to have a look around. Everybody wants to see a bit of the world at that age. It was while I was in Cairns that the war broke out and I enlisted from there. I was young and I thought I'd like to be in it.

He was indeed young, then just 18, but when he enlisted he added three years to his age. Richard, who was on the farm with 16-year-old George, wanted Leonard to be released from the army, but he refused to come home and was soon in Tobruk. In August 1942, George, aged 19, also joined the army. A few months later he received a telegram saying that his father's health had deteriorated. He applied for leave, which was not granted, so he went absent without leave and returned to the farm. When his father's health improved, he returned to the army, was court-martialled, and after three months' detention was posted to New Guinea. Leonard, who by that time had returned to Australia from the Middle East, learned of his father's ill health and applied for leave without pay. He too was refused, and also went absent without leave. The state of Richard's health was so bad that he was immediately hospitalised, while Leonard took over all work at the farm. It was a property of 364 acres; the main income came from the dairy, which meant that Leonard had to milk twenty cows by hand twice a day. The farm also had two hundred fowls, pigs, and horses, and the complete absence of running water meant that he had to drive stock to water 'four miles each and every day'. The work was a matter of survival for Leonard and his young family (in 1943 he married and had a baby), as the mortgage and other expenses were mounting. Leonard meant to return to the army and made four applications for George to be released. In September 1945 Leonard was arrested, charged with desertion, and court-martialled. He pleaded not guilty and his description of the situation was so honest and straightforward that the accusation was dismissed and he was discharged from the army.[150] Richard Gregorenko died in 1950.

Left: George Gregorenko (Courtesy of Gregorenko family)
Right: Leonard Gregorenko reunited with his sister Olga
and mother Vera during WWII (Courtesy of Gregorenko family).

Gregory Jakimov, like Richard Gregorenko, was not fit enough to join the AIF: he had been severely wounded at the Western Front, but his sons carried on the tradition. His elder son, Robert Roman, had died in a traffic accident 'at the northern approach to the [Sydney] Harbour Bridge' at the age of 16 not long before the war and we can imagine how anxious the Jakimovs were when their second son, Gregory, known as Mick, enlisted in the RAAF at the age of 19. In 1941, after training in Australia and Canada, he was sent as a pilot to Britain and Africa. He became a flight lieutenant and in 1943 was awarded the Distinguished Flying Cross, constantly exhibiting 'initiative and courage' in his attacks on the enemy. His attack on an enemy submarine, featured in the *Illustrated London News*, became particularly famous. Jakimov described the attack:

> We were on routine patrolling when we sighted, from 3,000 ft, the submarine cruising on the surface. Although visibility was bad, we got its position, and first attacked at an angle. Our bombs fell short of the target, so I circled for another attack.
>
> The Jerries by this time had manned a light anti-aircraft gun on the conning tower, but could not reach their deck guns before we again swept in. We let go our guns and saw strikes along the enemy craft.
>
> I again circled and we again attacked with all guns blazing, and straddled him with depth charges. They went off in a few seconds, and well – that's about all.

Mick's younger brother Roman Arnold could hardly wait to turn 18 and follow his brother into the RAAF, where he served as a guard.[151]

But not all would return home safely. Matfeus Oleinikoff's son Peter served in the RAAF as a pilot officer based in England. On 6 February 1945 his aircraft crashed in Sussex while flying in low cloud during an operational flight and all on board were killed. Peter had a de facto wife and a baby son in England.¹⁵² Stephen Surovsov did not return home either. In 1943 he attempted suicide while serving in the garrison battalion and died in hospital.¹⁵³

Besides Army service, our Anzacs became involved in the life of the country at war in a variety of ways. Even before the war, seeing the rise of Fascism in Europe, Wolfe Hoffman would help people fleeing from Europe to Australia by arranging invitations for them.¹⁵⁴ During the war Richard Gregorenko, farming at Tangool, supported the Patriotic Fund. Thomas Platonoff was involved in the campaign known as 'Sheepskins for Russia'.¹⁵⁵ Nicholas Fedorovich wanted to put his knowledge of languages to good use during the war. In 1939 he applied for an interpreter's position (Russian and Polish), 'willing to offer his services in an honorary capacity' if no paid position was available.¹⁵⁶

Peter Oleinikoff, RAAF, a son of Matfeus Oleinikoff (AWM)

When war began, several Ukrainian-born Anzacs who were not naturalised found that their status had once again caused them problems. It impelled many to regularise their situation, producing a third peak in the number of naturalisations. After the First World War, we could trace the movements of Nicholas Roomianzoff from one job to another in the Mackay area by means of the alien registration records. Now, at the beginning of the Second World War, he was still in Mackay and still not naturalised, so again had to register with the police as an alien in wartime: his occupation at that stage is recorded as 'waterside worker'. In 1939 he moved to Darwin, then back to Mackay, then to Townsville, then back to Mackay, repeating the same pattern again and again. From his photograph of that year on his registration form, on which his fingerprints are also impressed, a tired-looking, withdrawn man gazes out at us as if saying, 'You don't trust me – what do I care.'¹⁵⁷ Waterside employment was hard and dangerous. In 1946 alone Roomianzoff was twice taken to hospital by ambulance with injuries received at work. But in 1952 luck turned his way: he won 300 pounds in the Golden Casket lottery.¹⁵⁸ This allowed him to live the last period of his life a little more comfortably, and he did not hurry to obtain naturalisation, probably still hoping to return to his native Sabadash in Ukraine, where he had left his mother. He was naturalised only a few years before his lonely death in Cairns in 1974.

'Does it include me?'
Peter Komesaroff's story

Peter Komesaroff was one of the few who dared to say 'no' to the pervasive atmosphere of suspicion. At a public meeting held in August 1943 by the Carlton-Fitzroy sub-branch of the RSL, a resolution was put forward 'protesting against foreign-born persons and naturalised British subjects being permitted to sell any commodity' in the area. 'So-called naturalised aliens were only aliens after all,' the sub-branch president argued. Komesaroff, an active RSL member in a neighbouring branch, was present at this meeting and asked:

> 'This motion - does it include me?' …
> 'Of course it is not meant to include you', was the reply.
> 'I am not concerned whether it was meant to or not meant to', Mr. Komesaroff said. 'I am a naturalised British subject, born in Russia, served with the A.I.F. in the 1914-18 war, over four years, and I am crippled for life as a result. This resolution says you don't want so-called naturalised aliens in business. Does it include me?' …
> 'It does include you, but you know the Government may not carry it out.'

The resolution was quickly carried, after which Komesaroff again stood up.

> 'This is not a question of me, but of you', he said. … He moved up the aisle, and tearing his R.S.L. badge from his coat he tossed it up on to the chairman's table. 'I refuse to belong to a fascist-controlled organization', he said, 'and, therefore, I resign from the R.S.L.'

The Australian Council for Civil Liberties, in publishing an account of this case, warned Australians that 'The first sign of fascism is ordinarily an organised attempt to cancel those principles of justice that are the basis of democracy.'

Komesaroff, his daughter says: 'did not ever return as a member of the RSL after that, that was finished'.[159] It did not matter to him that the sub-branch's resolution received no support from RSL headquarters or the government.

Nevertheless, Komesaroff's experience with the RSL did not deter him from being passionately involved in community affairs; he had a reputation for being 'one of the few who knew how to implement ideas'. He worked hard for Jewish immigration in the late 1930s, at a time 'when Australia was not particularly interested in the fate of Hitler's victims', spending 'hours each day going from person to person obtaining the necessary guarantees for each Jewish permit'. During the Second World War he was involved in various committees instrumental in raising money for the war effort, and in 'Sheepskins for Russia'. After the war he worked with the 'Aid for Israel' committee. His friends used to say that he had become 'himself something like an institution'.[160]

Left: Frank Dynowski, 1950, migrating to Australia for the second time (NAA)
Right: The Age, 1950

Meanwhile in war-torn Europe, Ukraine, and Russia, the story of our Anzacs continued. One of them was Frank Dynowski, who came from a cultured Polish family in Kyiv and worked in outback New South Wales as an agricultural labourer. He married while serving in the AIF and stayed in France. Later he moved to Poland and, according to the *Age*, during the Second World War joined the Polish army with the rank of major, 'was taken prisoner by the Russians, escaped, and then helped organise the Polish underground movement'. He took part in the 1944 Warsaw Uprising, in which 'all my effects as well as the army documents were destroyed', he wrote when applying for replacements. Captured by the Germans, he was kept as a prisoner of war in a camp in Lubeck and after the war served in the Polish forces in Germany. In 1950 he returned to Australia in the wave of displaced persons. By that time he had trained as an engineer, but on settling in Hobart he had to turn again to waiting tables.[161]

The war brought an opportunity for a reunion to the Volkofsky/Wolkowsky family. In 1927 Theofil had attempted without success to get his younger brother Wojciech out of the Soviet Union. Then, Theofil's son explains, one day after the war, 'Dad got a letter from him addressed to "Volkofsky farmer, Australia".' Wojciech had ended the war in a displaced persons' camp in Germany, where he had been taken by the Germans; before that he had been in a Soviet labour camp. 'Dad paid Wojciech's fares from Germany … He came out in 1945 and did very well in Australia.'[162] Wojciech, who reached Australia in 1948, also brought the terrible story of the decimation of their family in Ukraine during Stalin's reign. Characteristically, as mentioned earlier, the experience of the horrors of the Soviet regime, associated with 'Russian' rule, made Wojciech identify firmly with the plight of the Ukrainians, while Cezar, who remembered only pre-revolutionary life, did not lose his sympathy for 'Russia'. Nevertheless, the fact that the letters he sent to his family there might have played a role in their arrests tormented Cezar to the end of his life. His granddaughter Carolyn wrote about the tragedy of this reunion in her poem (see the back cover of the book).

Marea, Cezar's daughter, expressed her response to the horrors and trials of the war in a short story, 'Mamma-Babushka comes home'. It shows life returning to a village which was liberated from the Germans just a week earlier, through the eyes of an old woman whose son is fighting in the army, while her daughter-in-law gives birth to her grandson. The story has interspersions of Russian and Ukrainian words and folk songs, which indicate that Marea was speaking of the land of her father. The end of the story is symbolic – the old woman comes to the burnt-out ruins of their village church and, 'kneeling among the shambles before the shattered remnants of an icon', thanks 'God in His Goodness'. 'Like a fire within, her spirit had fought for this as the spirit of all the people, unconquerable, had fought, accepting no defeat. … For one moment her face was transfigured with glory, the next it lay still forever more. Mamma-Babushka had come home'.[163] Although brought up in different traditions, Marea knew what religion meant to her father's people.

The life story of Alexander Sank was not so happy. In 1921 he left Australia for Harbin, where his mother lived, with plans to foster Australian-Russian trade relations. In 1922 he moved to Khabarovsk where he found a position as an interpreter in a commercial bureau. Later he married and moved to Novosibirsk, working as a procurement officer for Kuzbass Mining and other industrial enterprises. In 1938 he was convicted for illegal trading, but survived the ordeal. He was arrested a second time in 1951, at the time of Stalin's post-war anti-Jewish campaign. This time he was accused on political grounds and found guilty of a range of offences – from suppressing a non-existent Arab nationalist uprising to being naturalised in Australia, from sending Soviet newspapers to his friends in Harbin to disseminating anti-Soviet propaganda; the latter charge was endorsed by the housemaid of his family, who was an exile herself and in this way earned permission to return to Ukraine. During the investigation Sank was abused and beaten and made to confess to the charges against him. He was sentenced to 10 years in the camps. It took him several years to get his release after Stalin's death, when his health was already ruined in the camp. He was rehabilitated in 1996, most likely posthumously.[164]

The broken threads

With the fall of Stalinism, our Anzacs – those who were still living – had more opportunities to reunite with their families in Ukraine, but this remained difficult. One story documents such an attempt.

In 2008 the popular Russian television program 'Wait For Me' announced a search for the descendants of Silivon Kozachuk, accompanied by a beautiful photograph of his family. The data about him accurately matched that of Ksenofont Kozachuk, the Ukrainian Anzac, and I contacted Svetlana Vishnevaia, who was looking for him. She wrote,

> According to the documents he is indeed Ksenofont, at home they used to call him Silivon. In the 1960s granddad Ksenofont would regularly correspond with his brother (my grandfather) Overian Yakovlevich Kozachuk. From his letters we learnt that he obtained permission to come to visit us through the Red Cross. This was in about 1971-1973. We were informed that he had arrived in Moscow and then died there. His son collected his body and took it back to Australia. After that, we lost contact with them.[165]

Svetlana also said that once Ksenofont sent them a whole box of sea-shells and she kept one; listening to its murmur she often thought about her relatives in faraway Australia. She was a little girl when they were waiting for Ksenofont to arrive, and she still remembered the excitement as they refurbished her grandfather's house in Kosivka, which stood on the very spot where Ksenofont and his 15 siblings were born; and how upset they all were when the terrible news of his death in Moscow reached them.

It took me almost a year to trace the whereabouts of Ksenofont's descendants in Australia with the help of Michael Brunker, the Mayor of the Collinsville area, where the Kozachuks lived. Ksenofont's youngest daughter Hilda May was still living in a nursing home and passed the information to the younger generation. Unfortunately, some members of his family had not forgiven him for his abuse of his wife, although some of his grandchildren expressed interest in his history. But they were all astonished to hear that Ksenofont died in Moscow on the way to see his relatives. They had never heard about his trip to Ukraine and assured me that he had actually died peacefully in Bowen in 1987, aged 96. When I conveyed the news to Svetlana, she added, 'I remember how Ksenofont described all the efforts it took him to get permission to visit us. His letter was full of strong expressions towards the organisations which he had to contact.'[166] Clearly the Soviet authorities had found the ideal way to prevent the Ukrainian side of the family making undesirable contact. Now it was too late to renew those ties; the Australians never contacted Svetlana or her 85-year-old father Vasily, the nephew of Ksenofont, but I hope that one day the great grandchildren will be able to overcome the past and discover their Ukrainian heritage.

Left: Vasily Overianovich Kozachuk and his wife in Kosivka never had a chance to meet his Australian cousins (Courtesy of Kozachuk family)
Right: The Kozachuks' new house in Kosivka stands at the very spot where Ksenofont was born (Courtesy of Kozachuk family)

Reunions when members of the families were outside Ukraine were more successful. The American cousins of Betty Dorfman, the daughter of Wolf Dorfman, learnt about her through the website 'Russian Anzacs' and I was happy to connect them. 'I wish to thank you with all my heart for making it possible for me, through your book *Russian Anzacs*, to meet my American cousins and so fill a big gap in my life,' Betty wrote to me after their reunion in America.[167] Lion Harlap, whom we left in Palestine after the war, returned to Australia in 1963 for his sister's 80th birthday; they had not seen each other for forty-eight years.[168] We may hope that the relatives of Constantine Pinkevitch, who were looking for him via the Red Cross in 1952, did finally find him.[169]

For Australians, the re-discovery of their Ukrainian roots is not easy, either logistically or emotionally. The children often have little to go on when they start investigating their family history. Richard Gregorenko's granddaughter, Carol, who once wondered why she had such a strange name, went to Callide Valley, where her grandfather lived between the wars, and discovered a number of people who still remembered her family. Denis Papchuck's grandchildren were planning to go to Ukraine one day and I have recently heard from Ben Goffin's grandson, Richard, who has never met his grandfather and is about to set out on 'an amazing trail to follow back'.[170]

Left: Betty Dorfman (second from the right) at her reunion
with her American cousins (courtesy of Betty Dorfman)
Right: Lion Harlap reunited with his sister, 1963
(The Canberra Times, 1963)

Conclusion – the falling stars

The stories of the Anzacs from Ukraine that we have been following are a sample of prosopography – a history presented through the narratives of various members of one cohort. The historian's task is not to take sides or conceal dark issues, but to let the heroes be themselves. They were brought to Australia from different walks of life, thrown for several years into the melting pot of the Australian army, survived the bloody juggernaut of war, and then once again took different paths. But at least one thing united them all: they happened to live through difficult times, and they happened to be actors of a history which manifests itself not only through glowing official accounts but through the crowded, haphazard stories of 'ordinary' human lives. Venturing into history through these individual lives brings us to the understanding that the only objective truth is the motion of human life in the tragedy of its existence. These lives are like falling stars – brightly flashing through Ukrainian and Australian history and disappearing as if without a trace.

A new era, separated by a century from the youth of our heroes, brings new values and attitudes, and it is unjust to impose these wholly upon our Anzacs. Some did things of which we would not approve, but they lived in an extreme time and cannot be judged from our comfortable present. All we can do is love them as a mother loves her sons, whatever sideroads take them away from the 'right' path. Indeed, what unites them is that they are all forgotten sons of Ukraine, whose people are now mature and kind enough to accept them as they were.

The biggest injustice on our part would be to write off our Anzacs from the Ukrainian map of Australia as 'assimilated', or to declare, as the editors of the 'History of Russians in Australia' did, that the pre-First World War émigrés 'did not play any role in forming Russian communities in Australia'.[171] It is true that these men did not build a church in Australia; nor did they have a chance to establish a diverse communal life or to teach their children Ukrainian and Yiddish, yet they were without doubt a community: a community of people belonging to their Ukrainian motherland, where they could return only in their dreams; a community raised on Ukrainian and Russian literature concerned with social injustice, be it Shevchenko, Gogol, or Tolstoy; a community of Anzacs traumatised by the war, who never spoke about its horror and senselessness; a community of swagmen and farmers pioneering the harsh Australian outback; a community of aliens who managed to win the sympathies of their neighbours and make Australia their home; and, finally, a community of husbands of Ukrainian and Jewish, British and Australian women, all of whom did their best to heal their mental and physical wounds.

We may never know the exact locations where these falling stars ended their journeys, but it comes to us to remember the traces of their light. Visit the Australian War Memorial and place a poppy on the Roll of Honour for Nickefor Domilovsky from Kyiv or Moisey Kotton from Kremenchuk, finding them among thousands of Australian names. Or, perhaps, pause on Victoria Bridge in Brisbane, from which William Whynsky jumped to his death – his life was so short that we cannot with certainty establish his place of birth or even his name. Make your way further on, to South Brisbane, stop at Russell Street, and through the roaring of the traffic and chatter of commuters hurrying to the station, try to hear a mixture of Ukrainian, Russian, Yiddish, and English voices as these countrymen and their children pour onto the street in another time after a concert by the Russian, Ukrainian, or Jewish Association, just opposite Malinowsky's shop. Or visit the Botanical Gardens in Sydney where Koropets' life ended, and then travel to 35 Barton Road in Artamon, where a house named 'Kertch' once celebrated Kamishansky's motherland. Never mind that a block of flats now stands in its place – you can still imagine how he would open the inscribed gates on returning home from work and for a moment remember the salty smell of the sea in his childhood. Or perhaps, if you set off travelling across the country, use our digital map (*http://russiananzacs.net/map*) of places associated with the Ukrainian-born Anzacs who have charted their paths all across Australia, from coast to coast; you might even manage to find Volkofsky's Olino station among the sheep paddocks somewhere past Dubbo.

Notes

Introduction

1 Ivan Franko, 'Peredmova' [Introduction], *Literaturno-naukovyi vistnyk*, no. 5, 1910, pp. 318-320. See also Olga Zernets'ka, 'Pershyi perekladach avstraliis'koi literatury na Ukraini' [The first translator of Australian literature in Ukraine], *Vsesvit*, no. 5, 1983, pp. 151-152.

2 *Leader*, 16 November 1918, p. 37. Frederic Austin Ogg, 'The Ukraine, a New Nation', *Munsey's Magazine*, no. 1, October, 1918, pp. 1-13.

3 'Prussia', *Sydney Gazette and New South Wales Advertiser*, 24 July 1808, p. 1.

4 *Ukraintsi v Avstralii: materialy do istorii poselennia ukraintsiv v Avstralii* [*Ukrainians in Australia: materials for the history of Ukrainian settlement in Australia*], Melbourne, Nakladom Soiuzu ukrains'kykh orhanizatsii Avstralii, 1966.

5 Marko Pavlyshyn, 'How much do we know about Ukrainians in Australia?', in *First Wave Emigrants: The First Fifty Years of Ukrainian Settlement in Australia*, ed. by Halyna Koscharsky, New York: Nova Science Publishers, [2000], pp. 9-10.

6 Khrystyna Misko, 'The pre-DP wave: Rethinking the boundaries of the diaspora', in *First Wave Emigrants: The First Fifty Years of Ukrainian Settlement in Australia*, ed. by Halyna Koscharsky, New York: Nova Science Publishers, [2000], pp. 19-30.

7 Khrystyna Misko, *Faded footsteps, Forgotten graves: Queensland's Ukrainian Anzacs*, Brisbane: Boolarong Press, 2016.

8 Kalyna Kenez, 'Pershi vidviduvachi z Ukrainy' [The first visitors from Ukraine], *Ukraintsi Avstralii. Entsiklopedychnyi dovidnyk*, Sydney: Vilna dumka, 2001, pp. 32-37.

9 A.I. Savchenko, 'Ukrainskaia emigratsiia v Avstraliiu' [Ukrainian emigration to Australia], in *Tikhookeanskii put' razvitiia: kontseptsii i real'nost': tezisy XXII nauchnoi konferentsii po izucheniiu Avstralii i Okeanii*, Moscow: Nauka, 1996, pp. 35-38; O.I. Savchenko, 'Chisel'nyst' ta sklad ukrains'koi emigratsii v Avstralii na pochatku XX st.' [The numbers and composition of Ukrainian emigration in Australia in the early twentieth century], *Gileia: naukovii visnik*, no. 72, 2013, pp. 97-102; O.I. Savchenko, 'Diyal'nist' ukrains'koi emigratsii v Avstralii na pochatku XX st.' [The activities of the Ukrainian emigration in Australia in the early twentieth century], *Gileia: naukovii visnik*, no. 77, 2013, pp. 39-42.

10 Elena Govor, 'Russian perceptions of Australia, 1788-1919'. PhD Thesis, Canberra: ANU, 1996, pp. 224-235, 247-259; Elena Govor, *Australia in the Russian Mirror: Changing Perceptions, 1770-1919*, Melbourne: Melbourne University Press, 1997, pp. 119, 145-158; Elena Govor, *My Dark Brother: the Story of the Illins, a Russian-Aboriginal Family*,

Sydney: UNSW Press, 2000, pp. 109-122 (chapter 'Little Siberia'); Elena Govor, *Russian Anzacs in Australian History*, Sydney: UNSW Press & NAA, 2005.

11 'Peredmova' [Introduction], in *Ukraintsi v Avstralii = Ukrainians in Australia*, Melbourne: Australian Federation of Ukrainian organisations, 1998, pp. vii-xii.

12 Grigor Piddubnyi, *Midiani zagravy [Glow of the Copper Smelters]*, Kharkiv: V-vo Vseukr. rady politkatorzhan, 1933, p. 81.

13 'Ukrainian National transliteration', https://en.wikipedia.org/wiki/Ukrainian_National_transliteration/.

14 'Romanization of Ukrainian', https://en.wikipedia.org/wiki/Romanization_of_Ukrainian/.

Part One

1   Here and further all biographical details are based on data in service records, naturalisation applications, and alien registration. Their archival details and, in many cases, digitised files are available from the Russian Anzacs website (http://russiananzacs.net/). In some cases, further information is drawn from shipping records, the birth, death, and marriage records of the states, and electoral rolls available in the database of Ancestry.com (http://ancestry.com). These and all following links to other databases were accessed and verified in January 2016.

2   NAA: A659, 1941/1/4758, Oleinikoff, Matjeus – Naturalisation.

3   https://pamyat-naroda.ru/.

4   NAA: D2994, CHERPITER J.

5   NAA: A1, 1923/10281, J. John Sepscak Naturalisation.

6   Janice Hunter, interview, 21.11.2001, Elena Govor's archives, Canberra.

7   Tom Volkofsky, interview, 9.11.2001, Elena Govor's archives.

8   Peter Tilleard, interview, 20.01.2017; e-mail 23.01.2017, Elena Govor's archives.

9   NAA: PP14/1, 16/1/186, Gretchinsky JT; http://baza.vgdru.com/1/11230/.

10 NAA: B2455, MALISHEFF GEORGE.

11 https://pamyat-naroda.ru/.

12 NAA: A1, 1915/18561, Zacharias E. Pieven – Naturalization.

13 Piven-Large family archives, Sydney.

14 NAA: A1, 1921/23781, G. Gregory Jakimov Naturalization.

15 Charles Price, 'Russians in Australia: A demographic survey', in *Russia and the Fifth Continent. Aspects of Russian-Australian Relations*, ed. by J. McNair and T. Poole, St Lucia: University of Queensland Press, 1992, pp. 54–71; Elena Govor, *Australia in the Russian Mirror: Changing Perceptions, 1770-1919*, Melbourne: Melbourne University

Press, 1997, pp. 145-151; Elena Govor, 'Russians in Australia, 1804-1920: Convicts, Swagmen and Anzacs', in *Encounters under the Southern Cross: Two centuries of Russian-Australian Relations, 1807-2007*, ed. by Alexander Massov, John McNair and Thomas Poole, Adelaide: Crawford House Publishing, 2007, pp. 116-118.

16   Govor, *Australia in the Russian Mirror*, pp. 151–56.
17   Volkofsky, interview, 9.11.2001.
18   'A red page of life. Persecuted Russian in Sydney', *Sun*, Sydney, 16 June 1912, p. 12.
19   NAA: A1, 1924/28909, Perlman, Max – Application for naturalisation certificate.
20   NAA: B2455, HARLAP L; A1, 1934/1345, Lion (Leon) HARLAP – Naturalization.
21   NAA: B2455, LEBOVITZ ELIAS.
22   *Iz arkhiva S.Iu. Vitte. Vospominaniia. T. 2. Rukopisnye zametki* [*From S.Iu Vitte's Archive. Memoirs. Vol. 2. Manuscript Notes*], St Petersburg, 2003, p. 629.
23   Marriage certificate, in: NAA: B2455, NICHOLSON ROBERT.
24   M. Ankudinow, Statutory declaration, 1938, in: NAA: B2455, Ankudinow M.
25   Jan Rees, 'Michael Ankoodinoff', copy in Elena Govor's archives.
26   Jan Rees, 'George and Alessandra Ankoodinoff', copy in Elena Govor's archives.
27   Ibid.
28   Ibid.
29   NAA: B2455, ANKUDINOW M; A659, 1940/1/5657, Ankudinow, Michael – Naturalisation.
30   Dr Alexander Brodsky, 'Family Memoirs', p. 2, copy in Elena Govor's archives.
31   'New justices of the peace', *The Brisbane Courier*, 11 July 1901, p. 2. Queensland State Archives, naturalisation, Item ID 882273, no. 10442, TCHORZEIOSKI Marian Georgius.
32   M. French, 'Tardent, Henry Alexis (1853 – 1929)', *Australian Dictionary of Biography*, Vol. 12, Melbourne: Melbourne University Press, 1990, pp. 167-168; J. L. Tardent, *The Swiss-Australian Tardent Family History and Genealogy*, Southport, Qld, 1982, pp. 171-175.
33   'Russians as settlers', *The Brisbane Courier*, 23 February 1911, p. 5; 'Russian Immigrants' Association', *Brisbane Courier*, 5 July 1911, p. 12; 'Russian immigrants. A desirable acquisition', *Daily Standard*, Brisbane, 23 June 1913, p. 2.
34   Ego, 'Iz Avstralii' [From Australia], *Zheleznodorozhnaia zhizn' na Dal'nem Vostoke*, 1910, no. 1, pp. 11-13.
35   NAA: A1, 1913/14106, Lamotte Alexis Sage – Naturalization; B2455, SAGE LAMOTTE ALEXIS.
36   NAA: A1, 1934/2433, Christian DE RINK – Naturalization; B2455, RINK CHRISTIAN.
37   He also stated that he was born in Tobolsk in Siberia.
38   'Deserters from foreign warships', *Victoria Police Gazette*, 29 May 1901, p. 205.
39   Dorothy Lazarus, interview, 16.09.2001, Elena Govor's archives.

40 Leah Jas, e-mail, 6.09.2001, Elena Govor's archives.
41 'Mr. Thomas Lakovsky', *The Hebrew Standard of Australasia*, Sydney, 13 March 1931, pp. 3-4.
42 Chaim Freedman and Julie Ruth, 'The Interlocking Melbourne Russians', *Roots-Key Newsletter of the Jewish Genealogical Society of Los Angeles*, Spring 2005. http://kehilalinks.jewishgen.org/colonies_of_ukraine/articles/MelbourneRussians.htm
43 'Dr. Reuben Rosenfield', *Jewish Herald*, Victoria, 24 December 1897, p. 16.
44 'Local and general news. Longreach', *The Capricornian*, Rockhampton, 2 January 1915, p. 8.
45 NAA: A1, 1914/19250, M Moisey Koton, Naturalisation.
46 Work references from Piven-Large family archives, Sydney.
47 'Advertising', *Morning Bulletin*, Rockhampton, 21 August 1913, p. 2.
48 NAA: B2455, KIVOVICH YUR; PP14/2, REPORTS – INTELLIGENCE.
49 Volkofsky, interview, 9.11.2001.
50 Allegations by Russian, F. Kechelly, in: QSA: 16865, 318868. Correspondence, police. Russians 785M.
51 Ibid.
52 NAA: B2455, MANICHIN JOHN.
53 Grigor Piddubnyi, *Midiani zagravy* [*Glow of the Copper Smelters*], Kharkiv: V-vo Vseukr. rady politkatorzhan, 1933.
54 NAA: J34, C46673, COCHURA, James – Service Number – 2812; A446, 1961/4615, COCHURA James born 13 August 1885 – Russian.
55 NAA: A1, 1925/25206, Snegovoy, A – Naturalisation certificate.
56 State Archives of the Russian Federation, Moscow (GARF): P8131-31-28916, Tsank Aleksandr Abramovich.
57 NAA: ST1233/1, N4734, T Volkofsky [Applicant] Woicih Volkopsky [Nominee].
58 Volkofsky, interview, 9.11.2001.
59 Govor's database of Queensland arrivals from Russia.
60 Elena Govor, Russian perceptions of Australia, 1788-1919. PhD Thesis, Canberra, 1996, pp. 232–233.
61 *Rossiiskaia konsul'skaia sluzhba v Avstralii 1857-1917 (Sbornik dokumentov)* [*The Russian consular service in Australia 1857-1917 (A Collection of documents)*], Compiled by A.Ia. Massov and M. Pollard, Moscow: Mezhdunarodnye otnosheniia, 2014, p. 296.
62 This estimate is based on Govor's database of naturalised former Russian subjects arriving in Queensland between 1908 and 1917. It is close to Piddubny's estimate, that before the war Ukrainians numbered at least one third among Russian émigrés from the Far East (Grigorii Piddubnyi, 'Ukrains'ki robitnyky v Avstralii' [Ukrainian workers in Australia], *Zakhidnia Ukraina*, no. 7-8, 1930, p. 107). At the same time his total estimate of Ukrainians in Australia at four to five thousand people seems to be too high.

63 'Russians in Queensland', *The Brisbane Courier*, 28 December 1911, p. 5.

64 S. Stedman, 'From Russia to Brisbane, 1913', *Journal and Proceedings of the Australian Jewish Historical Society*, vol. 5, 1959, p. 23.

65 Characteristically, the Union's appeal to raise money started with the words 'To all Russian speaking people in Australia'. 'Power in Unity', in: QSA: 16865, 318868. Correspondence, police. Russians 785M.

66 Piddubny, 'Ukrains'ki robitnyky v Avstralii', p. 110.

67 *Izvestiia Soiuza russkikh emigrantov*, 18 March 1915, p. 4.

68 Piddubny, 'Ukrains'ki robitnyky v Avstralii', p. 111.

69 *Izvestiia Soiuza russkikh emigrantov*, 29 July 1915, p. 3; 5 August 1915, p. 3; Piddubny, Ukrains'ki robitnyky v Avstralii, pp. 110-111.

70 Censor reports Q235 and Q236, in: NAA: BP4/2, Q199-Q399; Q781, in: NAA: NAA: BP4/2, Q699-Q997.

71 *Izvestiia Soiuza russkikh emigrantov*, 8 April 1915, p. 3.

72 Ia. Senik, 'Grigorii Piddubnii: (Bio-bibliografichne esse)' [Grigory Piddubny: (Biobibliographical essay], in *Ukrains'ka zhurnalistika v imenakh: Materialy do Entsiklopedii ukrains'koi zhurnalistiki*, L'viv, 1996, vip. 3, pp. 247-249.

73 *Rabochaia zhizn'*, 1 August 1916, p. 4.

74 *Rabochaia zhizn'*, 22 January 1917, p. 3.

75 *Rabochaia zhizn'*, 1 August 1916, p. 4; 22 February 1917, p. 3.

76 *Izvestiia Soiuza russkikh emigrantov*, 8 May 1914, p. 4; Savchenko. 'Diyal'nist' ukrains'koi emigratsii v Avstralii na pochatku XX st.'

77 Stedman, 'From Russia to Brisbane, 1913', p. 27.

78 Data from advertisements in Russian newspapers published in Brisbane in 1912-1917.

79 Stedman, 'From Russia to Brisbane, 1913', p. 26; V. Nasedkin, *Piatnadtsat' let skitanii po zemnomu sharu* [*Fifteen Years Wandering the Globe*], 2nd ed., Moscow, 1933, p. 54.

80 Piddubny, 'Ukrains'ki robitnyky v Avstralii', p. 109.

81 Ibid.

82 Stedman, 'From Russia to Brisbane, 1913'.

83 NAA: B2455, ROSSOGGSKY IVAN P. 'War notes. Roll of Honour. Sergt. Ivan P. Rossoggsky', *The Scone Advocate*, 10 August 1917, p. 7.

84 'Russians' protest. Will join in the fight', *Port Pirie Recorder and North Western Mail*, 26 June 1914, p. 2.

85 Brodsky, 'Family Memoirs', pp. 9, 11.

86 NAA: B2455, SERENNIKOFF JACOB; 'Dairying at Templestowe', *The Australasian*, Melbourne, 8 July 1922, p. 5.

Part Two

1   Elena Govor, 'Latvian Anzacs', in Aldis L. Putniņš, ed., *Early Latvian Settlers in Australia*, Melbourne: Sterling Star, 2010, pp. 24-25.
2   'Military camp', *The Bathurst Times*, 7 April 1916, p. 4; 'Killed in action', *Leader*, Orange, NSW, 2 December 1918, p. 2.
3   Thelma Webberley, letter, 22.10.2001, Elena Govor's archives.
4   NAA: B2455, TRAGER SAMUEL.
5   NAA: B2455, SADAGOURSKY HERRY.
6   'Garden fete at Kedron', *The Brisbane Courier*, 2 June 1915, p. 7.
7   'The Belgian Band', *The West Australian*, 2 June 1915, p. 8; 'The Belgian Band', *The Daily News*, Perth, 2 June 1915, p. 5.
8   'Patriotic entertainment', *Punch*, Melbourne, 15 October 1914, p. 40.
9   'Cordalba', *Maryborough Chronicle, Wide Bay and Burnett Advertiser*, 9 August 1916, p. 8.
10 Brodsky, 'Family Memoirs', p. 20.
11 'Russian soldier in Grafton. Corporal Kleshenko's experiences', *Daily Examiner*, Grafton, 7 December 1915, p. 2.
12 NAA: MT1486/1, KLESHENKO/JOSEPH; B2455, NOYLAND JOSEPH; B2455, KLINETINKO JOSEPH; B2455, KLESHENKO JOSEPH.
13 NAA: B2455, DIDENKO G.; AWM: AWM15, 19764, 3577 Pte Didenko – Re memo from Russian Embassy concerning his ill-treatment. For investigation.
14 Correspondence with Central Army Record Office, 1983, Robyn Dryen's archives, Sydney.
15 NAA: MT1486/1, BELESHAPKA/PLONTON; B2455, BELESHAPKA P.
16 Piddubny, 'Ukrains'ki robitnyky v Avstralii', p. 109.
17 NAA: ST1233/1, N9495.
18 NAA: J34, C46673, COCHURA, James – Service Number – 2812.
19 NAA: A1, 1915/11795, Arrival of undesirable Russians in the Commonwealth.
20 I. Lukashevich, 'Koolamarra', *Rabochaia zhizn'*, 11 July 1916, p. 2.
21 "One of many", 'Letter to the editor', *Rabochaia zhizn'*, 12 September 1916, p. 4.
22 Raymond Evans, *The Red Flag Riots: A Study of Intolerance*, St Lucia: University of Queensland Press, 1988, p. 32.
23 NAA: B741, V/5333, Alex Nicolas D'Abaza – Ex Russian Consul General – and Estate of late Nickefor Domilovsky.
24 NAA: A659, 1940/1/5335, Naturalisation of French, Russian and Italian subjects of military age.
25 N. d'Abaza to Minister of Defence, 23.11/6.12.1915, in: NAA: MP367/1, 592/4/55,

Russians Enlisted, February 1916 & January 1918 – Returns, Monthly.

26 NAA: A659, 1940/1/5335.
27 'Russian enlistment. Shirkers regarded as deserters', *Cairns Post*, 13 January 1916, p. 3; 'Russians in Queensland. Enlistment with the A.I.F. Visit of the Consul-General', *The Brisbane Courier*, 15 March 1916, p. 7.
28 NAA: A1, 1916/19578, Russian seamen to have certificate of nationality before shipping.
29 NAA: A1, 1916/32105, Consul General for Russia – re Registration of Russians at Consulates.
30 'Concerning people', *The Register*, Adelaide, 7 April 1916, p. 4; 'Southern Slavs. Visit of Russian military attache', *Kalgoorlie Miner*, 13 April 1916, p. 4; 'Slavs and miners', *The Daily News*, Perth, 15 April 1916, p. 5; *Rossiiskaia konsul'skaia sluzhba v Avstralii*, p. 304 (note).
31 NAA: A659, 1940/1/5335.
32 NAA: A446, 1953/50472, VOLKOFSKY Theofil born 5 November 1885.
33 NAA: B2455, SHULAR MAXIM.
34 NAA: B2455, Volkofsky T.; Volkofsky, interviews, 8.11.2001, 9.11.2001.
35 NAA: B2455, LEVIN MYER; A471, 1134, [LEVIN Myer (Private): Service Number – 57683: Unit – Light Trench Mortar Battery, Australian Imperial Force: Date of Court Martial – 25 October 1917].
36 NAA: B2455, TRAGER SAMUEL.
37 'Industrial Council. Russian victimisation', *Daily Standard*, Brisbane, 4 February 1916, p. 3.
38 'Hun intrigues in Australia. The Russian Association. Experiences of a member', *Truth*, Brisbane, 12 March 1916, p. 6; 'Delo gazety Truth' [Case of the *Truth* newspaper], *Rabochaia zhizn*, 13 March 1916, p. 3.
39 Judah L. Waten, *Fiction, Memoirs, Criticism*, St. Lucia: University of Queensland Press, 1998, p. 78.
40 Peter Tilleard, interview, 26.01.2017, Elena Govor's archives; AWM: 1DRL/0415, Lesnie, Frank Bernard, Letter 1.11.1915.
41 NAA: B2455, PIVINSKI WALTER.
42 NAA: B2455, WOLKOWSKY CEZAR; Peter Tilleard, interview, 20.01.2017.
43 NAA: B2455, SAST ALEXANDER; 'Private Sast's escape', *The Advertiser*, Adelaide, 30 June 1916, p. 8; 'Broken Hill soldier's adventures', *Barrier Miner*, Broken Hill, 12 November 1916, p. 4; 'Port Pirie man's story', *The Advertiser*, Adelaide, 22 November 1916, p. 9; 'Anzac's strange story. Port Pirie to London via Archangel', *The Register*, Adelaide, 22 November 1916, p. 8.
44 Albert Krantz, Letter, 21.04.1967, in: NAA: B2455, KRANTZ ALBERT.
45 Joseph Zines, Letter, 22.03.1964, in: NAA: B2455, ZINES J M.
46 Violet Cotman, interview, 7.10.2001, Elena Govor's archives.

47 NAA: B2455, TKACHENRO SAVELIY; NAA: A471, 5771, [GIBBS J (Private): Service Number – 2/1678: TKACHENCO S (Private) 1004: Unit – 25th Battalion, Australian Imperial Force: Date of Court Martial – 10 November 1915].

48 NAA: B2455, KACHAN JOHN.

49 NAA: B2455, ROSENFIELD REUBEN LAMAN; AWM25, 481/135, [Medical] Notes on eye, ear, nose and throat work at No 1 Australian General Hospital, Heliopolis by Major R L Rosenfield AAMC; AWM25, 481/134, [Medical] Notes on eye, ear, nose and throat work at Sutton Veny Hospital, England by Major R L Rosenfield AAMC.

50 NAA: B2455, GRETCHINSKY J; MT1486/1, GRETCHINSKY/JAMES.

51 'Battle of the Wazzir', https://en.wikipedia.org/wiki/Battle_of_the_Wazzir/.

52 'Russian immigrants', *Newcastle Morning Herald and Miners' Advocate*, 20 December 1913, p. 5.

53 NAA: B2455, BRODSKY L.

54 NAA: B2455, NOWEETSKY LEONARD.

55 'Soldiers' letters. [...] Private W. Dorfman', *Barrier Miner*, Broken Hill, 2 July 1916, p. 2.

56 NAA: B2455, COCHURA J.

57 NAA: B2455, KIVOVICH YUR.

58 NAA: B2455, HOFFMAN W 2224.

59 NAA: B2455, LEBOVITZ ELIAS.

60 NAA: B2455, Harlap L.

61 NAA: B2455, SANK ALEXANDER PAUL; GARF: P8131-31-28916.

62 C.E.W. Bean, *The Official History of Australia in the War of 1914–1918,*, vol. III *The Australian Imperial Force in France, 1916*, Sydney: Angus and Robertson, 1937, p. 598.

63 Joseph Morris Zines, Recommendation for award, AWM: https://www.awm.gov.au/people/rolls/R1624257/; AWM: 23/69/5, 52nd Infantry Battalion, [Unit diary], August 1916, p. 3.

64 NAA: B2455, KOVALSKY VACHALAR.

65 NAA: B2455, POPOW ALEXANDER.

66 NAA: B2455, ILIN CONSTANTINE; A2487, 1922/7548, [Notification of death of Constantin Ilin in hospital].

67 NAA: B2455, FELIPOR J; A471, 5731, [FELIPOV Joseph: Service Number – 4326: Unit – 6th Australian Tunnelling Company: Date of Court Martial – 2 November 1916]; A471, 7383, [FELIPOV Joseph (Private): Service Number – 4326: Unit – 3rd Battalion, Australian Imperial Force: Date of Court Martial – 25 May 1917].

68 AWM: AWM28 1/20P1, page 29, 4965 Pte George Breatman [*sic*].

69 NAA: B2455, ANKUDINOW M.

70 NAA: B2455, CHERPITER J; D2994, CHERPITER J.

71 NAA: B2455, ROSSOGGSKY IVAN P.

72 Harry Willey, *Scone's Fallen ANZACs*, Scone, 2005, p. 153.

73   'In Memoriam', *Sydney Morning Herald*, 7 June 1918, p. 5, 7 June 1919, p. 15.

74   NAA: B2455, OUCHARENKO JOHN.

75   NAA: B2455, VURHAFT JOSEPH.

76   'Samuel Carl Richard Stasinowsky', South Australian Red Cross Information Bureau file, digital resource https://sarcib.ww1.collections.slsa.sa.gov.au/soldier/samuel-carl-richard-stasinowsky/.

77   'Russian Journalist. Experiences with the A.I.F', *Cairns Post*, 19 December 1919, p. 8; NAA: B2455, FEDOROVICH N.

78   'Acknowledgments', *Barrier Miner*, Broken Hill, 1 July 1917, p. 2.

79   AWM: AWM30, B14.5, [Prisoner of war statements, 1914-18 War:] 5th Australian Division, 54th Battalion, 10 to 21 July 1916 [… 4477 DORFMAN …].

80   AWM: AWM28 1/166 page 24, 2281 Pte Samuel Harold Krantz; Bean refers to the same episode, 'Cpl. S.H. Krantz (Perth, W. Aust.) of the 43rd Bn. … and an American rushed [the machine-gun] and bayoneted the crew', *The Official History of Australia in the War of 1914–1918*, vol. VI, *The Australian Imperial Force in France during the Allied Offensive, 1918*, St Lucia: University of Queensland Press, 1983, p. 290.

81   South Australian Red Cross Information Bureau, https://sarcib.ww1.collections.slsa.sa.gov.au/packet-content/56158#https://sarcib.ww1.collections.slsa.sa.gov.au/sites/default/files/packet_images/7543/SRG76_1_7543_100.jpg/.

82   AWM, Recommendation for award, digital resource: https://www.awm.gov.au/people/rolls/R1601161/.

83   Jules L. Tardent, *The Swiss-Australian Tardent family history and genealogy*, Southport, Qld, 1982, p. 477.

84   'Fritz on the run', *Telegraph*, Brisbane, 12 November 1918, p. 4.

85   Tardent, *The Swiss-Australian Tardent family*, p. 444.

86   NAA: B2455, KRANTZ SAMUEL HAROLD.

87   NAA: B2455, LEFFOW JACOB; AWM: AWM21, 1785/17, [Records of the Assistant Provost Marshal] 5013 Private J Lefow.

88   NAA: B2455, KOTTON MOISEY.

89   'Killed in action', *Leader*, Orange, 2 December 1918, p. 2.

90   NAA: A6286, 1/125, Q.F.3835, Mr Kotton, Harbin, to the Australian Workers Association, Brisbane, [1919].

91   NAA: B2455, SUROVSOV STEPHEN.

92   NAA: B2455, BREITMAN G.

93   Brodsky, 'Family Memoirs', p. 20.

94   Ibid.

95   'At Victoria Barracks', *The Sydney Morning Herald*, 16 March 1916, p. 5; 'Breaking camp', *The Sydney Morning Herald*, 6 April 1916, p. 9; NAA: A471, 1342, [GORBACH, Phillip (Private): Service Number – N/A: Unit – D Company, 4th Battalion Australian Imperial

Force: ANDERSON, Alex John (Private) C Company, 3rd Battalion Australian Imperial Force: Date of Court Martial – 15 March 1916].

96 'Central Queenslanders in England', *The Capricorn*, Rockhampton, 29 July 1916, p. 21.

97 'War notes. Roll of Honour. Sergt. Ivan P. Rossoggsky', *The Scone Advocate*, 10 August 1917, p. 7.

98 'Personal notes', *Telegraph*, Brisbane, 6 July 1918, p. 7; *The 7th F.A.B. Yandoo*, v.1, 19 June 1916, p. 3; *A Tale of two quotas: S.S. "Beltana", Devonport to Australia, June-July, 1919*, [Australia, 1919], p. 29.

99 Peter Tilleard, interview, 20.01.2017.

100 NAA: B2455, KAVITSKI VASITY; B2455, SEPSCAK JOHN; B2455, OLEINIKOFF MATFEUS; A659, 1941/1/4758, Oleinikoff, Matjeus – Naturalisation.

101 AWM: AWM15, 20574, 109 Pte LOOSGIC – Application to Russian Army not approved.

102 NAA: B2455, LOOSGIE STEPHEN; A471, 11515, [LOOSGIE S (Private): Service Number – 109: Unit – 26th Battalion, Australian Imperial Force: Date of Court Martial – 12 October 1917].

103 NAA: B2455, GULEVICH N.

104 NAA: B2455, RINK CHRISTIAN.

105 NAA: PP14/2, REPORTS – INTELLIGENCE.

106 NAA: B884, Q116182, Korotcoff Nicholas.

107 NAA: B2455, SNEGOVOY ANDREW; A471, 8592, [SNEGOVOY A (Private): Service Number – 2241: Unit – 49th Battalion, Australian Imperial Force: Date of Court Martial – 19 November 1918].

108 NAA: A471, 19905 PART 1, [FALLON Thomas J …: Date of Court Martial – 12 March 1917] see item note for other servicemen appearing at this court martial; A471, 10434, [TKACHENKO S (Private): Service Number – 1004: … Unit – 25th Battalion, Australian Imperial Force: Date of Court Martial – 20 October 1917]; A471, 10434, Proceedings of General Court-Martial of 1004 Private TKACHENKO, Sareely – 21 October 1917.

109 NAA: A471, 4621, Proceeding of a Field General Court Martial on Active Service – 5999, Sapper, JOHNSON T W & Sapper PAPCHUCK D – 3rd Aus Tunnelling Coy., AIF; A471, 9308, [PAPCHUCK D: Service Number – 2358: JOHNSON T W 5999: Unit – 3rd Australian Tunnelling Company, Australian Imperial Force: Date of Court Martial – 13 October 1918].

110 NAA: B2455, KUSMIN PETER.

111 NAA: B2455, GREGORENZ R.

112 'The Author of "Kismet"', *Cairns Post*, 22 December 1919, p. 4.

113 NAA: B2455, MALISHEFF GEORGE.

114 'Letters from soldiers', *Sunday Times*, Perth, 26 March 1916, p. 1.

115 'In the thick of it. Australian soldiers describe their experiences', *Sunday Times*, Perth, 16 December 1917, p. 1.

116 Peter Tilleard, interview, 20.01.2017.
117 NAA: A2481, A1918/6461, Free passage Ethel Kleshenko; 2455, ANKUDINOW M.
118 NAA: A471, 13467, [OUCHARENKO John (Private): Service Number – 6327: Unit – 39th Battalion, Australian Imperial Force: Date of Court Martial – 27 June 1918]; A2487, 1920/4000, [Applications for free passage to Australia – H Fletcher, A V King, P N Lacey, H C Prunty, J Ouchernko, E R Beaton, W H Saunders].
119 NAA: B2455, KUSMIN PETER.

Part Three

1 Raymond Evans, '"Agitation, ceaseless agitation": Russian radicals in Australia and the Red flag riots', in J. McNair and T. Poole (eds), *Russia and the Fifth Continent. Aspects of Russian-Australian Relations*, St Lucia: University of Queensland Press, 1992, p. 129.
2 NAA: BP4/1, 66/4/3660, File on Russians, Russian Association, Soviet of Souse in Brisbane; relating to meetings, demonstrations, deportations, prosecutions.
3 NAA: B741, V/197, Russians, Sydney. Returned Soldiers, War Records of.
4 NAA: A1, 1923/12211, C. Cezar Wolkowsky Naturalization.
5 NAA: A2487, 1920/2196, [Russian ex-serviceman].
6 L. Berk et al., 'Russian soldiers' protest', *Daily Mail*, 17 September 1918, p. 7; NAA: A1, 1919/14595, Walter Kalasnikoff Naturalisation.
7 NAA: A1, 1920/3694, J. John OUCHIRENKO – Naturalization; 'Notes and Notices', *The Australasian*, Melbourne, 17 January 1920, p. 30.
8 Gavin Brown and Robert Haldane, *Days Of Violence: The 1923 Police strike in Melbourne*, Ormond, Vic: Hybrid Publishers, 2009, p. 171; 'Short shrift to looters', *The Mercury*, Hobart, 10 November 1923, p. 9.
9 NAA: B741, V/197.
10 NAA: A1, 1923/12211.
11 'Bolshevik rule. The Russian Ideals', *Warwick Daily News*, 3 April 1919, p. 8.
12 NAA: J2773, 1282/1926, Henry Plumb, Ksinofont Kozachuk, …; 'Gold seekers', *Townsville Daily Bulletin*, 29 September 1926, p. 6; 'Collinsville notes', *Townsville Daily Bulletin*, 5 February 1941, p. 6.
13 Carol McKenzie, interview, 30.08.2001, Elena Govor's archives.
14 Alexander Ouchirenko, letter, 23 May 2002, Elena Govor's archives.
15 NAA: BP4/3, RUSSIAN RUDEZKY J.
16 NAA: BP4/3, RUSSIAN ROOMIANZOFF N; NAA: BP4/3, RUSSIAN SHULAR M.
17 'To be cleaned and fed. Out of work Russian gaoled', *Daily Standard*, Brisbane, 28 June 1921, p. 3; 'A Russian's "Million a day"', *The Telegraph*, Brisbane, 15 October 1921, p. 2; 'A capitalist vagrant. One month's hard labour', *Western Star and Roma Advertiser*, 31

May 1922, p. 3; '"I'm A Bolshevik!" Russian scares Glencoe. Barefooted Fowl-Chaser', *The Armidale Express and New England General Advertiser*, 15 April 1924, p. 3.

18   'Plotonoff. A thumb-nail history', *The Inverell Times*, 14 October 1924, p. 2.
19   *Queensland Police Gazette*, 16 February 1935, p. 59; 30 March 1935, p. 118; 15 June 1935, p. 217.
20   NAA: A659, 1940/1/5657, Ankudinow, Michael – Naturalisation.
21   Janice Hunter, letter, 13.11.2001; interview, 21.11.2001, Elena Govor's archives.
22   'Official correspondence', *Queanbeyan-Canberra Advocate*, 26 February 1925, p. 2; 'At the police court', *Queanbeyan Age and Queanbeyan Observer*, 22 September 1925, p. 3.
23   'Local land board', *The Wyalong Advocate and Mining, Agricultural and Pastoral Gazette*, 20 December 1916, p. 3; 'Moree land board', *Moree Gwydir Examiner and General Advertiser*, 11 September 1917, p. 1.
24   NAA: A1, 1921/17688, N. Nicholas Fedorovich – Naturalization.
25   A Land Fit for Heroes? A History of Soldier Settlement in New South Wales, 1916-1939, http://soldiersettlement.records.nsw.gov.au/case-studies/tober-albert-michael/.
26   'Settler killed at Walpole settlement', *Albany Advertiser*, 8 October 1931, p. 1.
27   'Bruce Rock Police Court', *Great Southern Leader*, Pingelly, WA, 20 April 1923, p. 5.
28   NAA: A1, 1921/23781, G. Gregory Jakimov Naturalization.
29   Violet Cotman, interview, 7.10.2001.
30   'Dairying at Templestowe', *The Australasian*, Melbourne, 8 July 1922, pp. 5, 7.
31   'The Boucault Bay Trading Co.', *Northern Standard*, Darwin, 12 August 1924, p. 2.
32   'Booyal', *Maryborough Chronicle, Wide Bay and Burnett Advertiser*, 5 January 1918, p. 6.
33   Ken White, 'History of Richard Gregorenko & Sons – Callide Valley', Carol McKenzie's archive, Canberra (copy in Elena Govor's archives).
34   N.I. Dmitrovsky-Baikoff, 'Russkie v Kvinslende' [Russians in Queensland], *Avstraliada*, 2005, no. 42, p. 12 (Dudarko); no. 44, c. 11 (Bessmertny, Makagon); 2006, no. 46, p. 8 (Gniliak); 2007, no. 51, pp. 9-12 (Babkoff, Demchenko).
35   Volkofsky, interview, 9.11.2001.
36   Warwick Mayne-Wilson, 'The frustrations of researching old gardens', *Phanfare*, no. 210, January – February 2005, pp. 8-11.
37   'Local railway inventions', *Sunday Times*, Sydney, 26 March 1916, p. 20.
38   'Alleged incendiarism', *The Sydney Morning Herald*, 16 October 1917, p. 7; 'Quarter sessions', *The Sydney Morning Herald*, 21 November 1917, p. 8.
39   'Goods worth £270. Foreigner for trial', *Evening News*, Sydney, 20 September 1923, p. 5.
40   'Ayr notes', *Townsville Daily Bulletin*, 24 January 1930, p. 5.
41   Suzanne Edgar, 'Cotton, Lewy (1894–1972)', *Australian Dictionary of Biography*, Vol. 13, Melbourne: MUP, 1993, pp. 509-510.
42   *New South Wales Police Gazette*, 23 April 1924, p. 220.
43   NAA: A2487, 1921/4182, [Application for permission to use the letters 'Australian

Imperial Force' for business purposes – Wolff Zmood].
44   '£840 Fur Haul in City Shop', *The Age*, Melbourne, 12 April 1948, p. 3.
45   NAA: B741, V/3847, Wolfe Hoffman – Application for friends to enter Australia [13 pp]; NAA: B2455, HOFFMAN W 2224.
46   'Reciprocal trade with East', *News*, Adelaide, 28 June 1924, p. 4.
47   Dorothy Lazarus, interview, 16.09.2001.
48   'O Susie! Says Vengert wouldn't marry her', *Truth*, Sydney, 6 February 1921, p. 4; 'Vanished. Vengert says wad went away', *Truth*, Sydney, 8 April 1928, p. 23; 'Building gutted. Tenants narrow escape', *Cairns Post*, 15 August 1936, p. 6.
49   'Electric shocks!!', *Albany Advertiser*, 14 May 1931, p. 3; 'Tampering with a meter. Hotel Licensee fined', *The West Australian*, Perth, 15 May 1931, p. 14; 'Christian de Rink. Strikes trouble in New Zealand', *Albany Advertiser*, 8 September 1932, p. 4.
50   '"Cow" for a car', *The Daily News*, Perth, 5 November 1930, p. 1; 'Bankruptcy Court. Husband employed by wife', *The West Australian*, Perth, 6 November 1930, p. 7; 'Bankruptcy case. Accountant's books', *The West Australian*, 24 December 1946, p. 14; 'Contempt of court. Accountant sent to goal', *The West Australian*, 1 May 1947, p. 11; 'Prison sentence. Appeal to High Court', *The West Australian*, 8 May 1947, p. 15.
51   'Trager's painful extractions', *Truth*, Brisbane, 20 March 1927, p. 19.
52   'Gunner George Kamishansky', *Reveille*, August 1934.
53   John J. Taylor. Alexander Barr Winning (1892-1963), 2013, Western Australian Architect Biographies, http://www.architecture.com.au/.
54   Biographical materials in database of http://ancestry.com and bibliographical data on WorldCat database at https://www.worldcat.org/.
55   'Stuart Town', *Wellington Times*, NSW, 14 March 1940, p. 5.
56   'Musical notes', *Sunday Times*, Sydney, 16 June 1918, p. 15.
57   'Mr. E.A. Tardent', *The Brisbane Courier*, 3 April 1933, p. 17; 'Death of Mr E.A. Tardent', *Queensland Times*, Ipswich, 3 April 1933, p. 6.
58   NAA: A446, 1961/4615, COCHURA James born 13 August 1885 – Russian; J34, C46673, COCHURA, James – Service Number – 2812.
59   'Industrial court', *Daily Mercury*, Mackay, 12 December 1929, p. 7; 'In the supreme court of Brisbane', *The Brisbane Courier*, 11 October 1930, p. 5; 'In the courts', *Daily Mercury*, 13 February 1931, p. 9; 'In the courts', *Daily Mercury*, 3 March 1931, p. 8; 'Important decision. Sugar worker's case', *Worker*, Brisbane, 29 April 1931, p. 11; 'In the courts', *Daily Mercury*, 23 July 1931, p. 2; 'Magistrates court', *Daily Mercury*, 20 August 1931, p. 6; 'Deductions from wages', *Worker*, 6 January 1932, p. 10; 'In the courts', *Daily Mercury*, 10 March 1932, p. 3; 'In the courts', *Daily Mercury*, 22 June 1932, p. 8; 'Magistrates court', *Daily Mercury*, 7 July 1932, p. 9; 'In the courts', *Daily Mercury*, 30 November 1932, p. 8.
60   Electoral rolls, Queensland, Kennedy, Cloncurry, 1937.
61   'Wharfie hit head, died', *The Courier-Mail*, Brisbane, 17 November 1954, p. 1.

62   Find My Past database (http://findmypast.com).
63   'Stories in divorce', *The Daily News*, Perth, 14 August 1928, p. 6; 'Unemployment. The march on parliament', *The West Australian*, 4 December 1930, p. 17; 'Knocked off bicycle', *The West Australian*, 15 March 1943, p. 5; 'Lumper steals chocolate', *The Daily News*, 1 May 1944, p. 5.
64   'Dead body found. Suspicion of murder', *The Advertiser*, Adelaide, 3 April 1920, p. 8; 'Probably suicide', *Sunday times*, Sydney, 4 April 1920, p. 2; 'A Russian's death', *Northern Star*, Lismore, 5 April 1920, p. 5; 'Murder suspected', *Albury Banner and Wodonga Express*, 9 April 1920, p. 31; 'Domain mystery. Russian found shot. Coroner thinks suicide', *Evening news*, Sydney, 14 April 1920, p. 4.
65   Matrofan Koropets Death Certificate 4721/1920, Registry of Births, Deaths and Marriages, NSW.
66   'Returned soldier missing', *The Sydney Morning Herald*, 22 January 1923, p. 9; *New South Wales Police Gazette*, 28 February 1923, p. 114.
67   'Leaped from bridge. Ex-soldier's tragic fate. "As well end it all"', *Daily Standard*, Brisbane, 20 December 1920, p. 6; 'Dive to death', *Daily Mail*, Brisbane, 21 December 1920, p. 4. 'The bridge tragedy', *Queensland Times*, 22 December 1920, p. 5; 'River tragedies. Man jumps over bridge', *The Week*, Brisbane, 24 December 1920, p. 19.
68   'News and notes. ... Attempted suicide', *The West Australian*, Perth, 5 July 1923, p. 8; 'News briefs. Head in oven', *The Courier-Mail*, Brisbane, 6 January 1944, p. 5.
69   'Man shot dead', *The Daily News*, Perth, 30 April 1934, p. 3; 'Russian ex-officer's death', *The Daily News*, 3 May 1934, p. 9.
70   'Broken Hill war volunteer dies in a Sydney hospital', *Barrier Miner*, Broken Hill, 5 June 1928, p. 1.
71   NAA: A2487, 1921/14926, [Eligibility for medical treatment – J Rudezky]. Violet Cotman, interview, 7.10.2001.
72   Simonoff's list is in the file NAA: A1, 1923/8359, Repatriation of Russians. Agreement between Imperial Government & Soviet Government.
73   NAA: A1/15, 1920/7356, Naturalised Russians leaving Commonwealth.
74   NAA: A2487, 1920/2196, [Russian ex-serviceman]. Another Ukrainian wishing to return home in this list was Mitrofan Koropets, who committed suicide.
75   'Memorial', http://lists.memo.ru, sourced from *Kniga pamiati Amurskoi oblasti* [*Book of Memory of Amurskaia oblast*].
76   NAA: A1, 1934/3737, Louis BRODSKY – Naturalization. 'Trade with Russia. Committee formed in Sydney', *Sunday Times*, Sydney, 9 March 1924, p. 7. 'Communist aims', *The Sydney Morning Herald*, 9 July 1928, p. 11. 'Transport workers', *Advocate*, Burnie, Tasmania, 15 December 1928, p. 5. 'Exploit new gold field', *The Central Queensland Herald*, Rockhampton, 13 May 1948, p. 17. Warwick Brodsky, interview, 1.09.2001, Elena Govor's archives.

77 E-mail from Ferber's granddaughter Dru West 20.08.2011, Elena Govor's archives.
78 1940 United States Federal Census at http://ancestry.com/.
79 New Kensington, Pennsylvania, city directory at http://ancestry.com/.
80 Barbara Scott, message via Ancestry.com, 13.11.2015, Elena Govor's archives.
81 'Through the 'Gabba in Scanty Attire... Russian Romance Crashes', *Truth*, Brisbane, 8 February 1925, p. 10.
82 Volkofsky, interview, 9.11.2001.
83 'Prohibited publications', *Daily Herald,* Adelaide, 19 January 1918, p. 6; 'Prohibited publications', *Truth*, Perth, 26 April 1919, p. 8.
84 NAA: A1, 1927/12409, Carl KILLS – Naturalisation certificate; A1, 1930/182, Afanacy KORNEIUK – Naturalisation certificate.
85 Barbara Scott, Ancestry.com message, 13.11.2015.
86 Volkofsky, interview, 9.11.2001.
87 NAA: ST1233/1, N3255, George Kamishawsky [Applicant] Mrs Mary Glovatsky [Nominee] [Box 13].
88 'A Russian drama. Seven years of torture', *Morning Bulletin*, Rockhampton, 6 December 1922, p. 10.
89 NAA: A446, 1959/31952, MAXIMENKO Akelina born 15 August 1895 – Russian.
90 Barbara Scott, Ancestry.com message, 13.11.2015.
91 'Help for Russia', *Daily Standard*, Brisbane, 17 May 1922, p. 5.
92 Piven-Large family archives, Sydney; NAA: A1, 1915/18561, Zacharias E. Pieven – Naturalization; Klavdia Piven, Registers of Coroners' Inquests, 1821-1937, NSW, http://ancestry.com; Zachariah Pieven, Death Certificate 7183/1917, Registry of Births, Deaths and Marriages, NSW.
93 NAA: A1066, IC45/23/2/36, Welfare Enquiries: Australian Legation, Moscow – Mrs & Miss Nejinzeva.
94 Nicholas Fedorovich, Probate of the Will, no. 341366, in New South Wales Will Books 1800-1952, State Records Authority of New South Wales (accessed via database 'Find My Past' http://findmypast.com/).
95 'Fedorovich', *The Courier-Mail*, Brisbane, 21 May 1946, p. 10.
96 NAA: B741, V/10434, Miss N. Maneekeena & Mr Paul Koslick.
97 NAA: B73, R44428, CHERPITER, John – Service Number – 2743.
98 NAA: B741, V/10434, Miss N. Maneekeena & Mr Paul Koslick.
99 'Foreigners' Brawl', *Sydney Morning Herald*, 8 February 1926, p. 12.
100 NAA: B741, V/10434, Miss N. Maneekeena & Mr Paul Koslick.
101 Ibid.
102 NAA: A12217, L3072, Mrs Poly Tchorzewski – purchase of property in Bundaberg Queensland.
103 Dorothy Tober, interview, 15.11.2001, Elena Govor's archives.

104 AWM43, A436. Official History, 1914–18 War: biographical and other research files. Kamishansky G.; Alexander Ouchirenko, letter, 23 May 2002, Elena Govor's archives.
105 Cotman, interview, 7.10.2001.
106 Thelma Webberley, interview, 27.10.2001.
107 Violet Cotman, interview, 7.10.2001.
108 'The Bulletin', *Townsville Daily Bulletin*, 9 June 1928, p. 4; 'Supreme court', *Townsville Daily Bulletin*, 8 May 1948, p. 2.
109 Solomon Stedman, 'A life was built', National Library of Australia, Papers of Solomon Stedman, 1920-1979, MS 6408, p. 99.
110 'Through the 'Gabba in Scanty Attire... Russian Romance Crashes', *Truth*, Brisbane, 8 February 1925, p. 10.
111 'Family Notices. Provaka', *The Courier-Mail*, Brisbane, 27 May 1942, p. 8; 'Fancy dress dance Holland Park School', *The Courier-Mail*, 14 April 1934, p. 21.
112 Interviews with Violet Cotman, 7.10.2001, Tom Volkofsky, 9.11.2001, and Carol McKenzie, 30.08.2001.
113 Janice Hunter, interview, 21.11.2001.
114 'Obituary. Mr. Joseph Rudezky', *Dalby Herald*, 10 February 1931, p. 3.
115 Volkofsky, interview, 9.11.2001.
116 Ibid.; Peter Tilleard, interview, 20.01.2017.
117 NLA: Papers of Curt and Marea Prerauer, MS 10040, Series 7, folder 35.
118 NAA: A435, 1946/4/2081, KIVOVITCH Judah Myer – born 4 October 1890 – Russian.
119 NAA: A1, 1918/10222, J. Joseph Vurhaft Naturalisation.
120 'Russian here 40 years is naturalised', *The West Australian*, 29 July 1952, p. 4.
121 NAA: A1, 1935/9095, J. Mikulicic. Naturalization Certificate; A1, 1936/8862, P. Komesaroff – Naturalisation.
122 NAA: A1, 1923/12211, C. Cezar Wolkowsky Naturalization.
123 NAA: A1, 1920/3694, J. John OUCHIRENKO – Naturalization.
124 NAA: B741, V/197, Russians, Sydney. Returned Soldiers, War Records of.
125 NAA: A1, 1936/8862, P. Komesaroff – Naturalisation. Thelma Webberley, interview, 27.10.2001.
126 NAA: A6119, 5795, KOMESAROFF, Peter (aka KOMESAROOK) Miscellaneous papers.
127 NAA: A1, 1921/3357, B. Ben Goffin – Naturalization.
128 'In the thick of it. Australian soldiers describe their experiences', *Sunday Times*, Perth, 16 December 1917, p. 1.
129 NAA: A1, 1922/605, A.P. Alexander Paul Sank Naturalization.
130 NAA: B2455, Afendikoff C. J34, C47935, AFENDIKOFF, Cim [aka Cemon] – Service Number – 6032. 'R.S.S.I.L.A. Gordonvale sub-branch', *Cairns Post*, 29 February 1940, p. 3.

131 *New South Wales Police Gazette*, 23 April 1924, p. 220.

132 'Posing as returned soldier. Charges against a Russian', *Ballarat Star*, 17 June 1920, p. 3.

133 'Soldiers' tribute. Labor government appreciated. Pre-election letter', *Daily Standard*, Brisbane, 30 April 1918, p. 3.

134 'R.S.L. Lag on Migration', *Newcastle Morning Herald and Miner's Advocate*, 17 February 1949, p. 4.

135 'First Stage for Riflemen on Saturday', *Newcastle Morning Herald and Miner's Advocate*, 10 February 1949, p. 8.

136 'Obituary. Mr. Joseph Rudezky', *Dalby Herald*, 10 February 1931, p. 3.

137 'Mr. E.A. Tardent', *The Brisbane Courier*, 3 April 1933, p. 17; 'Death of Mr E.A. Tardent', *Queensland Times*, Ipswich, 3 April 1933, p. 6.

138 *Australian Women's Weekly*, 28 January 1939, p. 20.

139 World War 2 Nominal Roll, http://www.ww2roll.gov.au/.

140 NAA: B2455, Brodsky L.

141 'Timoshenko's nephew, says man in court', *News*, Adelaide, 20 March 1943, p. 3; 'Marshal Timoshenko's 'nephew'', *The Age*, Melbourne, 22 March 1943, p. 5; Jan Rees, 'George and Alessandra Ankoodinoff', p. 9.

142 NAA: B884, Q187674, NICHOLSON ROBERT...

143 Alexander Ouchirenko, letter, 23 May 2002.

144 'Soccer football', *The Hebrew Standard of Australasia*, Sydney, 20 May 1932, p. 7; 'Another Maccabean victory', *The Hebrew Standard of Australasia*, 20 July 1934, p. 2.

145 P.D. Monteath, *P.O.W.: Australian Prisoners of War in Hitler's Reich*, Sydney: Pan Macmillan Australia, 2011, pp. 192-193.

146 'With the forces', *Daily Advertiser*, Wagga Wagga, 20 September 1944, p. 2.

147 L. Pinkevitch, Letter, 15 May 1987. – NAA: B884, N152205.

148 Don Hunter, interview, 21.11.2001, Elena Govor's archives.

149 Ken White, 'History of Richard Gregorenko & Sons'.

150 NAA: B883, QX3624, GREGORENKO LEONARD...; A471, 74275, [GREGORENKO Leonard...], B883, QX54245, GREGORENKO GEORGE; A471, 32563, [GREGORENKO George...].

151 NAA: A9300, JAKIMOV G.; A9301, 168001. 'Destruction of U-Boat. Sydney Pilot's Story', *The Sydney Morning Herald*, 24 May 1943, p. 5.

152 NAA: A9300, OLEINIKOFF P M; A705, 166/31/321, OLEINIKOFF, Peter Matthew.

153 NAA: B884, N387017, SUROVSOV STEPHEN.

154 NAA: B741, V/3847, Wolfe Hoffman – Application for friends to enter Australia.

155 'Sheepskins for Russia', *Morning Bulletin*, Rockhampton, 27 October 1942, p. 2.

156 NAA: A663, O130/2/3, N. Fedorovich – Offer of Services as Interpreter.

157 NAA: BP25/1, ROMANZOFF N RUSSIAN.

158 'Ambulance attention', *Daily Mercury*, Mackay, 8 June 1946, p. 2, 12 October 1946, p. 2;

'Golden casket', *Brisbane Telegraph*, 19 March 1952, p. 12.

159 [Australian Council for Civil Liberties], *It can happen here! the case of an A.I.F. soldier, a naturalised British subject*, Melbourne, ACCL, 1944; Thelma Webberley, interview, 27.10.2001.

160 B. Patkin, 'Peter Komesaroff', Thelma Webberley's archive; P. Ruskin, 'Peter Komesaroff', *Australian Jewish News*, 16 October 1953.

161 'First A.I.F. Man Returns as Migrant', *Age*, 26 September 1950, p. 2; NAA: B2455, Dynowski F.; P1185, DYNOWSKI; A12036, 18, DYNOWSKI Franciszek born 19 May 1894. Database of the 1944 Warsaw insurrection: http://www.1944.pl/historia/powstancze-biogramy/Franciszek_Dynowski/.

162 Volkofsky, interview, 9.11.2001. NAA: A261, 1946/5009, Applicant – VOLKOFSKY Theofil Thomas; Nominee – WOLKOWSKY Woiciech; nationality Polish; A261, 1947/2519, Applicant – VOLKOFSKY Theofil Thomas; Nominee – WOJCIECH Wolkowsky; nationality Polish.

163 NLA: Papers of Curt and Marea Prerauer, MS 10040, Series 11, folder 2.

164 State Archives of the Russian Federation, Moscow (GARF): P8131-31-28916, Tsank Aleksandr Abramovich.

165 Svetlana Vishnevaia, e-mail, 7 July 2008, Elena Govor's archives.

166 Svetlana Vishnevaia, e-mail, 13 May 2009, Elena Govor's archives.

167 Bett Arnold, e-mail, September 2009, Elena Govor's archives.

168 'A touching reunion', *The Canberra Times*, 27 August 1963, p. 18.

169 NAA: B2455, PINKEVITCH CONSTANTINE.

170 Richard Goffin, e-mail, 6 May 2015, Elena Govor's archives.

171 *Istoriia russkikh v Avstralii* [*History of Russians in Australia*], vol. 1, Sydney: 'Australiada', 2004, p. 130.

List of abbreviations

AWM – Australian War Memorial
NAA – National Archives of Australia
QP – *Queenslander Pictorial*
SL NSW – State Library of New South Wales
SL SA – State Library of South Australia
UK National Archives – The National Archives, Kew, UK

Appendix - Biographies

We have reconstructed the original names for Slavs and, where possible, for Jews, providing them in Ukrainian for Ukrainian Anzacs and in Russian for the others.

Ethnic background information takes into consideration cultural assimilation, although in some cases there is not enough data to attribute this information with absolute certainty. Religious denomination is presented as it was recorded by the enlisting clerks. In some cases it might have been inaccurate (see discussion in the chapter 'Ethnic complexities').

Date of birth derives, if available, from the official records, such as statutory declarations in naturalisation applications and alien registration documents, but their verification in the original Ukrainian records could only be conducted in a few cases.

The date of arrival also derives from statutory declarations and has mostly been verified for the arrivals to Queensland from the Russian Far East, and, in some cases, arrivals to Sydney, Melbourne and Fremantle.

Unless otherwise specified, the recruits served in the rank of Private.

Afendikoff Cemon
Афендиков Семен
Russian/Greek background
Born: 15.05.1888 in Odessa. Religion listed as Russian.

Arriving in Australia in September 1915, Afendikoff lived in Sydney, finding work as a seaman and labourer. He enlisted on 1.03.1916 in Sydney and served in the 20th Battalion on the Western Front from 1917 to 1919, where he was wounded three times. He was returned to Australia on 19.06.1919 and discharged three months later. After his discharge he moved often, from Sydney to Nimmitabel in the Snowy Mountains, NSW, to Gordonvale, Qld, where he died on 19.12.1939.

Ankudinow Michael
Анкудинов Михаил
Russian background
Alias: George Wilson; Callahan.
Born: 1.05.1886 (other variants 1879, 1880, 1885, 1896, 1901) in Odessa, although he also stated that he was born in St Petersburg and Vladivostok. Religion listed as Roman Catholic.

Ankudinow came from a well-educated, prominent family that moved from Odessa to Vladivostok. Prior to his arrival in Australia in October 1912, he served in the Russian army and then went seafaring, spending time in China, Japan, and the USA. Disembarking in Port Adelaide, SA, he worked as a seaman and labourer. He enlisted on 20.05.1916 in Adelaide and served in the 50th and 43rd Battalions on the Western Front from 1916 to 1918. Here, his courage was noted and he was Mentioned in Despatches.

Wounded twice, he was invalided to England, where he married Maggie Callaghan in 1918. During his remaining time in the army he was assigned to the Australian Provost Corps, and was discharged on 8.05.1919 in London. He returned to Australia with his wife in 1920. His police records indicate that he and his wife had difficulty settling in one place and committed a series of petty crimes such as larceny and theft aggravated by drunkenness. His wife returned to the UK and Ankudinow continued moving from state to state. He reenlisted during WWII on three occasions, but each time was discharged after a few months. In 1940 he married Lillian Crough in Victoria. Ankudinow died in 1951 in Heidelberg, Victoria.

Belfort Alexander Eisy
Бельфор Александр

Jewish background

Born: 25.02.1891 in Odessa in a Russified Jewish family. Religion listed as Hebrew.

In 1907 Belfort came to the USA and worked in New York on the American Line as an electrician and a marine mechanic. In 1915 he applied for naturalisation in the USA, and in 1917 tried to enlist in the US Army. Later he travelled to New Zealand and then to Australia, disembarking in Melbourne on 31.01.1918. Enlisting in Rockhampton, Qld, on 2.07.1918, he was assigned to the Depot. However, he was discharged six weeks later as medically unfit. After the war he returned to the USA and continued working on ships until 1926 when his ship visited Odessa. He deserted the ship there and stayed in the Soviet Union.

Beloshapka Platon
Білошапка Платон

Ukrainian background

Born: 27.07.1892 in Kyiv. Religion listed as Church of England.

Prior to his arrival in Australia, Beloshapka served in the Russian army. He disembarked in Brisbane on 10.11.1912, moved to NSW, and travelled around the state. Enlisting on 4.03.1915 in Kiama, NSW, he was assigned to the 19th Battalion. He was transferred to the Liverpool camp, NSW, for reattestation and after over-staying his leave was discharged, with the reason given that he displayed 'an incompatibility with comrades and inability to follow military commands'. Owing to his lack of English, he was subsequently incarcerated as a German on two occasions. In the following years, his life in Australia was marked by numerous jail terms for loitering. It appears that in the late 1920s he went to the USA and tried to settle there, but returned to Australia in 1930, and the pattern of jail terms continued. Beloshapka died in Rockhampton, Queensland, on 26.10.1962.

Boronow Alexander
Боронов Александр

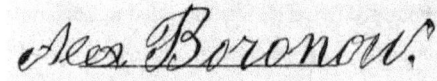

Russian background

Alias: Brown

Born: 1872 (enlistment) or 12.02.1859 (naturalisation) in Odessa. Religion listed as Roman Catholic.

Boronow arrived in Australia from Glasgow in about 1889. He found work as a cane cutter and labourer in the northern region of Queensland before enlisting in Townsville on 12.02.1916. He was assigned to the 9th Battalion but was discharged six months later as medically unfit and over-aged. He lived out his last years in Queensland, dying on 12.11.1925.

Borszcer David
Борщер Давид

Jewish background

Born: 1880 in Bershad, Podillia (now Vinnytsia region). Religion listed as Israelite.

Borszcer arrived in Australia from London with the Belgian Band under the patriotic endeavour of raising money for the Belgian Relief Fund; they disembarked on 1.06.1915 in Fremantle, WA. Moving to NSW, Borszcer enlisted on 28.04.1916 and was assigned to the Australian Light Horse Band in home service. He was discharged on 11.05.1917 and lived in Sydney, where he was the conductor of the Chatswood Orchestral Society. Later he moved to Tumut, where he died in 1939.

Breitman George
Брейтман Герш

Jewish background

Born: 1896 in Chechelnyk, Podillia (now Vinnytsia region). Religion listed as Jewish.

Breitman probably came to Australia from England, where his relatives lived. Enlisting on 31.08.1915 in Holsworthy, NSW, when he was 19, he served in the 3rd Battalion on the Western Front from 1916 to 1919. On 2.03.1917 at Ligny-Thilloy, France he exhibited bravery in the field, saving his officer's life and assisting in the capture of four enemy soldiers. He was awarded the Military Medal. In October 1917 he was wounded at Broodseinde, Belgium. In August 1918 in the move toward Peronne he was gassed but rejoined his battalion after recovery. On 4.04.1919 he contracted pneumonia and was transferred to a hospital in Andover, England, where he died a week later. Breitman received a full military funeral and was buried in Willesden Jewish Cemetery, Middlesex, England.

Brodsky Louis
Бродский Гедалия
Jewish background

Alias: David Lipschitz; Edward Marlen

Born: 25.12.1881 in Odessa. Religion listed as Jewish.

Brodsky worked at sea from his youth, arriving in Sydney on 7.03.1901. Here he met and married Sarah Marks in 1904 and they had two children, Isadore and Alexander. He worked cleaning and drying clothes. The family moved to Melbourne where Brodsky enlisted on 15.06.1915, being assigned to the 23rd and 14th Battalions. He deserted in Egypt and worked as a steward on various ships, eventually returning to Australia, where he gave himself up to the military authorities in 1918. He was not prosecuted. In the 1920s he served as Secretary on the Australia-Russia Trading Committee. Having divorced Sarah earlier, in 1942 Brodsky married Matilda Pearl Oldman. They had one child, Mark Anthony. Brodsky died on 29.08.1956 in Sydney.

Broon Hyman
Брун Хаим
Jewish background

Alias: Brwon, Brown

Born: 26.05.1873 in Kherson. Religion listed as Russian Jewish.

Broon arrived in Australia in May 1913. A tailor by trade, he enlisted in Liverpool, NSW, on 30.07.1915 and was assigned to the 1st Australian Dermatological Hospital. He was discharged on 5.04.1916, being convicted of theft. He enlisted again in Melbourne on 21.07.1917. While sick in hospital he developed delusions of persecution and attempted suicide. He was discharged on medical grounds a month later. Broom disappears from Australian records after the war; he probably left for Egypt to reunite with his wife Liebah Broon (Eliza Brwon), who was stranded there during the war.

Chain Isaac
Хаин (Хайкин?) Исаак
Jewish background

Born: 1878 or on 7.07.1886 in Odessa. Religion listed as Hebrew.

Chain arrived in Australia from Cape Town, South Africa on 4.03.1908, disembarking in Melbourne. He worked as a cigarette manufacturer in Melbourne and then in Sydney. By the time of his enlistment on 29.11.1915 in Casula, NSW, he was married to Sarah Bass. Their son Phillip was born soon after Chain's departure for the Western Front. Chain served in the 4th Battalion from 1916 to 1917. He was returned to Australia on 31.10.1917 and discharged seven months later as medically unfit. He reenlisted during WWII on 19.01.1941 in Sydney and served in the 7th Garrison Battalion. Chain was discharged on 12.08.1943 and died on 10.05.1945 in Sydney.

Cherpiter John
Черпіта Іван
Ukrainian background
Alias: Cherpita
Born: 1882 in Kamianets-Podilskyi. Religion listed as Greek Christian.

Cherpiter disembarked in Adelaide in 1912 and found work as a shoemaker, living with his de facto wife Anastasia and her daughter Lucy (Nadezhda). He enlisted on 29.10.1915 in Adelaide and served in the 10th and 50th Battalions on the Western Front from 1916 to 1917. He was killed on 2.04.1917 during the battle for Noreuil, France. Cherpiter's name is listed on the memorial panel at Villers-Bretonneux, France. Anastasia received an Australian pension after his death, moving to Melbourne. South Australian newspapers continued to commemorate his name on the day of his death up to the late 1920s.

Clesner Sam
Клезнер Саня
Jewish background
Born: 27.10.1892 in Odessa.

Clesner arrived in Australia on 6.01.1914, working in Sydney as a printer. Enlisting on 18.10.1915 in Liverpool, NSW, he was assigned to the Headquarters Staff Printers but was discharged three weeks later as his services were no longer required. After the war he lived in Brisbane and Melbourne from 1919 to 1920. Clesner was granted permission to leave Australia in April 1921.

Cochura James
Кочура Яків
Ukrainian background
Born: 1885 in Malomikhailivska *volost* (now Zaporizhia region). Religion listed as Russian.

Cochura served in the Russian foot guards for three years before coming to Australia via Vladivostok in 1913, disembarking in Sydney. Prior to his enlistment he moved around NSW, working as a miner and labourer. Enlisting on 21.01.1916 in Liverpool, NSW, he served in the 7th Light Horse Brigade in Egypt and Palestine from 1916 to 1919. Cochura was returned to Australia on 26.01.1919 and discharged seven months later. After his discharge he took up land under the Returned Soldiers Settlement Act 1916 in Temora, NSW, but during the Depression he moved to Sydney and then to Brisbane and Southport, Qld, where he worked as a wharf labourer. reenlisting during WWII in 1939 he served in the 1st Garrison Battalion and was discharged in 1945. Cochura died on 10.04.1961 in Queensland.

Cooper Roland Arthur
Купер Роланд Артур
British background

Born: 17.12.1897 in Mariupol. Religion listed as Congregational.

Cooper spent his early childhood in Mariupol in Ukraine and in Volsk in Russia, where his father worked as an engineer, but in 1909 the whole family moved to Sydney, which severed their Russian connections. Cooper was trained as a draughtsman, and with the outbreak of the war, served in the Militia in Sydney before his parents allowed him to enlist in the AIF on 15.02.1917 when he was nineteen. He served as a gunner and a driver in the artillery regiments on the Western Front in 1918. Returning to Sydney after the war, he worked as a newsagent, taking over his father's business. In 1932 he married Eileen Emily Moss.

Cotton Lewy
Котен Леви
Jewish background

Alias: Cotten

Born: 1894 in Odessa. Religion listed as Church of England.

Leaving Odessa in his youth, Cotton spent several years in France and England, where he was trained as a waiter. Coming to Australia in 1914, he worked as a waiter in Perth and Adelaide. Enlisting on 8.06.1916 in Perth as Cotten, he served on the Western Front from 1917-1918. Being transferred to London in February 1918, he served in the Australian Provost Corps. Cotton was returned to Australia on 18.12.1919 and discharged three months later. After the war he worked as chief waiter in the South Australian Hotel in Adelaide. He was married to Ivy Gertrude Jenkins and had a son.

Didenko George
Діденко Юрій
Ukrainian background

Born: 25.12.1884 in Akkerman (now Bilhorod-Dnistrovskyi). Religion listed as Orthodox.

Didenko disembarked in South Australia in 1911 and found work in Adelaide as a fireman and labourer. He enlisted in the AIF in Adelaide on 22.05.1916 but was discharged as medically unfit, owing to an untreated wrist fracture. On 30.11.1916 he reenlisted and served in the 5th Pioneer Battalion in England from 1917 to 1918. Discharged as medically unfit for a second time, he was returned to Australia on 12.05.1918. After the war, Didenko lived in Adelaide from 1919 to 1920 and most likely left Australia afterwards.

Domilovsky Nickefor
Доміловський Никифор
Ukrainian background

Born: 1892 in the village of Stavishche near Kyiv. Religion listed as Greek.

Working in Queensland as a labourer, Domilovsky enlisted in Cairns on 23.01.1915 and served in the 9th Battalion at Gallipoli in 1915 and on the Western Front in 1916, where he was killed in the battle for Pozières, France on 23.07.1916. Domilovsky's name appears on the Villers-Bretonneux memorial panel.

Dorfman Wolf
Дорфман Вольф
Jewish background

Born: 15.12.1886 in Rivne, Volhynia. Religion listed as Jewish.

Prior to his arrival in Sydney on 5.05.1915, Dorfman had served in the Russian army and travelled to Germany, Austria, the USA, China, Japan, and the Philippines. A few weeks after his arrival in Sydney he enlisted, and served in the 54th Battalion on the Western Front. In his first battle for Sugarloaf salient near Fromelles, France, in July 1916, he was taken prisoner of war by the Germans. Upon his release and return to Australia in 1919, he travelled around the world for work, setting up his own trading business in 1927 in Melbourne. Later he worked as a hotel keeper, manufacturer and merchant in Victoria and Western Australia. He married Emilie Cadwallander and they had one child, Betty. Dorfman died on 6.05.1969.

Dryen Edward
Друян Абрам
Jewish background

Born: 3.03.1882 in Pavlohrad in Katerynoslav province (now Dnipro).

Dryen arrived in Adelaide with his parents on 10.08.1894, moving later to Broken Hill, NSW, where he worked as a storekeeper. In 1914 he married Eva Bear and they had two children Ronald Gordon b.1916 and Betty b.1918. Enlisting on 28.08.1916 in Sydney, Dryen served in the Australian Instructional Corps as an acting staff sergeant major. He was discharged on 12.4.1917. During WWII Dryen reenlisted on 2.08.1941 and was assigned to the Australian Army Ordinance Corps, serving in Sydney. He was discharged on 16.09.1944. After the war Dryen lived in country NSW and Sydney, where he died on 27.02.1961.

Dynowski Frank
Дыновский Франк
Polish background

Born: 19.05.1894 in Kyiv. Religion listed as Roman Catholic.

Prior to his arrival in Sydney on 27.04.1914 Dynowski served in the Russian army. He worked as a labourer at Bugaldie, north of Dubbo, NSW, before enlisting on 22.01.1916 in Gulgong, NSW. He served in the 45th Battalion on the Western Front, attaining the rank of Acting Sergeant. While stationed in France he married Mary Antoinette Hue and stayed in France after the war ended. He was discharged on 27.07.1919. That same year he moved to Poland and took part in the 1944 Warsaw insurrection. Surviving, he served in the Polish forces in Germany from 1944 to 1950. Here he married Lissi-Henriette Lohrmann. In 1950 he returned to Australia in the wave of displaced persons, settling in Hobart. Although he was now an engineer, in Hobart he worked as a waiter. Dynowski died on 12.04.1970.

Fedorovich Nicholas
Федорович Николай
Russian/Polish or Belarusian background

Born: 27.07.1891 in Odessa. Religion listed as Greek.

Prior to his arrival in Brisbane on 21.08.1911 Fedorovich worked as a journalist for Russian and Manchurian newspapers in St Petersburg, Russia. In Queensland he worked as a cane cutter before enlisting in Cairns on 23.01.1915. He served in the 9th Battalion at Gallipoli where he was wounded. After being invalided to London, he visited his sick mother in Odessa, then re-joined the AIF, serving in the Administrative Headquarters in London. Returning to Australia, Fedorovich was discharged in 1918, and took up a soldier selection at Stanthorpe, Qld. His short story 'Kismet', about a wartime romance, was published in Australia in 1919. Visiting Russia in 1924, he married Eraida Nezhitseva. Fedorovich died on 18.05.1946 in Brisbane.

Feldman Israel
Фельдман Израиль
Jewish background

Born: 17.03.1889 in Odessa. Religion listed as Jewish.

Prior to his arrival in 1915 in Fremantle, WA, Feldman lived in Egypt and Palestine for 15 years. He was a widower and had a daughter, Betty. Feldman enlisted on 1.06.1916 in Perth and served in the 51st Battalion in England. He was returned to Australia a year later as medically unfit and was discharged on 11.03.1918. After the war Feldman lived in Perth, naturalising in 1925; he disappears from the records soon afterwards.

Felipor Joe
Филиппов Иосиф
Russian background

Born: 1888 in Odessa. Did not state religion at enlistment.

Prior to his arrival in Australia, Felipor had served in the Russian forces during the Balkan War. Arriving in Australia, he found work as a miner in WA in remote areas such as Meekatharra and Peak Hill. He enlisted on 9.03.1916 in Blackboy Hill, WA, and served in the 6th Tunnelling Company as a sapper on the Western Front. After a conflict with fellow servicemen in October 1916 he was court martialled and found guilty, but was returned to the trenches. On 29.12.1916 he was wounded and invalided to Australia on 26.09.1917. After his discharge Felipor remained in Western Australia, visiting London in 1924.

Ferber George
Фербер Самуил
Russian/Jewish background

Born: 13.06.1894 in Melitopol, Zaporizhia region. Religion listed as Roman Catholic and Church of England.

Ferber arrived in Australia in 1912 from Harbin, China, where his family lived. He lived in Brisbane and Sydney working as a draper. Enlisting in Brisbane on 20.01.1916 he was assigned to the 52nd Battalion but was discharged after failing to board his transport ship. He reenlisted on 3.10.1916 in Sydney, giving his occupation as a stockman, and served in the Camel Regiments in Egypt and Palestine from 1917 to 1918. After the war he returned to Australia where he was discharged on 24.01.1919. The same year he left for the USA, settling in California. He married Rose Cherkosky in Toledo, Ohio in 1920. Ferber died on 29.05.1941 in Los Angeles.

Goffin Ben
Гойхман Пинхас
Jewish background

Born: 10.05.1896 in Tulchin, Podillia (now Vinnytsia region). Religion listed as Lutheran.

As a child, Goffin and his family emigrated from Ukraine to the USA. From here, Goffin travelled to Australia, arriving in Melbourne on 18.02.1916. He enlisted on the same day, and served in the 22nd Battalion on the Western Front from 1916 to 1918; he was severely wounded thrice. Goffin was returned to Australia in 1919 and discharged on 14.05.1919. After his discharge Goffin lived in Melbourne, finding work as a plumber and ironmonger. In 1921 he married Anne Koodak and took up land in the soldiers' settlement near Albany, WA. They had three children: Maurice and Steven (b.1925) and Shirley (1928-1937). Goffin died on 5.10.1931 in a tragic accident on his farm.

Goldstein Frank
Голдштейн Франк
Jewish background
Alias: Frayam Yacker Zwillen Horstain
Born: 13.02.1887 in Ruzhyn, Kyiv province (now Zhytomyr region). Religion listed as Jewish.

Goldstein had lived in England with his family, who had moved there from Ukraine, for six years prior to his arrival in Sydney on 4.11.1907. He married Florence Rosa Saunders in 1910 and they had six children. Enlisting on 19.06.1916 in Sydney, he served in the 23rd Battalion on the Western Front, where he was wounded two times, losing his eye. Goldstein was returned to Australia on 19.10.1918 and discharged six months later. He lived with his family in Kogarah, working as an ice-cream vendor. Goldstein died on 31.07.1971 in Sydney.

Gorbach Phillipp
Горбач Пилип
Ukrainian background
Born: 23.12.1886 in Odessa. Religion listed as Church of England.

Gorbach worked at sea since his youth. Disembarking in Sydney on 28.11.1914, he enlisted two months later in Liverpool, NSW, and served in the 4th Battalion in Egypt. Gorbach was returned to Australia in 1915 as an escort on a troopship and was transferred to a training camp in Liverpool, NSW. While in the training camp, he joined a soldiers' protest about the poor conditions at the camp, which turned into riots. Gorbach was court martialled, sentenced to 90 days of hard labour and discharged with ignominy. He stayed in Sydney for a while working on coastal vessels and then left for San Francisco, USA where he was naturalised in 1917 and registered for Army service. By 1930 he was living in New York running a tin shop.

Gorodezky Ivan
Городецький Іван
Ukrainian background
Born: 1892 in the village of Lipivka, Kamianets-Podilskyi province. Religion listed as Roman Catholic.

Prior to his arrival in Australia Gorodezky served in the Russian army. Arriving in Australia he lived in Melbourne, found work as a mechanic and enlisted on 29.02.1916. Gorodezky served as a driver in the 3rd Divisional Supply Column and the Field Ambulance on the Western Front from 1916 to 1919. He was discharged on 31.08.1919 in London. After his discharge, he moved to Paris, where he married. He appears for the final time in Australian records in 1936, when he lost his passport.

Greenstein Wolfe
Гринштейн Вольф
Jewish background

Born: 25.11.1899 in Odessa. Religion listed as Jewish.

As a 14-year-old, Greenstein arrived in Australia with his family from England, where they had been living for thirteen years. They disembarked in Sydney on 25.11.1913 and settled in Canterbury, NSW. Wolfe gained an apprenticeship and worked as a printer until his enlistment on 4.06.1918, when he was assigned to the 2nd Battalion. He did not see active service and was discharged on 20.09.1919. After the war Greenstein married Jean Piraner and they had two children, Ester b. 1925 (served in the AIF in WWII) and Aaron b. 1927. Greenstein reenlisted during WWII and served in the 1st Battalion in Egypt and Greece as a Lance Corporal. He was captured by the Germans in Crete, but survived and during the 1940s worked as a newspaper compositor. He died in Sydney in 1962.

Gregorenko Richard
Григоренко Єрофей
Ukrainian background

Born: 04.10.1887 in Karapyshi, Kyiv province. Religion listed as Orthodox.

Prior to his arrival in Australia in 1910, Gregorenko lived in China and Japan. Before enlisting in Brisbane on 2.11.1915 he found work as a clerk and bookbinder. He served in the 7th and 14th Field Ambulances on the Western Front from 1916 to 1918. He was returned to Australia on 4.12.1918 and discharged two months later. After the war he married Vera Scriven in Brisbane and they had three children: Leonard Richard b. 1921; George b. 1923 and Olga b. 1925. Gregorenko's marriage did not last and he moved to Callide Valley, Queensland with his two sons to take up a cotton-growing selection. Both his sons served in WWII. Gregorenko died of tuberculosis in Brisbane on 7.07.1950.

Gretchinsky James Theodor
Гречинський Яків
Russian/Ukrainian background

Born: 23.10.1886 in Horodnia, Chernihiv. Religion listed as Greek Church.

Gretchinsky was educated as an electrical engineer in Moscow and Odessa. Prior to his arrival in Australia, he had served in the Russo-Japanese war as a sub-lieutenant. He disembarked in Brisbane on 25.04.1913 from Vladivostok. Enlisting in Longreach, Qld, on 24.12.1914, he served in the 9th Battalion in Egypt in 1915. He was invalided back to Australia on 10.06.1915 and discharged two months later. In 1915 he married Helen Whitfield, but the marriage did not last and later he married Violet Mary McMurdy. Failing to find work, he reenlisted on 13.03.1916 but was discharged two months later as medically unfit. After several years moving around Australia, he settled in Sydney where he gained work as an electrician. Gretchinsky died on 24.09.1956 in Queensland.

Gulevich Nicholas
Гулевич Николай
Russian/Polish background

Born: 1.12.1886 in Odessa. Religion listed as Greek Church and Roman Catholic.

Gulevich came to Brisbane via the Russian Far East, disembarking on 1.05.1910. He worked on the construction of the Kannagur and Blackbutt railway line, and farmed sugar cane in the Cairns area. Enlisting on 6.02.1915 in Cairns, Gulevich served in the 2nd Light Horse Regiment in Egypt and as a gunner on the Western Front from 1917 to 1918. On 6.11.1918 Nicholas was invalided back to Australia. He was discharged three months later. Recovering, he found work in the North Queensland shire council. Gulevich died on 18.01.1944 in Queensland.

Haiff Saul
Хаиф Саул
Jewish background

Born: 15.02.1886 in Odessa. Religion listed as Jewish.

Haiff arrived in Australia from Port Said, disembarking in Perth on 15.09.1909. He found work as a tailor in Perth and Sydney. Enlisting in Sydney on 3.04.1916, Haiff served in the 53rd Battalion on the Western Front in 1918. He was returned to Australia on 15.01.1919 and discharged a few months later. Settling in Canterbury, NSW, he married Yente (Jennifer) Pelmothe. Haiff died in 1949 in Canterbury.

Harlap Lion
Харлап Арие
Jewish background

Born: 21.07.1893 in Odessa (or Rehovot, Palestine). Religion listed as Jewish.

Harlap arrived in Australia from Palestine on 17.12.1910, disembarking in Fremantle, WA, to join his sister who had arrived two years earlier. Before his enlistment on 5.03.1915, he worked as a locksmith and engine fitter in Perth. He served in the 10th Light Horse Regiment in Egypt and Palestine from 1915 to 1919. Harlap was discharged in Egypt and reunited with his parents in Palestine. In 1924 he opened a cycle shop in Jaffa, Israel. He visited Australia in 1963.

Heselev Israel
Геселев Израиль
Jewish background

Born: 14.12.1889 in Huliaipole, Katerynoslav (now Dnipro region). Religion listed as Jewish.

Disembarking in Adelaide on 22.10.1906 Heselev moved to Broken Hill, NSW, and Melbourne. Prior to his enlistment he worked as a machinist and musician. He enlisted on 4.10.1916 in Melbourne but was discharged a month later. He remained in Melbourne, opened a furrier's store, and married Carrie Benness. Heselev died in 1963 in Caulfield, Victoria.

Hoffman Wolfe
Гофман Вольф
Jewish background

Born: 1.11.1892 in Khoshchevatoe, Podillia (now Vinnytsia region). Religion listed as Jewish.

Hoffman disembarked in Fremantle, WA, on 25.04.1910 and worked as a mill hand. Enlisting on 20.03.1915 in Perth, he served in the 16th Battalion at Gallipoli. In 1917 he was transferred to the 17th and 9th Field Ambulances on the Western Front. He was returned to Australia on 4.12.1918 and discharged four months later. In 1920 he married and settled in Melbourne, where he manufactured clothing. Reenlisting in the AIF during WWII, he served for six months as a Corporal at the Attestation Office in Caulfield, Victoria. Hoffman moved to Sydney in 1967 and died on 2.05.1976 in NSW.

Ilin Constantine
Ильин Константин
Russian background

Born: 1891 in Aleshki, Taurida (now Kherson region). Religion listed as Roman Catholic.

Enlisting on 13.03.1916 in Newcastle, NSW, Ilin served in the 1st Battalion on the Western Front. He was severely wounded at Flers, France, invalided to England, and on 13.11.1917 was returned to Australia and discharged. Ilin married Sarah Maud Fletcher in 1918 but died on 26.05.1922 in the Prince of Wales Hospital, Randwick. His wife died the same year from TB.

Jakimov Gregory
Якимов Григорій
Russian/Bohemian background

Born: 8.09.1894 in Kamianets-Podilskyi. Religion listed as Orthodox.

Prior to his arrival in Australia from Norway, Jakimov had lived in Bohemia (now the Czech Republic). Disembarking in Adelaide on 13.03.1911, he moved to NSW, where he worked on sheep stations. He enlisted on 18.01.1916 in Newcastle, and served in the 35th Battalion on the Western Front from 1916 to 1917, attaining the rank of Lance Corporal. He was invalided to England and returned to Australia on 21.12.1917, being discharged five months later. After his discharge, Jakimov returned to work on rural NSW sheep stations. In 1919 he married Marjorie Alice Hayne and they had four children: Robert Roman Jakimov (1920-1937); Gregory ('Mick') Jakimov, b. 1922 (served in RAAF in WWII); Majda Amy Marjorie, b. 1923; Roman Arnold Jakimov, b. 1927 (served in RAAF in WWII). The family moved to Smithfield, NSW. Jakimov died on 9.09.1971 in Sydney.

Kachan John
Качан Іван
Ukrainian background

Born: 1878 in Berdychiv, Zhytomyr. Religion listed as Greek Orthodox.

Prior to his arrival in Australia, Kachan had served in the Russo-Japanese war. He enlisted in Bundaberg, Qld, on 27.04.1915 and served in the 26th Battalion at Gallipoli. In December 1915 he was invalided back to Australia, being discharged on 28.06.1917. Kachan died in Sydney on 28.07.1918.

Kamishansky George
Камишанський Юрій
Russian/Ukrainian background

Born: 21.01.1890 in Kerch, Crimea. Religion listed as Greek Catholic.

The son of a St Petersburg prosecutor, Kamishansky took to the sea after his father's death and came to Australia on 10.10.1913, disembarking in Melbourne. He enlisted on 28.08.1914 in Sydney and served in the 1st Field Artillery Brigade at Gallipoli and the Western Front, where he was transferred to the 2nd Army Intelligence Staff. Returning to Sydney on 10.03.1918, he studied electrical engineering and accountancy. In 1921 he married an AIF sister, Jean (Janet) Elizabeth Smith. Kamishansky died in Sydney on 19.06.1934.

Kavitski Vasily
Кавітський Василь
Ukrainian background

Born: 1888 in Olshanskaia Slobodka in Kyiv province. Religion listed as Greek Catholic.

Kavitski arrived in South Australia in 1913 and worked as a sailor before enlisting in Keswick, SA on 2.06.1915, serving in the 27th Battalion on the Western Front from 1916 to 1917. He was returned to Australia on 26.09.1917 as medically unfit and was discharged three months later. After his discharge he worked as a boiler maker in Port Pirie, SA, then moved to Adelaide. In 1920 Kavitski received permission to leave Australia, and probably returned to Ukraine.

Kills Carl
Кілс Карло
Ukrainian background

Born: 29.07.1886 in Voskovtsy, Volhynia. Religion listed as Greek Orthodox.

Kills disembarked in 1910 at Port Adelaide, SA, arriving from South Africa. He found work as a blacksmith in Port Pirie and Melbourne, where he enlisted on 1.07.1915. He was assigned to the Depot but was discharged on 28.10.1915 as 'unlikely to become an efficient soldier'. Kills remained in Melbourne, working as a merchant, and married Mary Louisa Amy Todd in 1927. They had two children, Arie Amy b.1927 and Carl b. 1928. Kills died in Melbourne in 1969.

Kiva Nikalas
Кива Микола
Ukrainian background

Born: 1894 in Odessa. Religion listed as Russian and Roman Catholic. May have come from a Jewish family and was later baptised.

Disembarking on 23.03.1913 in Brisbane from the Russian Far East, Kiva enlisted in Townsville, Qld, on 21.02.1916 and served in the 9th Battalion on the Western Front. Kiva was killed on 22.04.1917 at Bullecourt, France. The AIF tried to locate and notify his mother in Odessa but she was never found. Kiva was buried in the Queant Road Cemetery, Buissy, France.

Kivovitch Yur
Кивович Юда
Jewish background

Alias: Judah Myer Kivovitch (naturalisation); Victor Michael Carmichael (changed name by deed poll)

Born: 4.10.1890 in Kherson. Religion listed as Jewish.

Kivovitch came from a large Jewish family which migrated to Palestine soon after 1905. From there Kivovitch travelled to China, India and Hong Kong. He arrived in Australia from Hong Kong on 8.12.1913, disembarking in Townsville, Qld, where he worked in the customs office. Enlisting on 31.08.1915 in Holdsworthy, NSW, Kivovitch served in the 18th Battalion, the Camel Transport Corps as a Sergeant, and the Censor's Office of the Australian Headquarters in Cairo. He served in Egypt and Palestine from 1916 to 1917 and was discharged on 21.03.1917. After the war Kivovitch married Rose Rivet Senez. He worked in South Australia as a merchant and manufacturer. In 1931 he left for Canada. Twenty years later he returned to Australia and lived in Sydney, working as a restaurant proprietor. Kivovitch died in 1965 in Sydney.

Kleshenko Joseph
Клишенко Йосип
Ukrainian background

Alias: Joseph Klesh

Born: 28.12.1892 in Dubno, Volhynia (now Rivne region). Religion listed as Roman Catholic.

Kleshenko disembarked on 20.07.1912 in Sydney from San Francisco, USA. Between 1914 and 1916 he enlisted seven times, usually being discharged after a few months as medically unfit or being considered 'unlikely to become an efficient soldier'. Initially he enlisted under the names Joseph Noyland, Joseph Klinetinko, and Joe Klestenko. The seventh enlistment was more successful, and he served in the 29th Battalion in England. While in England Kleshenko met and married 17-year-old Ethel Bateman. Returning to Australia in 1918, he was declared medically unfit. He worked in Sydney as a stevedore and died on 3.08.1947.

Kolesnikov William
Колесніков Володимир
Ukrainian/Russian background

Alias: Koles

Born: 7.03.1880 in Peretin, Chernihiv, although in official Australian documents Kolesnikov always added 'Kiev' to his place of birth. Religion listed as Church of England.

Kolesnikov arrived in WA in 1907 and worked in rural areas. In 1911 he moved to Sydney, enlisting on 24.05.1916. Kolesnikov served in the 1st and 55th Battalions on the Western Front from 1916 to 1917. On the 16.09.1917 at Polygon Wood near Ypres he was severely wounded. After months in English hospitals he was invalided back to Australia on 8.08.1918 and discharged six months later in Sydney. In January 1923 his coat and hat were found at a beach near La Perouse. Kolesnikov was never found, and it is assumed that he committed suicide by drowning.

Komesaroff Peter
Комисаров/Комисарук Пинхас
Jewish background

Born: 3.04.1899 in Andriivka, Taurida (now Zaporizhia region). Religion listed as 'Synagogue'.

Arriving in Melbourne with his family on 8.12.1913, Komesaroff worked in the family's drapery shop. Enlisting in Cootamundra, NSW, on 8.01.1916 he served in the 56th Battalion on the Western Front from 1916 to 1919. On 2.04.1917 during the advance on the Lagnicourt-Noreuil-Louveral line, France he was severely wounded. Invalided to England, he returned to the Western Front at the end of 1917. He was returned to Australia on 23.06.1919, settling in Melbourne, where he married Sarah Horowitz from Odessa. They had three children: Thelma b. 1924; Miriam b. 1926 and Judith b. 1930. Komesaroff worked as a travelling optician and was actively involved in Jewish community life. He died on 21.10.1971 in Heidelberg, Victoria.

Korniack Afanasey
Корняк/Корнюк Афанасій
Ukrainian background

Born: 5.07.1875 in Porytsk, Volhynia. Religion listed as Church of England.

Korniack fought in the Russo-Japanese war. Arriving in Australia, he left behind his son and daughter. He disembarked in September 1914 in Townsville, Qld. By this time he was nearly 40 years of age. He worked as a miner in Cloncurry and Friezland, Qld, (now called Kuridala). Enlisting in Townsville on 9.09.1915, he was assigned to the 26th Battalion, but was discharged without serving due to ill health on 6.04.1916. After his discharge he worked in North Queensland as a mechanic and fitter, later moving to Brisbane. Korniack died in Brisbane on 9.01.1960.

Koropets Mitrofan
Коропець Митрофан
Ukrainian background

Born: 1889, in Dobrotove, Krolevets, Chernihiv. Religion listed as Russian.

Koropets enlisted on 14.01.1916 in Casula, NSW. Having worked as a miner, he served as a sapper in the 1st Tunnelling Company on the Western Front from 1916 to 1918; he was gassed at Messines, Belgium on 14.03.1918. On 31.03.1919 he was returned to Australia and was discharged in September. Seven months later his body was found in the Domain Park, Sydney. The coroner found that he had probably committed suicide.

Kotton Moisey
Котон Моисей
Jewish background

Born: 8.06.1892 in Kremenchuk, Poltava. Religion listed as Church of England and Hebrew.

Arriving in Australia on 4.02.1912 from Harbin, China, Kotton disembarked in Brisbane, working in Millthorpe, NSW, as a carter. Kotton enlisted on 26.04.1916 in Bathurst, NSW, and served in the Light Trench Mortar Battery on the Western Front from 1917 to 1918. He was killed on 21.09.1918 in the assault on the Hindenburg line. Kotton was buried in Templeux-le-Guerard British Cemetery, St Quentin, France.

Koty George Herman
Коти Джордж
Jewish background

Born: 27.10.1897 in Kyiv. Religion listed as Jewish.

Koty moved with his family to the USA in about 1906. From there, he came to Australia, working in Adelaide on ships before enlisting on 6.07.1916. He served in the 43rd and 40th Battalions on the Western Front from 1916 to 1918, where he was wounded three times. He was returned to Australia on 18.01.1919 and discharged three months later. By the 1920s he had returned to the USA. Koty married Lilian Stilzner and had two children: Dolores Elaine b. 1929 and Glenda b. 1934. He died on 2.07.1966 in Brooklyn, New York.

Kovalevsky Andrew
Ковалевський Андрій
Ukrainian background

Born: 1888 in Blahovishchenka, Katerynoslav (now Dnipro region). Religion listed as Greek Orthodox Church.

Kovalevsky disembarked on 12.09.1913 in Brisbane from the Russian Far East and worked as a labourer in Bundaberg, Qld. Enlisting on 26.04.1916 in Bundaberg, he served in the 26th Battalion on the Western Front from 1917 to 1918. Kovalevsky was killed south of Peronne, France on 3.10.1918. He was buried at Prospect Hill Cemetery, Gouy, France. In his will he left his possessions to his mother in Ukraine, but she could not be found by the AIF.

Kozachuk Ksenofont
Козачук Ксенофон
Ukrainian background

Born: 26.01.1891 in Kosivka, Kyiv. Religion listed as Roman Catholic.

Prior to his arrival in Australia, Kozachuk lived in Canada and the USA. He disembarked in Sydney on 21.01.1914 and found work as a miner in NSW and Qld. He enlisted on 1.03.1916 in Cairns, but was discharged as medically unfit one month later. In 1921 he married Bessie Morris and they settled in Collinsville, Qld, where Ksenofont continued working as a miner. They had three children: Sybil b. 1919, Ksenofont William b. 1923 (served in RAAF in WWII), and Hilda May b. 1925 (served in RAAF in WWII). Kozachuk died in 1987 in Bowen, Qld.

Krantz Albert
Кранц Абрам
Jewish background

Born: 20.10.1892 in Novopavlovka, Katerynoslav (now Dnipro region). Religion listed as Hebrew.

At the age of 13 Krantz arrived in Australia with his brother Samuel. They disembarked in Adelaide on 1.02.1905 and then moved to Broken Hill, NSW, where Albert Krantz worked as a carpenter. Enlisting on 3.02.1915 in Liverpool, NSW, Krantz served in the 17th Battalion at Gallipoli in 1915 and on the Western Front from 1916 to 1918. On the 5.04.1918 he was wounded at the battle for Dernancourt and was returned to Australia. He was discharged in April 1920. After the war Albert learnt the trade of electroplating and worked in Sydney. He married Emily Eliza Adams (Bridge) in 1922 and they had two children: Hazel Rose b. 1923 and Maxwell Albert b. 1925. Krantz died on 20.09.1980 in Kogarah, NSW.

Krantz Samuel
Кранц Самуил
Jewish background
Alias: changed surname to Grant in 1919
Born: 6.02.1888 in Odessa. Religion listed as Jewish.

Krantz arrived in Australia on 1.02.1905 with his younger brother Albert. He worked in a hotel in Perth, WA. Here he married Jeanetta Loffman in 1916, and they had two children, Zelda and Sonia. Krantz enlisted in Perth on 28.02.1916 and served in the 43rd Battalion on the Western Front, receiving the Military Medal for bravery on 4.07.1918 and being promoted to Lance Corporal. Wounded, he was discharged on 10.09.1919 and returned to Perth. He worked as a draper and died in Perth on 7.02.1942.

Kusmin Peter
Задорожний Самуїл
Ukrainian background
Born: 20.07.1888 in Kyiv. Religion listed as Greek Catholic.

Kusmin disembarked in September 1913 on Thursday Island, arriving from Vladivostok. Prior to enlistment he worked as a miner in Newcastle, NSW. Enlisting on 20.06.1916, he served in the 2nd Australian Tunnelling Company as a sapper on the Western Front in 1917. He was wounded during the advance on the Lagnicourt-Noreuil-Louveral line and was invalided to England, where he met and married Mabel Louisa Kneller. Apprehended by the censor as a Bolshevik sympathiser, he was returned to Australia and discharged two months later. He left his pregnant wife in England. Kusmin died in Sydney on 13.03.1959.

Lakovsky David
Лаковский Давид
Jewish background
Born: 5.01.1898 in Katerynoslav (now Dnipro). Religion listed as Jewish.

Lakovsky arrived in Australia on 28.07.1903 from Odessa with his family when he was five years old. Disembarking in Fremantle, the family lived in Perth, Broken Hill and Sydney. Lakovsky enlisted on 28.12.1917, at age 17, in South Head, NSW, serving in the 36th Heavy Artillery as a gunner. He only reached the Western Front a few days before the Armistice of 11 November 1918, and was discharged on 31.07.1919 in London. After his discharge, he went to the USA and then returned to Sydney, working as the General Sales Manager of Metro-Goldwyn-Mayer Pictures. Lakovsky died on 5.03.1953 in Sydney.

Lakovsky Edward
Лаковский Эдуард
Jewish background

Born: 24.05.1893 in Iuzovo (now Donetsk), Katerynoslav (now Dnipro region). Religion listed as Salvation Army.

Edward, the older brother of David Lakowsky, enlisted in Oaklands, SA on 14.01.1915, serving in the 10th Battalion in Egypt. He was returned to Australia as medically unfit and discharged on 12.06.1916. Lakovsky moved to Melbourne, where he married Hilda Isabel Hooper on 15.12.1917. They had seven children: Lenard, Raymond, David, Isabel, Leah, Bonny and Gertrude. Lakovsky was employed by the Victorian Railways and then worked as a letter carrier and as a boot repairer. He died on 11.09.1977 in Creswick, Victoria.

Lebovich Morris
Лебович Морис
Jewish background

Born: 1895 in Maikop, Russia or Odessa. Religion listed as Jewish.

Lebovich arrived in Fremantle, WA, as a child with his family on 6.05.1903. The family lived in Perth and Sydney. Enlisting in Sydney on 31.10.1916, Lebovich served in the 2nd Battalion on the Western Front from 1917 to 1918. While working as a stretcher bearer at Amiens, France he was severely wounded on 5.05.1918 and died of his wounds. He was buried at the Caestre Military Cemetery near Hazebrouck, France.

Lebovitz Elias
Лебович Элие
Jewish background

Born: 2.01.1888 in Lviv, Austria, while his parents were Russian subjects born in Kyiv. Religion listed as Jewish.

Lebovitz grew up in Palestine and came to Australia on 7.11.1910 from Port Said. He lived in Perth and Melbourne working as a farmer and labourer. Enlisting in Perth on 27.03.1915, he was assigned to the 28th Battalion and served at Gallipoli in 1915. Being transferred to the Camel Corps after the evacuation from Gallipoli, he served in Egypt from 1916 to 1917. On the 19.04.1917 he was severely wounded near Gaza and was repatriated to Australia, being discharged on 5.10.1917. After the war he married Pearl Kozminsky and settled in Melbourne, working as a fruiterer.

Leffow Jacob
Лефов Яків
Ukrainian or German background

Born: 1893 in Chernihiv. Religion listed as Greek Chr[istian].

Enlisting on 13.12.1915 in Casula, NSW, Leffow served in the 19th, 36th and 38th Battalions on the Western Front from 1916 to 1918. On the 31.08.1918 he was killed in the assault on Mount St Quentin near Peronne, France. He was buried in the Peronne Communal Cemetery Extension.

Lemish Aaron
Лемиш Арон
Jewish background

Born: 24.08.1889 in Vyshnivets, Volhynia (now Ternopil region). Religion listed as Hebrew.

Prior to his arrival in Australia, Lemish had deserted from the Russian army. He arrived in Brisbane on 1.01.1911 via Harbin, China. Enlisting on 17.06.1915 in Brisbane, he served in the 3rd Field Artillery Brigade, but was discharged six months later as medically unfit. He found work as a labourer in Victoria and married Rachel (Rae) Cruchek, with whom he had five children: Esther b.1918; Annie b.1920; Lazarus b.1922; Myer b.1924 and Morris b.1931. Lemish reenlisted during WWII on 27.01.1942 in Victoria. His sons Lazarus and Myer also served in the AIF in WWII. After WWII Lemish moved to Victoria and died in 1965 in Ivan, Victoria.

Leneve Morris
Левин Майер
Jewish background

Alias: served as Levin Myer

Born: 24.08.1890 in Kyiv. Religion listed as Jewish.

Arriving in Australia from Liverpool, England, Leneve disembarked in Sydney on 14.11.1912, finding work as a tailor. He enlisted on 16.10.1916 in Sydney, serving in the 7th Light Trench Mortar Battery. He deserted on 12.03.1917 while training in Sydney, was apprehended in Bathurst, NSW, court marshalled and sentenced to 120 days of hard labour. He was then returned to the training camp at Liverpool, NSW, but deserted once again on 18.02.1918. The warrant for his arrest was withdrawn. Leneve returned to Sydney and continued to work as a tailor. He married Daphne Warren in 1935 and they had a son, Maurice Lionel, who served in the AIF in WWII. Leneve died in Sydney in 1967.

Loosgie Stephen
Лущик Стефан
Ukrainian background

Born: 9.03.1886 in Voloskivtsi, Chernihiv. Religion listed as Greek Church.

Loosgie disembarked on 2.01.1914 in Brisbane from the Russian Far East and found work as a labourer on railway construction sites in Queensland. Enlisting on 20.02.1915 in Cairns, Qld, he served in the 26th Battalion at Gallipoli in 1915 and on the Western Front from 1916 to 1918. He was wounded on 26.03.1917 during the advance on the Lagnicourt-Noreuil-Louveral line and was hospitalised in England. Returning to the trenches after recovery, he left his unit, was caught and court martialled as a deserter, but was found not guilty and returned to his unit. After being gassed and wounded again, he was finally invalided back to Australia, arriving on 20.10.1918. He returned to Brisbane, where he ran a fruit shop. In 1924 he made an unsuccessful attempt to return to Ukraine. Loosgie died on 30.08.1963 in Brisbane.

Mackomel Samuel
Мукомель Самуил
Jewish background

Alias: served as Muchomel

Born: 15.09.1893 in Odessa. Religion listed as Russian.

Arriving in Australia from Russia on 10.01.1911, Mackomel disembarked in Fremantle, WA. He moved to Perth, where he found work as a blacksmith. Enlisting on 1.10.1915 in Perth, he served in the 10th Light Horse Regiment and the 4th Divisional Ammunition Column, serving as a temporary farrier sergeant on the Western Front from 1916 to 1919. He was discharged in Australia on 1.06.1919 and married Celia Golding, with whom he had a daughter, Rose, b. 1920. Mackomel ran a café in Perth, and died on 20.01.1952, being buried in Karakatta Cemetery.

Malisheff George
Чекман Петро

Ukrainian/Russian background

Alias: in 1916 stated that his correct name was Petr Fedorovich Checkman

Born: 1884 in Odessa or Yampil, Podillia (now Vinnytsia region). Religion listed as Church of England.

Malisheff had served in the Russian army prior to his arrival in Australia. Arriving around 1911, Malisheff worked in railway construction and mining in Queensland. He enlisted on 14.08.1915 in Rockhampton, Qld, serving in the 25th and 9th Battalions on the Western Front from 1916 to 1918. In 1916 he suffered shell-shock at Pozières. He recovered only to be killed on 17.04.1918 at Hazebrouck, France. Malisheff was buried at the Borre British Cemetery in France.

Mamchin John
Мамчин Іван
Ukrainian background

Born: 27.05.1889 in Odessa. Religion listed as Church of England.

Arriving in Australia from Russia on 6.02.1911, Mamchin disembarked in Brisbane, where he worked on railway construction. Enlisting on 12.02.1916 in Brisbane he was assigned to the Depot but was soon discharged as medically unfit. He tried to enlist two more times. After the war Mamchin worked on ships and died on 6.08.1921 aboard the ship *Maori* in Lyttleton, New Zealand.

Maximenko Efim
Максименко Ефим
Ukrainian background

Born: 1891 in 'Russia' and was, judging by his surname, most likely a Ukrainian. Religion listed as Greek Roman Catholic and Roman Catholic (Greek).

Maximenko arrived in Sydney in 1909 and found work as an engine fitter, a trade he had learnt in Russia. In 1915 he married Cora B. Peterson. Enlisting on 21.03.1916 in Sydney he served as a sapper in the 9th Field Company Engineers on the Western Front from 1916 to 1917. On the 7.06.1917 at Messines, Belgium, he died of wounds. Maximenko was buried in the Bailleul Communal Cemetery Extension, France.

Micolazyk Isaac
Міколайчик Ісак
Possibly Ukrainian background

Born: Probably in Ukraine

Micolazyk enlisted in January 1916 and was discharged in 1916. No service records have been located.

Morozoff Albert Nickalay
Морозов Альберт Николай
Russian background

Born: 4.03.1882 in Odessa (also stated Lublin, Poland). Religion listed as Roman Catholic and Church of England.

Morozoff arrived as a seaman in Australia from the USA, deserting his ship in Port Adelaide, SA on 20.11.1914. Enlisting five months later in Keswick, SA, he served in the 10th Battalion and the 24th Howitzer Brigade; later he served in the 45th and 50th Battalions at Gallipoli in 1915 and on the Western Front from 1916 to 1917, being wounded twice. He was returned to Australia on 26.09.1917 and was discharged in January the following year. Three months later, on 9.04.1918, he reenlisted in Adelaide, but by the time he came to England the war was nearly over. He was returned to Australia on 18.01.1919 and was discharged two months later. After his discharge Morozoff worked as a farmer in South Australia. He then left Australia, working on ships in the Pacific, and travelled on to California, USA where he remained. Morozoff died on 14.12.1945 in San Francisco, USA.

Morozoff Alfroniza
Морозов Афанасий
Russian background
Alias: Aphonasiy Cardapolop [Afanasy Kargopolov]; John Morris
Born: 17.03.1876 in Tobolsk, Siberia or Odessa. Religion listed as Roman Catholic.

Prior to his arrival in Australia, Morozoff had served in the Russian Navy. When the Russian naval ship *Gromoboi* visited Australia during the Federation celebration in 1901, Morozoff (and Huon Pollejuke) deserted in Melbourne. He found work as carpenter in Gippsland, Victoria. By the time he enlisted in 8.05.1915 at Cloncurry, Qld, he had changed his name to Jack Morris. He was assigned to the 25th Battalion to serve in Egypt, but was returned to Australia four months later and was discharged on 12.04.1916. He reenlisted at Charleville, Qld, on 28.11.1917 but was discharged again. After his discharge he moved around Queensland. Morozoff died in 1954 in Queensland.

Morozoff Dermy
Морозов Дмитрий
Russian background
Born: 1.09.1897 in Kharkiv. Religion listed as Orthodox.

He arrived in Australia in 1915 and resided in Melbourne and in Mildura, Victoria, finding work as a clerk and a salesman. He enlisted on 4.09.1916 in Melbourne and was assigned to the 5th Australian General Hospital. He was discharged three months later at his own request. After his discharge he continued living in Melbourne working as a salesman, but later moved to Shanghai, China and then, in 1938, to California, USA.

Neborotchko Victor
Неборочко Віктор
Ukrainian background
Born: 26.10.1881 in Odessa.

Neborotchko enlisted in April 1916 and was discharged soon afterwards. No service records have been located. He then moved to the USA and England, where he worked as a seaman.

Nesterenko Afanasy
Нестеренко Афанасій
Ukrainian background
Born: 15.08.1888 in Odessa.

Nesterenko arrived in Australia in 1911. He enlisted in January 1916 and was discharged soon afterwards. No service records have been located. Nesterenko lived in Sydney and worked as an inventor; the NSW Railway Department showed interest in four of his inventions, but nothing eventuated. He opened a machinery store in Goulburn Street Sydney which burnt down, and was found guilty of maliciously starting the fire. He was sentenced to two years hard labour in Goulburn, NSW. Nesterenko later moved to Victoria, where he died in 1955 in Camberwell.

Nesterinko Phillip
Нестерінко Пилип
Ukrainian background
Born: 10.10.1891 in Konotop, Chernihiv (now Sumy region). Religion listed as Roman Catholic.

Nesterinko worked as a locksmith in Sydney before his enlistment on 3.02.1915 in Liverpool, NSW. He requested a discharge on medical grounds and this was granted a month later. Nesterinko emigrated to the USA.

Nicholson Robert
Посельников Борис
Russian background
Alias: Boris Poselnikoff (original name)
Born: 14.12.1890 in Odessa (WWI service records) or the Caucasus (WWII service records). Religion listed as Church of England.

Nicholson was the son of a Russian colonel, and with the death of his parents, he joined a Russian sailing ship as a seaman. Landing in Newcastle, NSW, he worked on farms, as a sailor, and as a scaffolder in Melbourne. He enlisted on 14.07.1915, serving in the 30th Battalion and the 15th and 16th Field Artillery Brigades as a gunner on the Western Front from 1916 to 1918. While in hospital in England, he met Bertha Henrietta Grabert and they married on 2.11.1918. He was discharged on 11.02.1919 in London, where they stayed a few years before returning to Australia. Nicholson reenlisted on 24.05.1940 in Cairns during WWII, serving in the 15 Garrison Battalion. He was discharged as medically unfit on 28.01.1943. He died on 14.07.1962 in Queensland.

Noweetsky Leonard
Новицький Леонард
Ukrainian background

Born: 1891 in Zmerynka, Podillia (now Vinnytsia region). Religion listed as Roman Catholic.

Enlisting on 8.04.1915 in Rockhampton, Qld, Noweetsky served in the 26th Battalion as a driver at Gallipoli in 1915. Noweetsky survived Gallipoli but was killed at Tel-el-Kebir Egypt on 24.01.1916 in an accident. He was buried at the Tel-el-Kebir War Memorial Cemetery.

Oleinikoff Matfeus
Олійників Матей
Ukrainian background

Born: 16.11.1879 in Poltava. Religion listed as Methodist.

Prior to his arrival in Brisbane, Oleinikoff had served in the Russian army. He disembarked with his family (wife Daria, children: Paul b.1905, Vera b.1907, Ida b.1909, Peter b.1910) on 4.09.1912. He and his family moved to Cordalba, Qld, where four more children were born (Lucy b.1912, George b.1914, Harry b.1916, Eva Jean b.ca.1918). He enlisted on 10.05.1916 in Brisbane and served in the 26th Battalion in England from 1916 to 1917, before being discharged as medically unfit on 27.10.1917. After his discharge he moved with his family to Brisbane, but in 1926 he and his wife separated. Oleinikoff died on 30.12.1944 in Woolloongabba, Brisbane. During WWII their son Peter died while serving in the RAAF in England.

Ostrinko Alexay
Острінко Олексій
Ukrainian background

Alias: Alik Osmirko (WWI service), Ostrin (business name)

Born: 1895 in Monastyrysche, Poltava region. Religion listed as Roman Catholic.

Arriving from Siberia on 11.10.1912, Ostrinko disembarked in Brisbane and then moved to NSW, where he found work as a labourer. Enlisting on 23.03.1915 in Liverpool, NSW, he was assigned to the 20th Battalion (Depot). Two and a half months later he deserted. The warrant for his arrest was cancelled in 1919 and Ostrinko opened a photographic studio, 'Ostrin Studios', in Ayr, Qld. He married Mabel Sievers on 16.06.1928. Owing to ill-health, Ostrinko sold his studio in 1938, but continued working as a photographer. He died on 1.06.1989 in Townsville.

Ouchirenko John
Овчіренко Іван

Ukrainian background

Born: 20.08.1895 in Odessa. Religion listed as Roman Catholic.

Ouchirenko disembarked in Melbourne in January 1915 from the USA and found work as a mechanic. Enlisting on 1.05.1916 in Melbourne, he served in the 5th and 39th Battalions on the Western Front from 1917 to 1918, where he was wounded twice. While on leave in England in 1917, Ouchirenko met and married Clara Lane. They had a daughter, Ruby, b.1919, but the marriage did not last. On his discharge from the AIF on 4.02.1919 Ouchirenko returned to Melbourne alone. Here he worked as a mechanic in workshops in South Melbourne and in the merchant navy. In 1927 he married Doris Robertson, and moved with her to Ballarat, Vic, where four children, Ivan, David, Alex and Stepanita were born. In 1941 the family moved to Queenscliff, Vic, where another daughter, Ann, was born. During WWII Ouchirenko enlisted again, serving in the 3rd and 9th Garrison Battalions and the Ordinance Depot until the end of WWII. His son Alex served in the Royal Australian Navy during the Korean War, while his son David served in the Vietnam War. Ouchirenko died on 21.08.1971 in Heidelberg, Victoria.

Papchuck Denis
Папчук Денис/Данило

Ukrainian background

Alias: Daniel Papchuck (after 1930)

Born: 3.09.1891 in Berezdiv, Volhynia (now Khmelnytskyi region). Religion listed as Orthodox.

Papchuck disembarked in Geraldton, WA, on 20.03.1913 and was working on farms by the time of his enlistment on 16.10.1915 in Blackboy Hill, WA. Papchuck served in the Mining Corps, 3rd Tunnelling Company, as a Sapper on the Western Front from 1916 to 1918, where he was gassed. Discharged on 18.07.1919 in England, he married Edith Agnes Fletcher in November 1919 in Liverpool, and returned with her to Western Australia in 1920. They lived in the outback and had three children, but the marriage did not last and in 1928 they divorced. Afterwards Papchuck worked as a waterside labourer, but also had times of unemployment. He married Annie Mabel Hannan in 1932 and had a large family with her, but Annie died in 1943, aged 31. Struggling to look after his six children, Papchuck remarried in 1949 to Olive Emily Ivey in Fremantle. He died in Fremantle, WA, in 1958.

Peachenoff Feodot
Печенов Федот

Ukrainian background

Born: 7.06.1883 in Bratske, Kyiv region. Religion listed as Greek.

Prior to his arrival in Australia, Peachenoff had served in the Russian army. He disembarked in Brisbane on 16.10.1911 and worked for nearly two years on railway construction before he had saved enough money to bring his wife Mary and daughter Nina to join him. They bought an agricultural farm in

Booyal, Qld. Their son Victor was born in 1920. Enlisting on 8.12.1915 in Brisbane, Peachenoff served in the 5th Field Ambulance on the Western Front from 1916 to 1919. He was returned to Australia on 8.04.1919, being discharged three months later. Returning to Booyal, he worked in cane cutting in the southeast of Queensland; in 1926 Mary died and he married Akelina Maximenko, with whom he had two children, Helen b.1928 and Valentine b.1929. During WWII Peachenoff moved to Sydney, where he died in 1968. His son Victor served in the 2nd AIF.

Perlman Max
Перельман Макс
Jewish background

Born: 1.10.1896 in Odessa. Religion listed as Jewish.

Perlman was three years old when his family moved to Jerusalem and then Palestine. He left Palestine when he was 16, arriving in Fremantle, WA, on 27.08.1911. He was working as a marine collector when he enlisted on 29.10.1916 in Perth, serving in the Depot, but was discharged as medically unfit two months later. After the war he moved within Western Australia from Geraldton to Perth, then to Claremont, working as a bag merchant. He married Mary in 1927. During WWII, Perlman reenlisted on 24.07.1942 in Claremont, being assigned to the Cooking School. He was discharged on 2.04.1943. Perlman died in 1959 in Melbourne.

Pesmany Thomas
Письменный Томас
Jewish background

Born: 28.06.1893 in Hlukhiv, Chernihiv region (also stated place of birth as Warsaw, Poland). Religion listed as Jewish.

Arriving in Australia from Manchuria, Pesmany disembarked in Brisbane on 12.11.1911. Prior to enlistment he moved from Brisbane to Sydney and then to Melbourne, working as a labourer and cook. Enlisting on 17.08.1915 in Warwick Farm, NSW, he served in the 9th and 11th Field Ambulances. He served on the Western Front from 1916 to 1919, returning to Australia on 2.06.1919. In 1920 he left for San Francisco, USA.

Pieven Zacharias
Півень Захар
Ukrainian background

Born: 18.09.1882 in Chernihiv, in a Cossack family. Religion listed as Russian Orthodox.

Prior to his arrival in Australia Pieven had been employed as a fitter in Odessa shipbuilding yards, mechanical workshops in Sormovo, Nizhni Novgorod, Russia, and railway workshops in Harbin, where he married Klavdia Kroloiski. They had a daughter, Nadya (Ida) b.1911. Pieven arrived in Australia from Japan, disembarking in Brisbane on 11.02.1911. He worked as a machinist and fitter in Maryborough,

Qld, and Sydney, where his wife and daughter joined him. Their son Harold was born in 1913, but on 4.08.1914 Klavdia died, aged 22. Pieven remarried Josephine Enzenross in 1916 in Sydney and enlisted on 28.11.1916, but was discharged as medically unfit on the same day. Pieven died on 30.04.1917 in Marrickville Cottage Hospital from heart disease, and was buried at the Church of England cemetery in Rookwood, NSW.

Pinkevitch Constantine
Пінкевич Константин

Ukrainian background

Born: 21.05.1889 in Kyiv. Religion listed as Greek Church.

Pinkevitch disembarked in Brisbane on 6.03.1911 from Harbin, China, and worked at Mt Morgan, Qld, as a turner. Enlisting in Brisbane on 16.04.1915 he served in the 7th Field Ambulance Unit at Gallipoli in 1915 and on the Western Front from 1916 to 1918. Pinkevitch was returned to Australia on 19.02.1919 and was discharged four months later. He married Ellen Reynolds in 1920 in Mt Morgan, where he was working in the mines. They moved to Newcastle, NSW, and had three children: Constantine James b.1921; Leo b.1923, and Mary. There he found work as a turner and mechanic in the railway workshops. Both of his sons served in WWII. Pinkevitch died on 19.10.1962, and was buried in the Anglican section of the Sandgate Cemetery, Maitland, NSW.

Pivinski Walter
Півінський Володимир

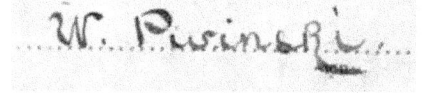

Ukrainian background

Born: 5.07.1887 (or 15.07.1882) in Odessa. Religion listed as Russian Church and Roman Catholic.

Prior to his arrival in Australia on 12.04.1914, Pivinski had served in the Russian navy. He enlisted on 4.05.1915 in Liverpool, NSW, serving in the 18th Battalion at Gallipoli in 1915, where he was heavily wounded in the Battle for Hill 971. He was returned to Australia in September 1915, reenlisted on 20.01.1916, but experiencing severe headaches on the boat and in Egypt, he was returned to Australia on 17.07.1916. He moved to London in 1917 and in 1919 he left for the USA, where he served in the US army in Manila. He later married and lived in Tacoma, Washington, USA. Pivinski died on 29.05.1943 in Tacoma.

Platonoff George
Платонов Юрій

Ukrainian/Russian background

Born: 3.05.1897 in Novoukrainka, Kherson region. Religion listed as Greek.

Platonoff disembarked in Brisbane on 12.11.1911 from the Russian Far East with his parents and older brother, Thomas Platonoff. The family settled at Booyal, Cordalba, Qld, where Platonoff worked with his brother as a labourer on the construction of the Cordalba-Dallarnil railway and on the family sugar cane farm in Booyal. Enlisting on 15.11.1915 in Brisbane, he served in the 25th Battalion on the Western Front from 1916 to 1919, where he was gassed at Passchendaele. He was returned to Australia on 20.05.1919. After his discharge Platonoff worked as a cane cutter and sawmill worker in the Childers and Innisfail areas of Queensland. He enlisted in the AIF in WWII, serving as a lance corporal in the 1st and 15th Garrison Battalions. He was discharged in 1943 and died on 23.08.1958 in Brisbane.

Platonoff Thomas
Платонов Тома
Ukrainian/Russian background

Alias: served as Platonaff, naturalised as Thomas Stephanus Platonoff

Born: 19.09.1892 in Novoukrainka, Kherson region. Religion listed as Roman Catholic.

Platonoff disembarked in Brisbane on 12.11.1911 from the Russian Far East with his parents and younger brother, George Platonoff. Enlisting on 17.01.1916 in Brisbane, a few months after his brother, he served in the 52nd Battalion on the Western Front from 1916 to 1917, being wounded twice. He was invalided to Australia and discharged on 29.11.1917. After his discharge Platonoff married Vera Kurtish in 1920 and they had three sons: Stanley b.1925, Thomas b.1927, and Peter b.1928. They resided in Booyal but then moved to Wundaru, where they continued the sugar cane business, but were evicted from their home during the Depression. During WWII the family moved to Rockhampton and then to Brisbane, where Platonoff worked as a wharf labourer and waterside worker. Platonoff died on 16.11.1954 in an accident on a ship in Brisbane.

Pollejuke Huon
Полещук Іван
Ukrainian background

Alias: Huon Pologouck (enlistment 1915); Jack Pollock

Born: 28.11.1878 in Ollenow, Podillia (possibly Olenevka, Vinnytsia region). Religion listed as Church of England.

Prior to his arrival in Australia, Pollejuke served in the Russian navy. Deserting the Russian navy ship *Gromoboi* in Melbourne in 1901, Pollejuke moved around Victoria, Tasmania, and New South Wales. In Melbourne he worked as a cook. Enlisting on 25.06.1915 in Liverpool NSW, he served in the 20th Battalion, but deserted three weeks later. He worked as a hawker in Surry Hills and died in Sydney on 13.07.1940.

Popow Alexander
Попов Александр
Russian background

Alias: In the USA changed his name to Peter Popow Alexander
Born: 21.11.1886 in Hlukhiv, Chernihiv region. Religion listed as Orthodox.

Popow, whose father was a general in the Russian army, studied in Belgium, receiving the Degree of Electrical Engineering at the University of Liege. Arriving in Australia from New Zealand in January 1914, he lived in Melbourne. He enlisted on 16.01.1915 in Melbourne and served in the 2nd Field Company Engineers as a sapper at Gallipoli in 1915, where he was wounded, and on the Western Front in 1916. Severely wounded at the Somme, Popow underwent multiple operations in England, being discharged in London on 4.06.1917. In 1919 he left for New York, settling in Boston, USA, where he married Eleanor Peirson in 1922, and had two children: Paul b.1924 and Lois. In the USA Popow worked in the field of electrometallurgy. Popow died on 24.01.1962 in Beverly, Massachusetts, USA.

Provaka Stephen
Проявка Стефан
Ukrainian/Russian background

Alias: Served under his original name Stepan Proiavka
Born: 14.09.1893 in Surazh, Chenihiv. Religion listed as Greek Church.

Provaka arrived in Australia from Russia via Harbin, China, disembarking on 30.07.1914 in Brisbane and working as a miner in Mount Morgan, Qld. Enlisting in Rockhampton, Qld, on 17.02.1916, he served in the 25th Battalion in England from 1916 to 1917. He was returned to Australia on 27.09.1917 and was discharged three months later. After the war he returned to Mount Morgan, then moved to Cairns and Newcastle, NSW, working as a labourer before settling in Brisbane. Provaka married Bertha Finnimore in 1927, and they had one child, Joyce, b.1928. Provaka died on 27.05.1941 in Brisbane.

Pshevolodskey Marian
Пшевлодский Марьян
Polish background

Alias: Mirien Millers
Born: 1881 in Bilka, Novohrad-Volynskyi region. Religion listed as Roman Catholic.

Prior to his arrival in Australia, Pshevolodskey had served in the Russian army in the Russo-Japanese War. He probably came to Queensland via the Russian Far East, and worked in Brisbane as a carpenter. Enlisting on 18.12.1914, Pshevolodskey served in the 15th Battalion at Gallipoli. On 9/10.05.1915, when his battalion was attacking the Turkish trenches facing Quinn's Post, he was killed. Pshevolodskey's name is commemorated at the Lone Pine Memorial on Gallipoli. His mother Paulina in Ukraine was never found.

Radetsky Sebastian
Радетський Севастян
Ukrainian background

Born: 1884 in Lidykhiv, Volhynia (now Ternopil region). Religion listed as Roman Catholic.

Prior to his arrival on 25.06.1912 in Brisbane via Japan, Radetsky had served in the Russian army. Enlisting on 18.12.1914 in Oaklands, SA, he served in the 10th Battalion at Gallipoli in 1915 and on the Western Front from 1916 to 1918, being wounded three times. He was returned to Australia on 21.03.1919 and discharged four months later. After his discharge, he lived in NSW. Radetsky died on 18.04.1935 in Sydney.

Rappeport Lionel
Раппепорт Леон
Jewish background

Born: 24.08.1885 in Nikopol, Dnipro region. Religion listed as Jewish.

Prior to his arrival in Australia, Rappeport had worked as a tailor in Russia. Disembarking in Fremantle, WA, on 10.01.1902 he remained in Fremantle, where he sold boots. His brother Samuel arrived in Fremantle two years later. Before enlisting, he was working as the keeper of a wine and soft drink saloon. Rappeport enlisted on 3.09.1917 in Perth and was assigned to serve in the Depot, but was discharged four months later. He married Miriam and they had four children: Sydney b.1911, Rachel b.1913, Gilbert b.1921, and Phillip b.1924. They lived in Perth, where Rappeport worked as fruiterer and greengrocer. He died in 1960.

Rappeport Samuel
Раппепорт Самуил
Jewish background

Born: 8.07.1890 in Nikopol, Dnipro region. Religion listed as Jewish.

Rappeport disembarked in Fremantle, WA, on 17.10.1904 when he was 14, joining his older brother Lionel who had arrived two years earlier. He found work in Perth as a bootmaker. Enlisting on 23.05.1916 in Melbourne, he served in the 43rd Battalion on the Western Front from 1917 to 1918. He was gassed and was discharged in Australia on 7.03.1919. He returned to Perth, then moved to Mount Lawley, WA. In 1925 he married Clara Dabscheek. He reenlisted during WWII and was assigned to the 10th Garrison Battalion. In 1946, while crossing a road in Mount Lawley, Rappeport was hit by a car. He was taken to the Royal Perth Hospital, where he died on 4.09.1946.

Rayzner Alexander
Райзнер Александр
Jewish background

Born: 3.07.1888 in Odessa. Religion listed as Protestant.

Prior to his arrival in Australia, Rayzner had lived in Hong Kong for four years. Disembarking in Brisbane on 9.04.1913, he soon moved to Sydney, where he worked as a tailor. Enlisting on 15.02.1917 in Sydney, he was assigned to the Light Trench Mortar Battery, serving in a Depot, but was discharged on 15.08.1917 as medically unfit. After his discharge Rayzner moved to Victoria, living in Melbourne and Armadale, where he settled with Ethel Bennett in 1918. They had a son, David b.1921. Rayzner died in 1964 in Melbourne.

Rink Christian
Ринк Кристиан
French/Russian background

Born: 16.01.1872 in Odessa (enlistment, alien registration) or Bordeaux, France (naturalisation). Religion listed as Orthodox.

Rink disembarked in Sydney from the USA, in September 1899 or in September 1905, moving around NSW from Broken Hill to Newcastle to Sydney, working as an electrician and mechanic. He enlisted in Sydney on 16.02.1916, serving in the 8th and 7th Field Company Engineers as a sapper and in the Australian Flying Corps on the Western Front from 1916 to 1917. After being court martialled for insubordination, Rink was returned to Australia on 12.03.1918 and discharged three months later as 'undesirable', as it was suspected that he was of German origin. After his discharge he married Teressa Tobin in 1919 in Brisbane. He then moved to the southern region of Western Australia, to Collie and Albany, where he was a part-licensee of a hotel. In 1931 he moved to New Zealand, where he was sentenced to 12 years imprisonment for discharging a firearm to resist arrest. After his release he married Clare and stayed in New Zealand, working as a mechanic, wine agent and builder. Rink died on 4.02.1961 in Christchurch, New Zealand

Roomianzoff Nicholas
Румянцев Микола
Ukrainian/Russian background
Alias: Romanzoff

Born: 8.01.1892 in Sabadash, now Cherkasy region. Religion listed as Russian Church.

Roomianzoff disembarked in Brisbane on 24.02.1914 from the Russian Far East. Enlisting in Rockhampton, Qld, on 1.04.1915, he served in the 9th Battalion and 49th Battalions at Gallipoli and on the Western Front. Wounded two times, he was returned to Australia on 5.04.1919 and discharged three months later. After his discharge Roomianzoff moved between North Queensland and the Northern

Territory for many years, working as a labourer on the railway in the Mackay area and as a waterside worker. Roomianzoff was naturalised not long before his death in Cairns in 1974.

Rosenfield Reuben Laman
Розенфельд Рубен

Jewish background

Alias: in 1933 changed name to Rosefield

Born: 1872 in Raiseinai, Lithuania. Religion listed as Jewish.

Rosenfield's family moved to Simferopol, Crimea, where his younger siblings were born and where he studied at a Government school. In 1888 the family came to Melbourne, where Rosenfield trained as a saddler and attended classes in the Working-man's College. He enrolled at the University of Melbourne, studying medicine. Graduating from the university, he worked as a medical practitioner in Whitecliff, NSW, and Melbourne. In 1899 he married Harriett Witkowski in Melbourne and had two sons, Albert Lister b.1901 and Clifford Leslie b.1903. Enlisting in the AIF on 27.07.1915, he served in the Australian Medical Corps, attaining the rank of major. During his first service in 1915-1916 he worked in hospitals in Egypt. Being reappointed in 1917, he served in Britain. After the war he continued his medical practice in Melbourne. Rosenfield died in Melbourne in 1958.

Rossoggsky Ivan
Росовський Іван

Ukrainian background

Alias: Rossovsky (most likely the correct name)

Born: 1894 in 'Vyndery' (likely Bendery, now Moldova) or in Odessa. Religion listed as Roman Catholic.

Prior to enlistment Rossoggsky worked at Glenrock Station (near Scone, NSW). Enlisting on 9.02.1916 in West Maitland, he served in the 34th Battalion on the Western Front from 1916 to 1917, attaining the rank of lance sergeant. Wounded in 1917, Rossogsky rejoined his battalion and was killed a week later, on 12.07.1917 at Messines, Belgium. Having no known grave, his name is recorded on Menin Gate Memorial, Ypres, and the Scone War Memorial. The Army were unable to contact Rossoggsky's mother to notify her of his death.

Rothman Leon
Ротман Леон

Jewish background

Born: 6.02.1896 in Odessa. Religion listed as Jewish.

Rothman arrived in Australia from Harbin, China on 1.01.1914 with his parents. The family disembarked and lived in Brisbane, where Rothman worked in jewellery. Enlisting on 6.09.1915 in Brisbane, he was discharged a month later as he was underage and did not have the consent of his parents. In

1917 he married Elsie Meerkin from Melitopol and they had six children: Samuel b.1918, Aaron b.1919, Samuel b.1921, Rose Ray b.1923, Phillip b.1925, and Abraham b.1930. During WWII Aaron and Samuel served in the AIF and Rose Ray served in the RAAF. Rothman worked in Brisbane as a salesman, but by 1930 the family moved to Sydney, where he found employment as a painter. Rothman died on 21.02.1953 in Sydney.

Rothstein Morris
Ротштейн Морис
Jewish background

Born: 1898 in Cherkavosk (Cherkasy?). Religion listed as Jewish.

Rothstein came to Melbourne in 1915 as a seaman, working there as a steward. Enlisting on 18.11.1916, he served in the 2nd Pioneer Battalion and the 5th Field Artillery Brigade on the Western Front from 1918 to 1919. Rothstein was returned to Australia on 19.06.1919. After his discharge he lived in Coburg, Victoria, and then in Sydney. He married Rachel Glick and had three children: Sarah, Deborah and Bella. Rothstein died in Sydney on 4.05.1953.

Rudezky Joseph
Рудецький Йосип
Ukrainian background

Born: 04.04.1890 in Skvyra, Kyiv region. Religion listed as Greek Church.

Prior to his arrival in Townsville, Qld, on 16.08.1913, Rudezky had served in the Russian army. He worked as a chauffeur in Queensland and on Thursday Island; he enlisted on 1.04.1915 in Rockhampton, serving in the 26th Battalion at Gallipoli in 1915 and on the Western Front in 1916. Being wounded, he was returned to Australia on 4.05.1917 and discharged three months later. After his discharge he returned to Queensland, moving to Brisbane, then Halifax, Townsville and Ingham in North Queensland, cutting sugar cane. He became ill from tuberculosis and in the sanatorium in Stanthorpe he met and married Agnes Annie Burns in 1920. They had five children: Lilly, Violet, Tanya, Doris and Tamara. The family later moved further north to the drier climate of Dalby, where Rudezky died on 7.02.1931.

Rudovsky Joseph
Рудовский Иосиф
Croatian background

Alias: surname: Mikulicic (original name); naturalised as 'Mikulicic (known as Rodd)'
Born: 19.03.1894 or 1895 in Susek, Yugoslavia, although enlisting in the AIF he gave his place of birth as Odessa. Religion listed as Church of England.

Arriving in Port Pirie, SA on 16.08.191, Rudovsky deserted his ship. He stayed in Port Pirie, then moved to Adelaide and from there to NSW, from Broken Hill to Newcastle, Sydney and Scarborough. He worked in mines and as a barman. Enlisting on 16.11.1915 in Casula, NSW, he served in the 1st

Tunnelling Company as a sapper on the Western Front from 1916 to 1918. He suffered gas poisoning at Messines and was returned to Australia on 2.03.1919, where he was discharged. After the war he lived in Sydney, where he married Neredah Victoria Withers and furthered his education. In 1937 he was appointed honorary consul for Yugoslavia, using the name Joseph Mikulicic-Rodd. After the death of Neredah, he married Gwendolin Hawkins in 1945. Rudovsky lived in Sydney until his death in 1980.

Sadagoursky Harry
Садогурский Пинхас
Jewish background
Alias: in the 1920s changed name to Harry Leon.
Born: 19.08.1897 in Odessa. Religion listed as Jewish.

Sadagoursky arrived in Australia with his parents from Palestine, where the family had moved. They disembarked in November 1912 in Fremantle, WA. Sadagoursky enlisted on 6.07.1916 in Perth, but was discharged a few months later as he was found to be underage. He found work as a horse breaker and then as a carter of bread for a bakery. On 9.01.1918 in Perth, he again enlisted but was rejected, owing to an injury sustained at work. Sadagoursky married Sadie Leon and in the 1920s moved to Melbourne, working as a fruiterer at the Victoria, Prahran and Dandenong markets. He died in 1959.

Saffar Morris
Сейфер Мойше
Jewish background
Born: 20.05.1887 in Volhynia (WWI attestation) or Ostrow, Poland (consul's information) or Paris, France (naturalisation and WWII attestation). Religion listed as Jewish (WWI) and Roman Catholic (WWII).

Saffar disembarked in May 1912 in Fremantle, WA, and then moved to Perth. Enlisting in Perth on 15.03.1916, he served in the 3rd Division Cyclist Company and the 51st Battalion on the Western Front in 1918. Being wounded, he was invalided to England then returned to Australia on 11.12.1918. He was discharged three months later. After his discharge Saffar moved to Brisbane and Melbourne, where he worked as a mechanic, a panel beater, and a chef. In 1922 he helped his wife Sarah and daughters Ella and Freda come to Australia from Ukraine after ten years apart; their daughter Millie was born in Australia. Saffar enlisted during WWII and served in the 3rd District Ordnance workshops. He moved to the Soldiers' Home in Myrtlebank, SA in 1947. Saffar died on 12.09.1947 in Adelaide.

Sage Lamotte Alexis
Саж Ламоте Алексис
French/Russian background
Born: 12.03.1874 in Odessa. Religion listed as 'Slav'.

Before landing in Albany, WA, on 11.11.1898, Sage served for three years in a 'Cossack Regiment' in

Russia. He worked in railway line construction in Albany. Enlisting in his forties on 18.01.1915 in Perth, Sage served in the 1st and 3rd Divisional Ammunition Columns and 3rd Field Artillery Brigade as a gunner and driver at Gallipoli in 1915 and on the Western Front from 1916 to 1918. While in a British hospital, he met Rosa Hales and they married before Sage was sent to the Western Front. On 9.07.1919 he returned to Australia with his wife and young daughter, Lillian b.1917. Their son Frank was born in 1923, but died in 1927. The family lived in Western Australia where Sage took up farming.

Sank Alexander Paul
Цанк Александр
Russian/Jewish background

Born: 4.08.1895 in Aleksandrovsk (now Zaporizhia). Religion listed as Greek and Russian Jewish.

Sank's family moved to Harbin, China in 1906, and Sank served in the Russian army. In 1913 Sank followed his brother to Australia, disembarking on 9.10.1913 in Brisbane. A motor mechanic by trade, he worked in Rockhampton, Qld, as a labourer and driver before enlisting on 24.07.1915 in Rockhampton, serving in the 25th and 9th Battalions on the Western Front in 1916. Being wounded, he was invalided to England for treatment and returned to Australia on 31.08.1916, being discharged a few months later. Sank reenlisted on 28.08.1917 and was on home service for seven months. After the war he remained in Queensland, working as a motor driver and tram guard. In 1921 he returned to his family in Harbin and in 1922 moved to Khabarovsk, Russia, working as an interpreter on the Ussury Railway, later marrying and moving to Novosibirsk, Russia, where he worked as an industrial supply agent. In 1951 he was arrested and sent to the GULAG for 'espionage' and 'anti-Soviet agitation', being released after Stalin's death.

Sast Alexander
Саст Александр
Russian background

Born: 27.10.1888 in Odessa. Religion listed as Church of England.

Sast fled Russia in his late teens to avoid military conscription, arriving on 3.08.1912 in Port Adelaide, SA. Sast worked in South Australia, in Port Pirie and Kilkenny, then Broken Hill, NSW, as a motor mechanic and fitter. Enlisting on 31.08.1914 in Morphettville, SA, he served in the 10th Battalion at Gallipoli in 1915. He was wounded twice, and was taken prisoner of war by the Turkish army in July 1915. He escaped captivity, reaching the British Army in Archangelsk, Russia. Smuggled to the UK, he was screened by the Court of Enquiry and continued his service on the Western Front, in the 3rd Australian Ammunition Sub Park and the 3rd Mechanical Transport Company from 1917 to 1918. He returned to Australia on 24.09.1919. After his discharge, Sast moved to Melbourne, where he met and married Charlotte Elizabeth (nee Hodkinson) Collidge in 1926. The family then moved to Sydney. Sast died on 2.06.1928 in the Prince of Wales Hospital in Randwick, NSW, of heart failure.

Sepscak John
Сепшак Іван
Ukrainian/Polish (?) background

Born: 13.10.1883 in 'Hopszywnica, Russia' (naturalisation interview); 'Romen, Russia' (newspaper advertisement). The former place could correspond to Koprzywnica in Poland, the latter to Romny in Ukraine. Religion listed as Greek Church.

Sepscak disembarked in Brisbane in December 1911 from Russia. He worked on farms in Albury, NSW, and Mahonga Station, NSW. Enlisting on 21.01.1916 in Cootamundra, NSW, he served in the 56th Battalion and the Anzac Light Railway on the Western Front from 1916 to 1917. He was heavily wounded, was returned to Australia on 24.01.1918, and discharged six months later. After his discharge Sepscak moved from Sydney to somewhere 'in the mountains'. He then settled on land in Bilboa near Kingaroy, Qld, under the Soldiers' Settlement scheme, working as a farmer. He committed suicide in Queensland in 1946.

Serebrennikoff Elias Jacob
Серебренников Яков
Russian/Jewish background

Alias: served as Serennikoff

Born: 28.05.1878 in Mikhailivka, Melitopol region. Religion listed as Greek Orthodox.

Serebrennikoff was well-educated and served in the Russian army as a sergeant-major. He arrived in Australia in 1915 and worked as a clerk in Mordialloc, Victoria. His profession was a botanist. Enlisting on 22.03.1915 on board the troop ship *Runic* in Colombo, he served in the 6th Battalion at Gallipoli. Two days after landing at Gallipoli he was wounded, and was returned to Melbourne, where he was discharged on 22.03.1916. After his discharge, Serebrennikoff worked for the Russian Consul-General Alexander Abaza, promoting enlistment among Russian emigrants in the AIF. Serebrennikoff married Alice Maud Swanson in 1917 and took up farming in Victoria. He was also involved in the exploration of oil deposits on Elko Island in the Northern Territory. Serebrennikoff died on 19.06.1927 in Dandenong, Victoria.

Shular Maxim
Шуляр Максим
Ukrainian background

Born: 10.08.1885 in the village of Paralub (?), Sosnytsia, Chernihiv region. Religion listed as Greek Church.

Arriving in Australia on 25.11.1914, Shular worked around North Queensland as a labourer. Enlisting on 10.05.1916 in Rockhampton, Qld, he was assigned to a Depot but was discharged as medically unfit four months later. Shular reenlisted on 10.04.1917 in Townsville, Qld, but was again discharged as medically unfit. He then lived in Brisbane.

Smoisen Abraham
Смойшен Абрам
Jewish background

Born: 1894 in Kherson. Religion listed as Jewish.

Arriving in Australia, Smoisen worked as a tailor in Sydney and married Bertha Landes in 1912. By the time of his enlistment on 7.01.1916 in Liverpool, NSW, they had two children. Smoisen served in the 1st and 2nd Light Horse Field Ambulance and the 2nd Australian Stationary Hospital in Egypt and Palestine from 1916 to 1918. He was returned to Australia on 26.01.1919 and was discharged three months later. After his discharge Smoisen returned to Sydney, but his marriage ended in divorce in 1927, and he moved to London.

Snegovoy Andrew
Снеговой Андрей
Russian background

Born: 1881 in Odessa. Religion listed as Church of England.

Snegovoy arrived in Brisbane on 3.04.1910 from Harbin, China. He worked in Brisbane as a motor driver, and on 9.03.1916 he enlisted, serving in the 49th Battalion on the Western Front from 1916 to 1918, being wounded twice. Returning to the field, he left his battalion on 12.09.1918 and was found guilty of desertion. His sentence was remitted at the end of the war and he was discharged on 11.10.1919, returning to Brisbane, then living in Newcastle and Sydney.

Sologub Egnaty
Сологуб Гнат
Ukrainian background

Born: 1883 in Konotop, Chernihiv. Religion listed as Roman Catholic.

Prior to his arrival in Australia, Sologub had served in the Russian army. Leaving his wife Domna and two children in Sosnovka, in the Russian Far East, Egnaty disembarked in Brisbane on 10.11.1912. He enlisted in Cloncurry, Qld, on 26.08.1916, serving in the 11th Field Company Engineers as a sapper on the Western Front from 1917 to 1919. He was returned to Australia on 8.05.1919 and was discharged four months later. Egnaty likely returned to the Russian Far East, as he had applied for permission to travel there in 1921.

Spisbah Alexander
Списбах Александр
Russian/German background

Born: 12.04.1877 in St Petersburg, Russia or Kharkiv, Ukraine. Religion listed as Orthodox.

Prior to his arrival in Australia, Spisbah had served in the Russian army headquarters. Moving to England, he married Lydia Batoulina (b. Orenburg) in 1911 in Liverpool. They had a son, George. The family disembarked in Albany, WA, on 16.03.1911. Spisbah worked as a miner in Kurraway and Boulder, WA. Enlisting on 13.11.1916 at Blackboy Hill, WA, he was discharged a few months later as medically unfit. After his discharge the family moved to Perth, then to Harvey and Mornington, WA, where Spisbah worked in a sawmill. When the mill closed, Spisbah was unable to find work, and committed suicide on 29.04.1934.

Steinberg Jack
Стейнберг Джек
Jewish background

Born: 1882 in Odessa (enlistment) or Brest, Belarus (naturalisation). Religion listed as Jewish.

After several years in Palestine, Steinberg came with his wife Ethel to Perth, where he worked as a cabinet-maker. Enlisting on 18.05.1917 in Perth, Steinberg was discharged as medically unfit two months later. Steinberg and his wife continued living in Perth, but by 1940 they had moved to Brisbane. Steinberg committed suicide on 5.01.1944 in Queensland.

Surovsov Stephen
Суровцев Степан
Russian background

Born: 2.08.1891 (WWI enlistment) or 2.08.1882 (WWII enlistment) in Klimov, Chernihiv region. Religion listed as Roman Catholic (WWI enlistment) and Greek Orthodox (WWII enlistment).

Prior to his arrival in Australia from the Russian Far East, Surovsov had served in the Russian army as a Corporal. He disembarked on 23.05.1914 in Brisbane, working as a miner at Balgowan Colliery near Oakey, Qld. Enlisting on 9.10.1915 in Toowoomba, Qld, he served in the 1st Tunnelling Company as a Sapper on the Western Front from 1916 to 1918, being promoted to Corporal, and was Mentioned in Despatches in 8.11.18. He was returned to Australia on 20.04.1919 and discharged three months later. After his discharge he moved to the Newcastle area, marrying Lily Kathleen Harrison in 1925. They lived in NSW, and then moved to Willoughby, where Surovsov worked as a gardener. They divorced in 1939. Surovsov reenlisted during WWII, serving in the 7th Garrison Battalion. Surovsov died on 17.01.1943 while on service, and was buried at the Lutwyche Cemetery, Brisbane.

Tardent Emile Augustus
Тардент Эмиль Август
Swiss background

Born: 9.04.1880 in Mykolaiv. Religion listed as Roman Catholic.

The Swiss family of Tardent came to Australia on 10.12.1887. Tardent's father, Henry, had studied at Odessa University. The family initially settled in Roma, Qld. Prior to enlisting, Tardent worked as a land ranger in Nanango, Qld. He married Marguerite Agnes Eva Doyle and they had 5 children: Enid Margaret b.1909; Leslie Vivian b.1911; Irene May b.1913; Esme Agnes b.1914; Ronald b.1922. Enlisting on 16.10.1916, Tardent served in the 9th and 42nd Battalions on the Western Front from 1917 to 1918, attaining the rank of corporal and receiving the Military Medal. Severely wounded, Tardent was returned to Australia on 16.03.1919 and discharged three months later. After his discharge, Tardent worked as a journalist and served for some years as an alderman of Wynnum Council, Qld. Tardent died in Wynnum on 1.04.1933.

Tchorzewski George Marion
Чоржевский Георгий Марьян
Polish background

Born: May 1870 in Ukraine or 'Russian Poland'. Religion listed as Roman Catholic.

The Tchorzewski family disembarked on 23.08.1882 in Rockhampton, Qld, settling at Bingera Plantation near Bundaberg, where they established a sugar cane farm. Tchorzewski enlisted on 27.03.1916 in Brisbane, serving in the 52nd Battalion in England from 1916 to 1917. He was returned to Australia on 8.04.1917 and discharged three months later. After his discharge, Tchorzewski moved to South Kolan, Bundaberg, Qld, where he worked as a farmer, and in 1924 married Polly Sakaranko. Tchorzewski died on 22.10.1944 in Queensland.

Tkachenko Saveliy
Ткаченко Савелій
Ukrainian background

Born: 03.10.1894 in Husiatyn, Kamianets-Podilskyi region. Religion listed as Greek Church.

Tkachenko disembarked in Townsville, Qld, on 27.10.1913, arriving via Siberia. He worked as a labourer in Townsville and Brisbane. Enlisting in Townsville on 08.03.1915, he served in the 25th and 26th Battalions at Gallipoli and on the Western Front from 1916 to 1918. He was court martialled for wounding himself and for being absent from his post on several occasions, being sentenced to 'penal servitude for life'. The sentence was suspended soon afterwards and he was sent back to the trenches. Returning to Australia on 28.03.1919, he attempted to return to Ukraine, but finally settled in Brisbane, working on the railways. Tkachenko was over 90 years of age when he died on 24.10.1985.

Tkachuk Peter
Ткачук Петро
Ukrainian background

Born: 06.08.1894 in Dubno, Volhynia (now Rivno region). Religion listed as Russian.

Tkachuk arrived in Brisbane on 15.10.1916, moving to Sydney, where he worked as a blacksmith before enlisting two months later. He served in the 7th and 2nd Light Horse Regiments and the 9th Battalion in Egypt and Palestine from 1917 to 1918 and on the Western Front from 1918 to 1919. Tkachuk was returned to Australia on 18.07.1919 and was discharged two months later. He moved to Newcastle in 1921 and worked as a sailor, but in 1922 was hospitalised in Gladesville Mental Hospital, NSW, where he died in 1926.

Tober Albert Michael
Тобер Михаил
Russian/German background

Born: 17.03.1890 in Volhynia. Religion listed as Russian Church and Church of England.

A seaman, Tober arrived in Australia in June 1913, disembarking in Port Adelaide, SA. He worked a blacksmith, motor driver and mechanic in Adelaide before enlisting on 27.02.1915 in Keswick, SA. He served in the 10th Battalion at Gallipoli in 1915, He became ill, was invalided back to Australia in March 1916, and discharged on 4.07.1916. After his discharge he moved to Melbourne. He married Lily Teresa Lawler in 1917 and they had four children: Albert b.1920, Patrick James b.1921, Mary Joan b.1923, and Olga. reenlisting on 24.01.1917 in Melbourne, Tober was assigned to the Engineers Reinforcements Unit, serving at the Depot. He was discharged seven months later as medically unfit. After the war the family moved to different areas of NSW and the ACT, with Tober working as a carpenter on various construction projects. Tober died in July 1960 in Sydney.

Trager Samuel
Траер Ешуа
Jewish background

Born: 1899 in Mykolaiv. Religion listed as Jewish.

Trager came to Brisbane with his parents and four siblings in 1911. The family settled in Brisbane, where Trager received the profession of a boot clicker. He enlisted in Sydney on 4.11.1915, but was discharged a month later as medically unfit. In 1917 he reenlisted but after a conflict with his CO he ran away from the unit. In the years after the war he was involved in petty crime, finally settling in Brisbane. He died on 15.11.1950 in Sydney.

Vengert Jack
Венгерт Иван
Russian/German/Jewish (?) background

Born: 2.05.1891 in Kyiv or Odessa. Religion listed as Russian and Church of England. His headstone in Rookwood Cemetery has Jewish denomination, which is doubtful, as Vengert never appeared in Australian records as Jewish.

Arriving in Australia from Russia via China, Vengert disembarked in 1913 in Brisbane. He moved from Brisbane to Sydney and then to Wyong, NSW, where he worked as a cook before enlisting on 16.02.1915 in Liverpool, NSW. Vengert served in the 18th Battalion at Gallipoli. Wounded, he was returned to Australia on 2.02 1916 and was discharged four months later. Vengert moved to Dora Creek near Newcastle, NSW, where he worked as a railway watchman. He married Emma Adeline Gudshus in 1917, and they had two children, Rita and Elsie, but the marriage later ended in divorce. Vengert reenlisted on 24.05.1918 in Gosford, NSW, and was assigned again to the 18th Battalion to serve on the Western Front. He sailed to England in July 1918 but arrived on the Western Front after the Armistice. Returning to Australia on 9.08.1919, he was discharged a few weeks later. He ran an illicit wine bar in Sydney before moving to Brisbane, where he opened a fruit shop. He later returned to Sydney, renting out flats. Vengert died on 17.12.1963 in Sydney.

Volkofsky Theofil
Волковські Теофіль
Polish/Ukrainian background

Born: 5.11.1885 in Lypky, now Zytomyr region. Religion listed as Roman Catholic.

Arriving in Brisbane on 21.08.1910 via China and Japan, Volkofsky moved from Brisbane to Sydney, and to Bourke, NSW, working in river fishing. Volkofsky's younger brother Cezar Wolkowsky arrived in Australia in 1914. Enlisting on 8.06.1916 in Dubbo, NSW, Volkofsky was assigned to the 33rd Battalion, but was discharged six months later suffering from pulmonary tuberculosis. Moving to Mount Boppy near Cobar, NSW, he worked in an apiary, becoming later a grazier at Olino Station, Cobar. He married Thelma McKean in 1928 in Cobar and they had 3 children: John b.1929; Anita b.1931 and Thomas b.1933. Volkofsky died on 6.06.1974 in Hornsby, NSW.

Vurhaft Joseph
Вургафт Иосиф
Jewish background

Born: 10.02.1893 in Odessa. Religion listed as Church of England.

Arriving in Cairns, Qld, on 29.12.1912 from China, Vurhaft remained in Queensland, where he worked as a gardener. He enlisted on 25.01.1916 in Rockhampton, serving in the 9th Battalion on the Western Front from 1916 to 1917. He was severely wounded at the battle for Menin Road, losing his arm, and was invalided back to Australia on 11.02.1918, being discharged nine months later. He left Australia in 1919 for Hong Kong and from there travelled to San Francisco, USA, where he remained. Vurhaft died in San Francisco on 29.12.1969.

Whynsky William
Винський Володимир
Ukrainian or Polish background
Alias: Whensky, Whinsky; served as Whnsky

Born: 1881 in Vehesky (?). Religion listed as Roman Catholic.

Whynsky came to Australia in about 1910 and worked as a stone dresser in Helidon near Toowoomba. Enlisting on 10.03.1915 in Brisbane, he served in the 25th Battalion at Gallipoli and on the Western

Front in 1916. He was severely wounded at Pozières, France, was returned to Australia on 13.02.1917, and was discharged three months later. He resumed his work as a stone dresser at Helidon and then moved to Brisbane in December 1920. A few days after moving to Brisbane, Whynsky committed suicide on 18.12.1920.

Winning Alexander Barr
Виннинг Александр Бар
British background

Born: 17.09.1892 in Kharkiv. Religion listed as Presbyterian.

Winning's Scottish father, a mining engineer, died in Kharkiv when he was three years old, and his mother moved to Glasgow with her infant sons. Winning was educated in Glasgow, undertaking an apprenticeship and studies in building construction. He migrated to Australia on 11.06.1912, arriving in Albany, WA, and moving to Perth, where he worked as an assistant in an architectural firm. Enlisting on 2.07.1916 in Perth, he served in the 11th Battalion on the Western Front from 1917 to 1919. After his discharge in Britain on 5.06.1920, he stayed in Glasgow, undertaking further studies. Returning to Perth, he resumed work in the same architectural firm where he had worked before the war, as a chief assistant. He married Dorothy Major in 1923 and they had three children: Olga Patricia b.1924, Ian Stewart Barr b.1926, and George Alexander b.1934. Winning became an architect, being involved in the design of many buildings in Perth. In 1945 he was elected as the President of the WA Charter of the Royal Australian Institute of Architects. Winning died 20.03.1963 in Perth.

Wolkowsky Cezar
Волковські Цезар
Polish/Ukrainian background

Born: 19.04.1894 in Lypky, now Zytomyr region. Religion listed as Roman Catholic.

Prior to his arrival in Sydney on 1.08.1914, Wolkowsky studied in a military school in Russia for three years. He sailed to Australia on the invitation of his elder brother, Theofil Volkofsky, who had settled in Bourke, NSW. Enlisting on 26.05.1915 in Liverpool, NSW, Wolkowsky served in the 19th Battalion at Gallipoli in 1915, being wounded two weeks after landing. He was invalided to Australia on 11.04.1916 and discharged eight months later. Returning to Sydney, Wolkowsky worked as a tram conductor and married Gwynnyth Rhodee Woodberry in 1919. They had two children, Marea Victusya and Sonia Mae. Wolkowsky died in 1970 in Sydney.

Woolf Isaac
Вульф Ісаак
Jewish background

Born: 1870 in Uman, Cherkasy region. Religion listed as Jewish Russian.

He arrived in Australia some time before 1892 and found work as a shoemaker in Adelaide. Enlisting in

Morphettville, SA on 5.10.1914, he was assigned to the 4th Field Ambulance, however his application was cancelled a week later, perhaps because of his age (he was nearly 45).

Zines Joseph Morris
Цинес Иосиф Морис
Jewish background

Born: 1895 in Kamianets-Podilskyi (also stated he was born in St Petersburg). Religion listed as Jewish.

Zines was thirteen when he arrived with his family in Australia from Port Said, Egypt. They disembarked in Fremantle, WA, on 6.12.1907. Living in Perth, Zines learnt the trade of a tailor. Enlisting on 19.11.1914 in Blackboy Hill, WA, he served in the 12th and 52nd Battalions at Gallipoli in 1915 and on the Western Front in 1916. He was wounded at Mouquet Farm, France on 3.09.1916 and was recommended for an award. Zines was returned to Australia on 20.12.1917 and discharged four months later. After the war he moved to Sydney, where he worked as a tailor. Zines died in 1971 in Sydney.

Zmood Woolf
Жмуд Зеев
Jewish background

Born: 2.01.1893 in Andriivka, Taurida (now Zaporizhia region). Religion listed as 'Synagogue'.

Zmood disembarked on 19.01.1910 in Melbourne, where his sister lived, later working as a commercial traveller. He enlisted on 16.12.1915 in Cootamundra, NSW, and served in the 2nd Battalion on the Western Front from 1916 to 1919, being wounded twice. Zmood was returned to Australia on 20.05.1919 and was discharged three months later. After his discharge Zmood lived in Victoria, moving from Shepparton to Wangaratta and then to Melbourne, where he started a drapery business in Lonsdale Street. He married Anne Rosenthal and they had two children, Diana and Rachel. Woolf died in Melbourne on 2.12.1964.

Index

Illustrations are indexed in **bold type**.

A

Abaza, Alexander, 33, 54, 55-57, 115
Adelaide, 42, 80, 96, 97, 120, 140
Afendikoff, Cemon, 10, 39, 52, 56, 79-80, 86, 90, 153, 188
Akkerman (Bilhorod-Dnistrovskyi), 12, 193
Albany, 24, 43, 114, 121
Aleksandrovsk. *See* Zaporizhia
Aleshki, 77, 200
Alimoff, Sergey, 35
Amiens, 85, 86, 88
Andriivka, 27, 203, 232
Ankudinov, Georgy, **20**
Ankudinow (Callaghan), Maggie, 103, 112
Ankudinow, Michael, 19, **20**, 21, 79, 83, 85, 103, 112-113, 154, **155**, 188-189
Armentières, 74, 78
Arnold (Dorfman), Betty, v, 165-**166**
Averkoff, William, **44**-45, **81**

B

Babkoff, Nikolai, 116
Ballarat, 119
Barcan, Benjamin, 37
Bathurst, 60, 117, 204, 208
Bean, C.E.W., 75
Belfort, Alexander, 19, 39, 52, **129**, 189
Beloshapka, Platon, 52-54, 58, 60, 96, 111-**112**, 130, 133, 189
Benarkin, 31
Bendery, 40, 81, 221
Berdiansk, 27, 135
Berdychiv, 29, 201
Berezdiv, 97, 214
Bershad, 48, 190
Bessarabia, 12, 14, 22, 154
Bessmertny, Vlas, 116
Bilhorod-Dnistrovsky. *See* Akkerman
Bilka, 29, 218
Bingera Plantation, 22, 30, 32, 82
Bjelonoshka, Theodor, 125
Blahovishchenka, 31, 205
Boileau, Angus Herbert, 79
Boon, Lexie, 159
Boronow, Alexander, 24, 47-48, 190
Borszcer, David, 48, 122, 190
Bourke, 33, 40, 60, 117-118
Bowen, 110, 165
Bratske, 31, 214
Breitman, George, 49, 79, 83, 89, **90**, 91, 132, 190

Brisbane, 15, 23, 29, 30, 31, 33, 34-39, 47, 48, 61, 80, 90, 106, 108, 110-111, 114, 116, 119, 121, 122, 123, 126, 133, 137, 139, 144, 145-146, 147, 148, 168
Brodsky (Marks), Sarah, **50**
Brodsky, Alexander, 21-22, 42, 49-**50**, 91, 157-**158**
Brodsky, Isadore, **50**, 157-**158**
Brodsky, Louis, v, 19, 21-22, 42, 49-**50**, 58, 69-70, 91-92, 129-130, 154, 157, 191
Brodsky, Vivien, v
Brodsky, Warwick, v, 130
Broken Hill, 24, 25-26, 27, 32, 35, 74, 84
Broodseinde, 83
Broon, Hyman, 42, 191
Brovkoff, Panteleimon, 37
Browne, Roland S., 139-142
Brunker, Michael, 165
Bugaldie, 40
Bullard, R.W., 141
Bullecourt, 80, 152
Bundaberg, 22, 24, 31, 32, 41
Bungonia, 53
Bur (Tilleard), Carolyn, v, 163, back cover

C

Cairns, 32, 33, 35, 36, 42, 49, 64, 82, 109, 159, 161,
Callide Valley, 116, 166
Canberra, 113-114
Chain, Isaac, 42, 154, 156, 191
Chechelnyk, 79, 190
Checkman, Petr. *See* Malisheff, George
Cherkasy, 220, 222, 231
Chernihiv, 8, 11, 12, 13, 14, 19, 29, 30, 31, 32, 39, 42, 94, 96, 124, 198, 203, 204, 208, 209, 212, 215, 218, 225, 226, 227
Cherpiter, John, 9, 42, 80, 91, 139-141, 192
Chita, 16-17
Chomley, M. E., 84
Clesner, Sam, 51, 128, 192
Cloncurry, 31, 32
Cobar, 32, 36, 42, 117-118, 148
Cochura, James, 29, 32, 54, 72, 114, 123, **156**, 192
Collinsville, 109-110, 165
Coolgardie, 25
Cooper, Roland Arthur, 10, 42, 47, 90, 120, 193
Cootamundra, 47, 120
Cordalba, 31, 33, 47, 49, 94
Cotman (Rudezky), Violet, v, 67, 115, 144, 147, 153
Cotton (Cotten), Lewy, 120, 193
Crafti, Efim, 37
Crimea, 16, 28, 135, 201, 221

D

Dalby, 115, 138, 143, 144, 147, 148, 153
Dee Why, 118, 156

Demchenko, Samuel, 116
Dernancourt, 85
Diachkoff, Constantine, **44**-45
Didenko, George, 12, 51, 119, 128, 193
Dimbisky, Stephen, 37
Dnipro. *See* Katerynoslav
Dobrotove, 42, 124, 125, 204
Domilovsky, Nickefor, 32, **43**, 49, 64, 74, 75, 91, 167, 194
Dorfman, Wolf, v, 29, 31, 70-72, 74-75, 84, 99, **121**, 165-166, 194
Douglas, Alexander and Serafima, 37
Drachuk, Paul, 12
Dryen, Edward, v, 26, 51-**52**, 157, 194
Dryen, Robyn, v, 52
Dryen, Ronald Gordon, 157
Dubbo, 16, 40, 61, 168
Dubno, 40, 50, 51, 52, 72, 202, 228
Dudarko, Pavel, 116
Dynowski (Hue), Mary, 103
Dynowski, Frank, 40, 103, 163, 195

E

Egypt, 25, 26, 63-65, 67-73, 92, 97, 156-157
England, 43, 51, 66-67, 76, 77, 78, 80, 82, 83, 85, 89, 91, 94-96, 98, 99, 100, 103, 123, 142, 148, 156, 161
Evans, Raymond, 55
Everitt, Herbert John, 125

F

Fedorovich (Nezhintseva), Eraida, 139
Fedorovich, Nicholas, 30, 32, 49, 64, 83-84, 98-99, 108, 114, 139, 161, 195
Feldman, Israel, 26, 195
Felipor, Joe, 42, 74, 77-78, 93, 115, 196
Ferber, George, v, 29, 31, 32, 72, **130**, 196
Figtree Creek, 33
Fisher, Andrew, 94-95
Franko, Ivan, 1
Freedman, Chaim, 27
Friezland (Kuridala), 31-32, 55

G

Gallipoli, 49, 50-51, 57, 63-69, 72, 73, 75, 83, 91, 93, 94, 97, 103, 105, 139, 151,
Glavasky, Usten, 49
Glen Innes, 111
Glenrock, 40, 80, 92
Gniliak, Semen, 116
Goffin, Ben, v, 19, 39, 52, 80, 88, **89**, 114, 152, 166, 196
Goffin, Richard, v, 89, 166
Goldstein, Frank, 18, 42, 80, 86, 119, 132, 197
Gorbach, Phillipp, 52, 69, 92, 130, **131**, 197

Gorbun, Mrs, 35
Gordonvale, 153
Gorodezky, Ivan, 42, 49, 74, 90, 130, **131**, 197
Govor, Elena, 2
Grechinsky, Fedor, 11
Greece, 156, 157
Greenstein, Esther, 157, **158**
Greenstein, Wolfe, 18, 42, 47, **48**, 119, 154, **156**-157, 198
Gregorenko (Scriven), Vera, 116, **160**
Gregorenko, George, 116, 147, 159-**160**
Gregorenko, Leonard, 116, **158**-**160**
Gregorenko, Richard, v, 30-31, 74, **97**, 98, 110, 116, 132, 147, 159-160, 161, 166, 198
Gretchinsky, James Theodor, 11, 29, 30, 32, 48, **69**, 110, 114, 120, 198
Gueudecourt, 78
Gulevich, Nicholas, 13, 30, 31, 33, 73, 93, **96**, 199

H

Habaeff, Thomas, 49
Haiff, Saul, 26, 120, 199
Halychyna, 1, 22
Hammersley, Ellen, 99
Harbin, 3, 15, 28-31, 34, 38, 46, 89, 128, 138, 142, 154, 164
Harchenko, Gregory, 35
Harlap, Lion, 18, 26, 72-73, **166**, 199
Hazebrouck, 85, 99
Helidon, 126
Heselev, Benjamin, 27, 48
Heselev, Israel, 26-27, 48, 120, 199
Hlukhiv, 19, 32, 215, 218
Hoffman, Wolfe, 8, 26, 64, 73, 74, 120-121, 156, 161, 200
Holsworthy, 49, 53
Horodnia, 11, 29, 198
Hughes, W.M., 107
Huliaipole, 27, 199
Hull, Geoffrey, v
Hull, Oksana, v, 5, 125
Hunter, Don, v
Hunter, Janice, v, 113, 147
Husiatyn, 228

I

Ilin, Constantine, 77, 78, 81, 127, 200
Illman, Jukka, vi, 89
Inverell, 111-112
Ipswich, 35, 48, 123
Ivanychi, 9

J

Jabinsky, Andrew, 49
Jakimov, Gregory (Mick), Jr., 160

Jakimov, Gregory, 13, 82, 115, 160, 200
Jakimov, Roman Arnold, 160
Jarrahdale, 26
Jas, Leah, v, 25
Jones, Harold, 107

K

Kabo, Raphael, vi
Kachan, John, 29, 32, 67, 68, 201
Kalasnikoff (Kalashnikoff), Walter, 108
Kalgoorlie, 25, 26, 40, 123
Kamianets-Podilskyi, 9, 13, 26, 37, 42, 80, 192, 200, 228, 232
Kaminer, Jackie, v
Kamishansky (Smith), Jean, 143, 201
Kamishansky, George, 19, 40, 48, 63, 64, 73, 122, 132, 135, 143, 147, 168, 201
Kamishansky, Petr, 19
Karapyshi, 30, 116, 198
Katerynoslav (Dnipro), 14, 18, 25, 26-27, 29, 31, 72, 194, 199, 205, 206, 207
Kavitski, Vasily, 13, 42, 67, 78, 93-94, 119, 128, 201
Kelemnuk, George, 37
Kenez, Kalyna, 2
Kerch, 19, 148, 168, 201
Khabarovsk, 30, 70, 164
Kharkiv, 14, 31, 35, 39, 42, 43, 116, 122, 130, 155, 211, 226, 231
Khashchuvate, 8
Kherson, 9, 12, 14, 42, 116, 191, 200, 202, 216, 217, 226
Kiama, 53
Kills, Carl, 9, 42, 58, 132, 134, 153, 201
Kingaroy, 114
Kishinev, 12
Kiva, Nikalas, v, 30, **44**-45, 74, 80, **81**, 91, 202
Kivovitch, Yur, 31, 33, 49, 72, 73, 97, 132, 150, 202
Kleshenko (Bateman), Ethel, 103
Kleshenko, Joseph, 19, 40, 50-51, 60, 103, 107-108, 109, 125, 132, 151-152, 202
Klimov, 13, 227
Kogarah, 32, 119
Kolesnikov, William, 12, 40, 82, 125-126, 132, 203
Komesaroff (Isaacman), Sarah, 143
Komesaroff, Peter, v, **27**, 46-**47**, 80, 120, 143, 151, 152, 162, 203
Konotop, 29, 212, 226
Korniack, Afanasey, 9, 29, 30, 31, 55, 119, 132, 134, 203
Koropets, Mitrofan, 42, 74, 84, 124-125, 168, 204
Koscharsky, Halyna, v
Kosivka, 41, 165, 205
Koslick (Cherpiter), Anastasia, 139-**142**
Koslick, Paul, 139-142
Kotton, Moisey, 29, 33, 46, 89-90, 91, 167, 204
Kotton, Samuel, 29, 90, 167
Koty, George, v, 39, **78**, 85, 86, 130, **131**, 204

Kovalevsky, Andrew, 31, 32, 74, 76, 90, 91, 132, 205
Kovalsky, Viacheslav, 76
Kozachuk (Morris), Bessie, 144-**145**
Kozachuk, Hilda May, 157, **158**, 165
Kozachuk, Ksenofont William, **145**, 157
Kozachuk, Ksenofont, v, 19, 41, 55, 109-110, 133, 144-**145**, 146, 157, 164-165, 205
Kozachuk, Overian, 164
Kozachuk, Vasily, 165
Krantz, Albert, 26, **64**, 67, 85, 119, 205
Krantz, Samuel Harold, 26, 85-86, 88-89, 132, 206
Kremenchuk, 29, 167, 204
Kremenets, 9
Kumok, Viktor, vi
Kurri Kurri, 41
Kusmin (Kneller), Mabel, 103
Kusmin (Zadorohney), Peter, 13, 30, 42, 74, 79-80, 98, 103, 107, 206
Kyiv, 1, 8, 11, 12, 13, 14, 24, 29, 30, 31, 35, 39, 40, 41, 42, 49, 52, 60, 98, 116, 117, 163, 167, 189, 194, 195, 198, 201, 204, 205, 206, 207, 208, 214, 216, 222, 229

L

Lakovsky, David, v, 18, 25, 26, 47, 121, 132, 206
Lakovsky, Edward, v, 18, 25, 26, 47, **69**, 207
Lakovsky, Tom, 25-26
Lawgi, 116, 159
Lazarus, Dorothy, v, 25
Lebovich, Aaron, 26
Lebovich, Morris, 26, 47, 85, **86**, 91, 207
Lebovitz, Elias, 8, 18, 67, 72-73, 207
Leffow, Jacob, 8, 10, 39, 89, 91, 208
Lemish, Aaron, 29, 156, 157, 208
Lemish, Lazarus, 157
Lemish, Myer, 157, **158**
Leneve, Maurice, 157, **158**
Leneve, Morris, 42, 60, 157, 208
Lesnie, Frank, 64, 65
Lidykhiv, 29, 219
Lighting Ridge, 32
Lipivka, 42, 197
London, 76, 83-84, 92, 94, 95, 103, 122, 129, 130, 156
Loosgie, Stephen, 31, 67, 74, 79, 83, 86, 94-96, 128, 132, 209
Loss-Pavlenko, Paulina, 30
Lviv, 8, 14, 18, 207
Lypky, 11, 16, 17, 117

M

Mackay, 110, 111, 116, 161
Mackomel, Samuel, 26, 73, 90, 122, 132, 210
Makagon, Ivan, 116
Malinowsky, Simon, 37, 168

Malisheff (Checkman), George, 9, 12, 29, 31, 74, 75, 85, 91, 99, 209
Malomikhailivka, 29, 192
Mamchin, John, 31, 127, 210
Maneeken, Marjory (Lucy, Nadezhda), 139-**142**
Maneeken, Vasily, 140
Mariupol, 42, 120, 193
Marsden, Victor, 98
Maximenko (Peterson), Cora, 81-82
Maximenko, Efim, 8, 13, 42, 73, 81-82, 91, 210
Maximenko, Peter, 137
McKenzie (Gregorenko), Carol, v, 147, 166
Melashich, Gordon, 35-36
Melbourne, 24, 27-28, 32, 35, 38, 39-40, 46-47, 57, 68, 108-109, 110, 115, 120, 121, 136, 139-142, 148, 151, 155
Melitopol, 32, 37, 43, 196, 222, 225
Messines, 80, 81, 82, 84, 85, 152
Micolazyk, Isaac, 8, 210
Mikhailivka, 43, 225
Mikulicic-Rodd, Joseph. *See* Rudovsky, Joseph
Mirgorodsky, Joseph, 37
Misko, Khrystyna, 2, 13
Moldova, 12, 154, 221
Momba, 115
Monastyryshche, 30, 213
Moonan Flat, 40, 80-81
Mornington, 43, 127
Morozoff, Albert, 19, 40, 42, 52, 67, 75, 78, 115, **131**, 210-211
Morozoff, Alfroniza, 24, 49, 69, 132, 211
Morozoff, Dermy, 42, 130, 211
Morris, Jack. *See* Morozoff, Alfroniza
Moscow, 8, 11, 35, 76, 139, 164-165, 198
Mount Chalmers, 31
Mount Morgan, 32, 41, 54-55, 58, 92, 111, 119
Mouquet Farm, 75, 76, 111
Muchomel, Samuel. *See* Mackomel, Samuel
Mykolaiv, 22, 47, 86, 122, 153, 227, 229

N

Nasedkin, Vladimir, 38
Naughtons Gap, 33, 46, 89
Neborotchko, Victor, 130, **131**, 211
Nesterenko (Nester), John, 61
Nesterenko, Afanasy, 119, 212
Nesterinko, Phillip, 212
New Guinea, 110, 157, 159
New South Wales, 39, 41, 47, 53, 57, 62-63, 111, 114, 122, 138, 163
New Zealand, 19, 121-122, 127, 129
Newcastle, 24, 32, 39, 40, 41, 42, 69, 72, 77, 103, 110, 114, 116, 119, 153, 157
Nicholson (Grabert), Bertha, 103
Nicholson (Poselnikoff), Robert, 19, 39-40, 48, 56, 73, 103, **110**, 132, 156, 212
Nikopol, 26, 219

Noreuil, 79, 80
Novopavlivka, 26, 205
Novosibirsk, 164
Novoukrainka, 12, 13, 216, 217
Noweetsky, Leonard, 30, 32, 49, 67, **70**, 91, 213

O

Odessa, 3, 8, 9, 12, 13, 18, 19-21, 22, 24, 25, 26, 28, 30, 31, 37, 39, 40, 42, 47, 51, 52, 57, 62, 65, 73, 74, 77, 80, 82, 83, 97, 98, 120, 126, 128, 129, 139, 148, 155, 156, 188, 189, 190, 191, 192, 193, 195, 196, 197, 198, 199, 202, 203, 206, 207, 209, 210, 211, 212, 214, 215, 216, 220, 221, 222, 223, 224, 226, 227, 229, 230
Ogg, Frederic Austin, 1
Oleinikoff, Daria, 144, 145-**146**
Oleinikoff, Ida (Nadezhda), 144, 146
Oleinikoff, Matfeus, 8, 29, 33, **49**, 94, 108, 116, 133, 136, 137, 144, 145-**146**, 161, 213
Oleinikoff, Peter, 144, **161**
Olino, 117, 168
Olshanskaia Slobodka, 42, 201
Osmirko, Alik. *See* Ostrinko, Alexay
Ostrinko, Alexay, 30, 60, 119-120, 132, 148, 213
Oucharenko (Lane), Clara, 82
Ouchirenko (Robertson), Doris, 143, 144
Ouchirenko, Alexander, v, 144, 156
Ouchirenko, John, v, 19, 52, 82, 83, 103, **108**, 110, 119, 132, 143, 144, 148, 151, 156, 214

P

Palestine, 18, 26, 68, 72, 73, 153, 166, 195, 199, 202, 207, 215, 223, 227
Papchuck (Fletcher), Edith Agnes, 123
Papchuck (Hannan), Annie Mabel, 123-124
Papchuck, Denis, 19, 74, 85, 97, 110, 123-**124**, 148, 151, 166, 214
Pashinsky, Anthony, 23
Passchendaele, 83
Pavlova, Anna, 120
Pavlyshyn, Marko, 2
Peachenoff (Maximenko), Akulina, 137
Peachenoff, Feodot, v, 29, 31, 33, 49, 74, 90, 116, 133, 134, 136, **137**, 157, 214-215
Peachenoff, Helen, 134, 137
Peachenoff, Maria, 137
Peachenoff, Valentine, 137
Peachenoff, Victor, 137, 157, **158**
Perlman, Max, 18, 28, 156, 215
Péronne, 88-90
Perth, 25, 26, 40, 42, 47, 97, 120, 122, 123, 152
Pesmany, Thomas, 32, 49, 59, 74, 93, 215
Piddubny, Gregory, 4, 31, 35, 38, 53
Pieven, Klavdia, **138**
Pieven, Zacharias, v, 12, **30**, **138**-139, 215-216

Pinkevitch, Constantine, 30, 32, 33, 55, 67, 74, 90, 106, 119, 153, 157, 166, 216
Pinkevitch, Leo Carson, 157
Piven-Large, Harold, 138, **139**
Piven-Large, John, v
Pivinski, Walter, 42, 52, 64, 65, 69, 130, 216
Platonoff (Kurtish), Vera, 116, 123, 136
Platonoff (Odarchinko), Tatiana, 12, 116
Platonoff (Platonaff), Thomas, 11-12, 13, 31, 47, 49, 82, 115-116, 123, 128, 136, 161, 217
Platonoff, George, 11-12, 13, 31, 47, 49, 74, 83, 115-116, 123, 136, 156, 216-217
Platonoff, Stephan, 12, 29, 31, 33, 116
Podillia, 8, 9, 12, 14, 19, 26, 29, 30, 37, 39, 48, 67, 114, 190, 196, 200, 209, 213, 217
Poleshchuk, Ivan. See Pollejuke, Huon
Pollejuke, Huon, 24, 49, 132, 217
Pollock, Jack. See Pollejuke, Huon
Pologouck, Huon. See Pollejuke, Huon
Poltava, 8, 14, 20, 29, 30, 37, 60, 116, 204, 213
Polygon Wood, 82, 83, 130
Popow, Alexander, 19, 48, 64, 65, 73, 76, **77**, 122, 132, 218
Port Pirie, 35, 42, 119, 140
Porytsk, 9, 29, 203
Poselnikoff, Boris. See Nicholson, Robert
Pozières, 75, 76, 110, 126
Prerauer, Curt, 149
Prokop, Yulia, vi
Provaka (Finnimore), Bertha, 146
Provaka (Proiavka), Stephen, 12, 32, **49**, 59, 74, 132, 146, 218
Pshevolodskey, Marian, 29, 30, 33, 64, 91, 218

Q

Queensland, 10, 22-23, 24, 28-39, 41-42, 47, 62-63, 67, 74, 83, 86, 92, 94, 110, 111, 112, 115-116, 120, 126, 127, 130, 133, 140, 147, 153, 156, 157

R

Radetsky, Sebastian, 29, 42, 64, 67, 75, 80, 88, 119, 219
Rappeport, Lionel, 26, 219
Rappeport, Samuel, 26, 86, **157**, 219
Rayzner, Alexander, 31, 220
Rees, Jan, v, 20
Rehovot, 18, 72, 73, 199
Rennenkampf, Paul, 17
Rink, Christian, 10, 24, 48, 73, 96, 121, 220
Rinkevich, Osiph, v, **44**-45, 80, **81**
Rivne, 29, 70, 194
Robilliard, Dane, v
Rockhampton, 22, 32, 47, 49, 58, 67, 70, 74, 75, 82, 85, 92, 93, 116, 123
Rodenko, Daniel, 39

Roomianzoff, Nicholas, 12, 32, 49, 64, **67**, 74, 75, 85, 90, **104**-105, 110, 111, 161, 220-221
Rosenfield, Reuben Laman, 28, 68, 133, 221
Rossoggsky, Ivan, 40, 41, 80-81, 91, 92, 221
Rothman, Aaron, 157
Rothman, Leon, 29, 33, 47, 157, 221-222
Rothman, Rose Ray, 157
Rothman, Samuel, 157, **158**
Rothstein, Morris, 8, 39, 52, 73, 90, 222
Rudezky (Burns), Agnes Annie, 143, 144, 148
Rudezky, Joseph, v, 30, 49, 67, 74, 75, 110, **111**, 115, 127, 143, 144, 147, 148, 153, 222
Rudezky, Tamara, 144, 147
Rudovskaya (Rudovsky), Mary, 35, 108
Rudovsky (Mikulicic-Rodd), Joseph, 10, 42, 57, 74, 84, 151, 222-223
Russian Far East, 14, 18, 28-30, 34, 52, 76, 82, 94, 128, 138, 140, 154,
Ruzhyn, 18, 42, 197

S

Sabadash, 161, 220
Sadagoursky, Harry, 18, 26, 47, 223
Saffar, Morris, 42, 85, 135-136, 156, 223
Saffar, Sarah, 135-136
Sage (Hales), Rosa, 100
Sage, Lamotte Alexis, 10, 24, 64, 67, 73, 90, 100, 152, 223-224
Saint Petersburg (Petrograd, Leningrad), 19, 20, 43, 53, 83, 98, 141, 226
Saltykova Divitsia, 12
Sank, Alexander, 29, 30, 33, 47, 74, 92, 128, 152, 164, 224
Sast, Alexander, 10, 42, 48, 63, 64, 65-67, 73, 127, 224
Savchenko, Oleksandr, 2
Scott, Barbara, v, 137, 158
Sepscak, John, 9, 83, 94, 114, 225
Serebrennikoff (Swanson), Alice, 115, 148
Serebrennikoff, Jacob, 43, 48-49, 57, 64, 115, 148, 225
Serebrennikov, Josif, 43
Sevastopol, 37
Shirochin, Dmitry, vi
Shlensky, Nicholas, 37
Shouiupoff, John, 37
Shular, Maxim, 32, 55, 56, 58, 60, 111, 225
Siberia, 3, 12, 14-17, 28, 30, 38, 98, 122, 140, 211
Simferopol, 28, 221
Simonoff, Peter, 128
Skvyra, 11, 30, 41, 222
Smith, Annie, v
Smith, Maree, v
Smoishen, Abraham, 42, 72-73, 120, 130, 153, 226
Snegovoy, Andrew, 30, 32, 74, 80, 85, 90, 97, 128, 132, 226

Sologub, Egnaty, 29, 30, 32, 52, 55, 73, 90, **128**, 129, 226
Sologub, Stepan, 129
Sosnovka, 30, 129
Sosnytsia, 32, 225
South Australia, 24, 39, 40, 42, 62, 115, 120
South Brisbane, 37, 39, 106, 110-111, 121, 126, 139, 168
Spisbah (Batoulin), Lydia, 43
Spisbah, Alexander, 10, 43, 127, 157, 226-227
Spisbah, George, 43, 157, **158**
Stanthorpe, 114, 127, 143, 144
Stasinowsky, Samuel Carl Richard, 83
Stavishche, 43, 49, 194
Stedman, Solomon, 145
Steinberg, Jack, 126, 227
Stoopachenko, Paul, 37
Stuart Town, 122
Surazh, 12-13, 218
Surovsov, Stephen, 13, 32, 74, 90, 118, 132, 153, 154, 156, 161, 227
Svinaboy, Maxim, 28
Sydney, 10, 16, 24, 25, 26, 33, 35, 36, 39, 40, 42, 48, 77, 81, 92, 97, 100, 107, 109, 110, 116, 119, 120, 121, 122, 124-126, 127, 128, 129, 137, 138-139, 148, 149, 156, 157, 168

T

Tangool, 116, 161
Tardent, Edward Felix, 88
Tardent, Emile Auguste, 10, 22-**23**, 48, 86-**88**, 122-123, 153, 227-228
Tardent, Henry Alexis, 22-**23**, 48, 227
Tardent, Jules, **88**
Tardent, Oswald Urbin, 88
Taurida, 14, 18, 27, 77, 78, 200, 203, 232
Tchorzewski (Sakaranko), Polly, 142
Tchorzewski, George Marion, 22, 47, 142, 228
Tchorzewski, Ignacy, 22
Temora, 114, 123
Tereshchenko, Valerie, v, 43
Ternopil, 219
Tilleard, Alyn, v, 11, 64, **149**
Tilleard, Peter, v, 40, 93, 102
Tkachenko, Saveliy, 59, 67, 74, 90, 97, 128, 148, 228
Tkachuk, Peter, 52, 72-73, 127, 228-229
Tober (Lawler), Lily, 113, **143**
Tober, Albert Michael, v, 8, 10, 64, 67, **113**-114, 142, 144, 147, 157, 229
Tober, Albert, Jr., 157, **158**
Tober, Dorothy, v
Tober, Mary, 157, **158**
Tobruk, 159
Tolmachev, Gregory. *See* Piddubny, Gregory
Tolstoff, Vladimir, 116
Toowoomba, 23, 32, 126

Townsville, 31, 33, 58, 110, 111, 161
Trager, Samuel, 29, 47, 61, 122, 229
Tulchyn, 39, 114, 196
Tumut, 122
Tupikoff, Nicholas, 52

U

Uman, 24, 231
USA, 18, 19, 35, 39, 52, 70, 112, 121, 122, 129, 130, 165-166
Uspenivka, 27

V

Vasilieff, George, 49
Vengert (Gudshus), Emma Adeline, 103
Vengert, Jack, 8-9, 10, 31, 64, **65**, 103, 121, 128, 132, 229-230
Veselaya, 26
Villers-Bretonneux, vi, 85
Vinnytsia, 190, 196, 200, 209, 213, 217
Vishnevaia, Svetlana, v, 164-165
Vladivostok, 9, 16, 17, 19-21, 28, 29, 30, 32, 79, 103, 188
Volhynia, 8, 9, 10, 29, 40, 42, 75, 97, 194, 202, 202, 203, 208, 214, 219, 223, 228, 229
Volkofsky, Theofil, v, 11, 16-17, 31, 32, 33, 34, 40, 58, 60, 61, **117**-118, 123, 133, 134-135, 147, 148-149, 163, 168, 230
Volkofsky, Tom, v, 11, 16, 31, 33, 60, 117-118, 133, 134-135, 147, 148-149, 163
Voloskivtsi, 31, 96, 209
Voskovtsy, 9, 201
Vurhaft, Joseph, 31, 74, 82, 130, 150, 230
Vyshnivets, 29, 208

W

Wallumbilla, 23
Walpole, 114
Wanalta, 40
Warsaw, 64, 163
Waten, Judah, 61-62
Webberley (Komesaroff), Thelma, v, 47, 152
Wee Waa, 53, 111
Welch, T.A., 53, 54, 56
West, Dru, v
Western Australia, 18, 24, 25-27, 39, 42, 57, 62-63, 100, 114, 115, 123-124, 127
Wheeler, H. G., 92
Whynsky, William, 8, 67, 74, 75, 126, 168, 230-231
Willey, Harry, 80-81
Windle, Kevin, v
Winning, Alexander Barr, 10, 42, **132**, 157, 231
Winning, Ian, 157
Wolkowski, Wojciech, 11, 163, back cover
Wolkowsky (Tilleard), Sonia Mae, 144, **149**

Wolkowsky (Woodberry), Gwynnyth, 100-**102**, 109, 144, 151
Wolkowsky, Cezar, v, 11, **40**, 61, 64, 65, **93**, 100, **101**-**102**, 107, 109, 119, 144, **149**, 151, 163, 231, back cover
Wolkowsky, Marea Victusya (Prerauer, Maria), 144, **149**, 153, 163-164
Wollongong, 53
Woolf, Isaac, 24, 231-232
Woolloongabba, 37, 111, 144
Wynnum, 123, 153

Y
Yampil, 9, 209
Ypres, 76, 77, 152

Z
Zadorohney, Samuel. *See* Kusmin, Peter
Zaporizhia, 192, 196, 203, 224, 232
Zhytomyr, 197, 201, 230, 231
Zines, Joseph Morris, 26, 47, 64, 67, 76, 232
Zmerynka, 30, 213
Zmood, Woolf, 27, 78, **79**, 85, 90, 120, 232

www.ingramcontent.com/pod-product-compliance
Lightning Source LLC
LaVergne TN
LVHW061213060426
835507LV00016B/1909